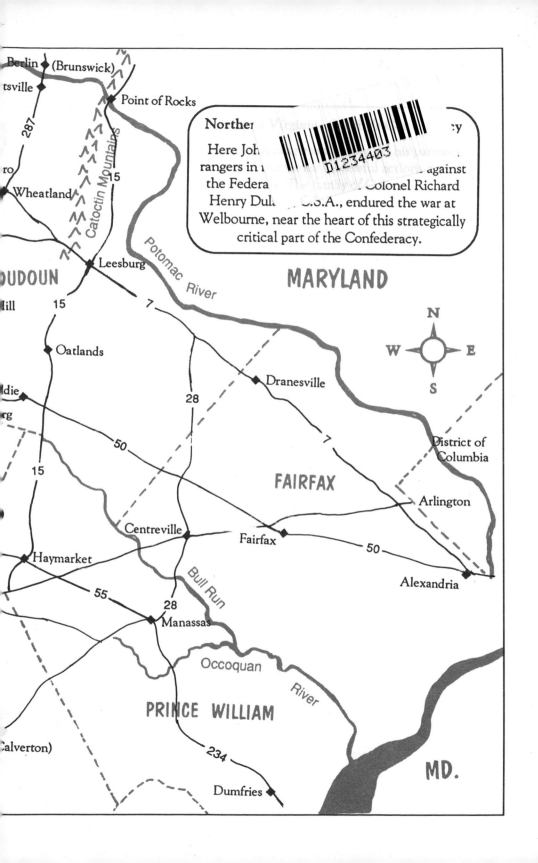

Berlin (Brunswick)

tsville

287

ro

Wheatland

Point of Rocks

15

Catoctin Mountains

Potomac River

Leesburg

MARYLAND

DUDOUN

Iill   15   7

Oatlands

Idie

rg

50

15

28

Dranesville

N
W   E
S

7

District of
Columbia

FAIRFAX

Arlington

Centreville

Fairfax

50

Haymarket

Bull Run

55

28

Manassas

Alexandria

Occoquan

River

PRINCE WILLIAM

alverton)

234

Dumfries

MD.

The Dulanys of Welbourne

A FAMILY IN MOSBY'S CONFEDERACY

The Dulanys of Welbourne

A FAMILY IN MOSBY'S CONFEDERACY

Margaret Ann Vogtsberger

Rockbridge Publishing Company
Berryville, Virginia

Published by Rockbridge Publishing Company
P.O. Box 351
Berryville, VA 22611
(540) 955-3980

Photographs courtesy of Nathaniel H. Morison III with these exceptions:
Plate 14 (bottom) Sheila Cochrane; Plate 15 (top), Plate 16 (top &
bottom), Plate 18 (top) Daniel deButts; Plate 17 (all 3) Richard Lundgren;
Plate 3 (bottom), Plate 6 (top) Katherine Tennery; Plate 1 (top), Plate 15
(bottom), Plate 20 (top & bottom) Stephen Wagner.

Library of Congress Cataloging-in-Publication Data

Vogtsberger, Margaret Ann
      The Dulanys of Welbourne : a family in Mosby's confederacy /
Margaret Ann Vogtsberger
              p.   cm.
      Includes bibliographical references and index.
      ISBN 1-883522-03-X
      1. United States—History—Civil War, 1861-1865—Personal narratives,
Confederate. 2. Virginia—History—Civil War, 1861-1865—Personal
narratives. 3. Dulany family—Correspondence. 4. Dulany, Richard
Henry, 1820-1906—Correspondence. 5. Middleburg (Va.)—Biography.
I. Title
E605.V64   1995
975.5'03'0922—dc20
[B]   95-45379
                                              CIP

*To my mother and father
who made everything possible*

Contents

Preface

In 1934, the novelist Thomas Wolfe, at the recommendation of his editor, Maxwell Perkins, visited for a time with Perkins's friend, Miss Elizabeth Herbert Lemmon, at Welbourne, the home of her sister, Mrs. Nathaniel Morison. Wolfe was much taken with the place and took special note of an inscription scratched into a windowpane that was attributed to John Pelham, a Confederate officer who had been there seventy-two years earlier. Sometime in the late 1970s I came across this item in Wolfe's biography and recalled "the gallant Pelham" of Douglas Southall Freeman's *Lee's Lieutenants*.

In 1980 I visited Welbourne during the annual Garden Week tour of the Garden Club of Virginia, where my hostess graciously showed me the spidery writing. Much to my delight, Welbourne was a bed-and-breakfast, and I arranged to stay one night—one night that grew to dozens in the past fifteen years.

The owners of Welbourne, Mr. and Mrs. Nathaniel Holmes Morison III, are a rarity in the Old Dominion—the sixth generation of a family that has occupied the same house for almost two hundred years. The Morisons are the guardians of a treasury of letters and other papers of Mr. Morison's great-great-grandfather, Colonel Richard H. Dulany, 7th Virginia Cavalry, C.S.A., and other family members. It is through the friendship and generosity of the Morisons that I have enjoyed the opportunity to organize, research and finally edit this collection.

Assembling the letters was a major undertaking in itself as over the years they had been scattered throughout the family. A major cache was made available when Pelham, another Dulany family home, was sold out of the family in 1989, and eventually other papers surfaced through careful searches of the attics, nooks and crannies at Welbourne. Unfortunately, some letters were found only in part; in one instance, a page missing from a letter in an historical society's archives turned up amid the dusty file cabinets and old shoeboxes. A few letters remain incomplete; where this is the case, it is so noted in the text. In some cases where an original is missing, there exists a typescript copy, made by the late Mary Dulany Lemmon White, who transcribed many of the letters. A comparison of extant originals with her typescripts show her to have been a meticulous and accurate copyist.

Spelling, punctuation and grammar in the original letters is generally good but somewhat erratic, which may be attributed to the hurried, sometimes pressured, circumstance of their creation as much as the writer's literary skill. At age thirteen young Richard, never a crack speller, wrote to his sister Mary from Dickinson College in Carlisle, Pennsylvania:

> I suppose you would like to know how my time est imployed. ... I get up in the morning at six oclock & go to college to prayers & then return & eat breakfast at seven, at eight we go the grammar school as soon as I go in I recite my latten tutor and grammar. at nine I say my reader and parsing. at eleven we have recess for twenty five minutes, at two oclock I say geography. at three our history and greek grammar, at four we let out of school, at seven we go in and study our taskes for the next day at nine we to bed which I am going to very soon....

Although the later letters do not share this degree of error, inconsistencies in spelling where the meaning is clear—such as Moseby in one place, Mosby in another—have been corrected. The name deButts was generally capitalized; today it is not. For the sake of clarity, punctuation has been added in some places, especially in long letters, where periods have replaced overused dashes and long blocks of text have been broken into paragraphs.

The physical condition of the letters has created some challenges to modern readers. Some letters consist of two sets of sentences, one set horizontally on the page and one set vertically, designed to wring double duty from scarce writing paper. Many of the letters are in pencil, which Dulany's father complains are almost illegible when received. This, plus years of folding and refolding, has rendered some words undecipherable; where this is the case, the reader is so advised.

Most of the letters quoted herein are in the Morisons' personal collection, and I am grateful for permission to use others from the deButts Family papers at the Virginia Historical Society, Richmond.

Much of the work on this collection took place at Welbourne, a wonderful environment for any writer. It was especially satisfying to know that Thomas Wolfe and F. Scott Fitzgerald also found inspiration there.

Acknowledgments

In such an undertaking as this, many people need to be thanked. To Nat and Sherry Morison, my heartfelt gratitude for allowing me the privilege of working with these letters. Their patience, understanding and great trust and confidence encouraged me in this project. In opening their home to me so generously, they have redefined the term "Southern hospitality."

Mrs. G. Howard White, formerly of Pelham and now of Washington, D.C., lent her support to this project and helped put me in contact with other family members, including Mr. and Mrs. William Tayloe and Arthur deButts. Daniel deButts of Wicklow, near Upperville, answered endless questions on Dulany and deButts family genealogy. My thanks to all of the Dulany and deButts families for their support.

Special thanks to John Divine, for sharing with me his unmatched scholarship of the history of Loudoun County and cavalry operations; William H. Strong, Jr., whose knowledge of Colonel Mosby and the activities of Mosby's Rangers proved most helpful, especially in identifying names and places; Garland Hudgins, who gave me a personal tour of the cavalry battlefield of Toms Brook; Bryce Suderow, whose papers on cavalry operations at Trevillian and Hawes Shop were provided most generously; Scott C. Mauger, for a personal tour of the route of Wade Hampton's "Beefsteak Raid"; Dr. D. Gardiner Tyler, for sharing his vast knowledge, especially identifying place names, of Charles City County, Virginia; and C.J. Cochrane, for helping me try to decipher many illegible parts of letters and keep my filing system straight.

I humbly took guidance from some fine professional historians: Robert K. Krick, chief historian at the Fredericksburg and Spotsylvania National Military Park, provided invaluable advice on the search for Confederate records; Christopher M. Calkins, historian at the Petersburg National Battlefield, helped in the research on Reams Station; Michael P. Musick of the National Archives, author of the 6th *Virginia Cavalry,* and Richard Armstrong, author of the *7th Virginia Cavalry,* offered much help with research. Credit and thanks are also extended to Jeffrey D. Wert, Col. Donald L. Stumbo, Robert Driver, Robert O'Neill, Richard J. Lundgren, David Roszel, Wes Peppinger, John K. Gott, Nancy C. Baird, Robert deT. Lawrence, Stephen Wagner, and Beverly Young.

The staffs of the following institutions were particularly helpful: the National Archives; Library of Congress; Virginia State Library; Virginia Historical Society; William Perkins Library, Duke University; Southern Historical Collection, University of North Carolina at Chapel Hill; Alderman Library, University of Virginia; Swem Library, College of William and Mary; Dickinson College, Carlisle, Pennsylvania; Handley Library, Winchester, Virginia; Charles H. Taylor Library, Hampton, Virginia; Thomas Balch Library, Leesburg, Virginia; Loudoun County Court House; Fauquier County Court House; Clarke County Historical Society and Museum; and the Fauquier County Historical Society.

I am blessed with many friends who advised and listened to me, whose opinions I respected and whose encouragement I needed. They include Charles H. Hooper, who embodies the spirit of "the gallant Pelham"; Joan and Tom Brzustowicz; Mr. and Mrs. Scott Bowers; the late June A. Mitchell; the late Cheryl Y. Fales, head of the Virginiana Room in the Hampton Public Library; Jennifer Young; William E. Potter; and Gene Jones. Two writers who showed me it could be done are Robert J. Trout, who "follows the plume" still, and Mary Elizabeth Sergent, who has the "spirit of Old West Point."

I cannot help but thank my publisher and editor, Kathie Tennery, for giving me this opportunity to share the letters of a very special family in an especially beautiful part of Virginia and can only hope the world will be a little richer for having read them.

Introduction

The Dulanys—1687-1833

The Dulany Family was prominent in the Maryland Tidewater in the early 1700s. Daniel Dulany (1687-1753) was born in Queens County, Ireland, attended the University of Dublin and in 1703 arrived at Port Tobacco, Maryland, indentured to Colonel George Plater as a clerk in his law office. In 1710 he was admitted to the bar and within ten years was a respected lawyer and landowner in Prince Georges County, Maryland. He married well. His first wife was Plater's widowed daughter, Charity Courts; no children, if any, survived this marriage. His second wife was Rebecca Smith, the daughter of Colonel Walter Smith of Calvert County. Dulany, known as "the Elder" to distinguish him from his son, held many important offices: commissary general of the Court of Probate (1721); attorney general (1722); judge of the admiralty; agent and receiver of the proprietary; and burgess for Annapolis. He is buried at St. Anne's Church, Annapolis.

Daniel Dulany "the Younger" (1721-1797) was educated at Eton and Clare College, Cambridge, and admitted to the Maryland Bar in 1747. He married Rebecca Tasker, daughter of Benjamin Tasker. Like his father, he held many important offices: secretary of the province of Maryland from 1761 until the Revolution and, with Benjamin Tasker, commissary general. He was the mayor of Annapolis in 1764.

The younger Daniel was a great lawyer, orator and writer. "It was the constant practice of the courts of the Province to submit to his opinion every question of difficulty which came before them: and so infallible were his opinions considered that he who hoped to reverse them was considered as 'hoping against hope'," wrote the eminent lawyer, John V.L. McMahon.

Family lore tells us that the younger Dulany may have been indirectly responsible for the American Revolution when he ordered a carriage to be built for him while on a trip to London. Lord North strolled in to check on the progress of his own carriage and spotted Dulany's. "And whose splendid carriage is this?" he asked. When told it belonged to an American, North sniffed, "If Americans can afford to ride in such fine carriages as that, they are able to pay more taxes!" True or not, the Revolution effectively ended Dulany's public career. He and his wife sat out the war at their estate, Hunting Ridge, outside of Baltimore, and afterward he resumed the practice of law.

In the next generation, one son, Daniel Dulany III, and his sister, Ann, returned to England, being unsympathetic to the Revolution. The third son, Benjamin Tasker Dulany, stayed in the new country.

Benjamin (1752-1819) was the clerk of the Frederick County, Maryland, court and later justice of the Fairfax Court, Virginia. Like his father and grandfather, he married well. Elizabeth French (1757-1824) was the daughter of Penelope Manley and Daniel French. French deeded the land and was the contractor for the building of Pohick Church. He owned two estates, Claremont and Rose Hill near Alexandria, and also held land on Wankopin Creek, in what would later become Loudoun County, Virginia. Elizabeth was the ward of George Washington and an heiress, "of whom half the world was in pursuit," noted her guardian, who attended the wedding.

Benjamin and Elizabeth owned a townhouse in Alexandria and a country estate called Shuter's Hill, where they often entertained. One rowdy party was celebrated in poetic parody by the psuedonymous A.X. in a piece entitled "The Ball at Shooter's Hill." Despite producing twelve children, their marriage was not a happy one and ended in divorce in 1808. As part of the large settlement, each of their children received a handsome estate in northern Virginia.

John Peyton Dulany (1787-1878) was Benjamin and Elizabeth's third son and seventh child. He received five hundred acres in Loudoun County from his parents on December 26, 1811. On May 18, 1812, he married Mary Ann deButts (1786-1855) of Mount Welby (now the Oxon Hill Children's Farm) in Prince Georges County, Maryland. She was born at Welbourne Hall in Lincolnshire, England, the daughter of Mary Welby of Denton Manor and Dr. Samuel deButts (1756-1814) of County Sligo, Ireland. When John and Mary Ann moved to his farm, they called it Welbourne, after Mary Ann's birthplace. The word is Old English, *wel* meaning a well or spring of water and *boume* meaning a boundary or destination point.

In February 1813, Mary Welby deButts described her son-in-law's farm and the original Welbourne—a log cabin that still stands in 1995, albeit in woefully dilapidated condition—in a letter to her brother:

> Mr. Dulany's farm is a fine level spot, the land is very rich, has many excellent springs upon it and two fine streams of water run through it—plenty of wood and stone for building. 4 miles distant there is a long range of the Blue Ridge Mountains which I think a beautiful object. The house is very small, consisting only of two little rooms below and the same above. Mr. D hopes in a few years by industry and attention to his Farm to be enabled to Build a more commodious residence. The Neighbourhood chiefly consists of plain industrious but independent People chiefly Quakers, there are very few Slaves in that part of Virginia and the whole time I was there I never saw a poor Person. Doct. DB [deButts] & I rambled frequently about when we could leave Mary Ann for an hour or two & we introduced ourselves to several of the Neighbors & were never suffered to depart without partaking of some good country fare, such as excellent Bread, butter, cheese, Honey, apples, pastry, Pumpkin puddings, etc. etc.—and were generally laden on our return with vegetables for Neighbour Dulany as they know [he] had no garden that year.

According to the Loudoun County deed book, Dulany added significantly to his land holdings in the 1800s in several transactions. On October 28, 1833, he bought eighty acres of land from widow Joanna Lewis, including a stone house with two rooms on two floors, believed to date from 1770, situated in a park-like setting and surrounded by huge old trees. This became the core of present-day Welbourne, also known as Welbourne Hall. Some of the original woodwork can be seen in the present dining room and a second floor bedroom. The property with the log cabin then became known as Old Welbourne.

In the 1830s Dulany made several alterations to Welbourne. He added a two-story front—a simple rectangular block of five bays with gable roof and interior end chimneys connected to the earlier section by a traverse hall containing the stair—from brick kilned from the farm, which was later stuccoed. On what was once the outer wall there is a message, written in pencil, that can be easily read today: "Elizabeth D. Herbert, August 18, 1836." Elizabeth, called Mittie, (1822-1901), was one of John and Mary Ann's nieces.

Welbourne

$\mathscr{T}$oday a visitor's impression of Welbourne is not of a manor, but of a country house in the grand sense, designed for a huntsman and rider. In June 1884, Major Heros von Borcke, a Prussian who had served on the staff of General J.E.B. Stuart, returned to America to visit his old comrades. He wrote of Welbourne:

> It was a glorious morning when I awoke from a refreshing sleep and walked out of my bedroom upon the veranda, before me a park with fine old trees in which the birds were merrily singing a morning song, and in the distance the blue outline of the Blue Ridge Mountains. Such an old Virginia plantation gives one an impression of most delightful ease and comfort. The house, of which the main building was two stories high and the wings, in one of which I stayed, only one story, was surrounded by a broad veranda, and stood in the midst of handsome old trees with luxurious foliage.

More than one hundred years later, very little has changed. A guest at Welbourne today is immediately struck by a sense of seamless history. Generations of ancestors look down from the walls: Benjamin Dulany of Fairfax County and his beautiful wife, Elizabeth French; their son, John Peyton Dulany, the progenitor of the family in Loudoun County; and his son, Richard Henry Dulany, colonel of the 7th Virginia Cavalry, Confederate States Army. Although filled with priceless memorabilia and antiques, Welbourne survives as a home, still lived in and meant to be enjoyed.

The architectural evolution of Welbourne charts the changing tastes and lifestyles of succeeding generations. In the 1830s, two one-story wings were added and in the 1840s, a long veranda with Italianate columns, two stories high, plain and graceful. A two-story addition to the back was added in the late Victorian era, and dormer windows added in the early part of this century face the driveway. Somehow it all meshes together so the eye sees nothing out of place in the overall structure.

The Dulanys of Welbourne

$\mathcal{O}$f the nine children born to John Peyton and Mary Ann deButts Dulany, only three survived into adulthood. Julia Bladen Dulany (1816-1865) married her first cousin, Samuel Welby deButts (1814-1839). The wedding was held in the parlor at Welbourne, but her father, who opposed the match, refused to attend. Two sons were born, John Peyton deButts (1837-1912) and Samuel Welby deButts, called Welby (1839-1912). Widowed in 1839, Julia married the Rev. Samuel S. Roszell in 1845.

Mary Ann Dulany (1818-1895) married George William Carlyle Whiting (1809-1864), a direct descendant of merchant John Carlyle. Whiting, who was called Carlyle, was beset with business problems. He bought a bank in Washington, D.C., only to have an employee steal most of the money and force him into bankruptcy; he retained only what the Dulanys were able to buy back at public auction. He once owned the Oakley plantation near Upperville, but claimed the soil to be too poor to work. The Whitings lived at Richland in Stafford County, and their support seems always to have been dependent upon the Dulanys.

The only son to survive was Richard Henry Dulany, who was born at Old Welbourne on August 20, 1820. In childhood he was influenced by the religious devotion of his parents, who were devout Methodists. His mother once wrote to him: "[M]y darling and beloved Son neglect not your religious duties—always live and act—knowing and ever bearing in mind this awful recollection, 'Thou God seest me.' To the Christian it is a most delightful thought—that even our motives and thoughts as well as our actions are ever open to His sight." These beliefs Richard Dulany passed on to his own children.

Richard was sent to Dickinson College in Carlisle, Pennsylvania, which at that time was a Methodist school. Yet he proved an indifferent student, and his grades fell to the point that the president of the college, John Price Durbin, notified his father. Richard received this letter from his father, written on January 21, 1839:

> My dear Richard
> On my arrival at Home I found Mr. Durbin's letter with one from you. How deeply I was disappointed and mortified to hear that you would not, for I will not say you could not, sustain yourself in your class; none but a devoted Father can know or

feel—I am confident that if you had studied as I certainly had a right to expect you would, you would not only have done credit to yourself but to your parents also—this letter will be accompanied with one in reply to President Durbin. I have requested him, if he thinks best to supply you with a private tutor, if by that means you will be enabled to keep up with your class. If not, you will have to fall back in the Freshmens. Without an education, my dear Richard, you never can sustain a respectable standing in Society, I have however urged you so frequently on this subject that I feel it needless to say anything more. Let me hear immediately what Mr. Durbin's determination is on this painful subject and whatever it may be I shall expect you will bow with submission. It is now so dark that I cannot see what I have written.

Farewell my dear Richard.

Believe me as ever your devoted father,

John P. Dulany

Detailed school records are unavailable; Richard is listed as a non-graduate of the Dickinson College law school, class of 1842.

Despite his apparent scholastic difficulties, Richard, who enjoyed fox hunting, assembled his own pack of hounds in 1840, at the age of 20. Officially recognized in 1904, just before his death, the Piedmont Hunt is the oldest in America.

In 1840, Julia's three-year-old son, John Peyton deButts, inherited the estate of Millicent Welby Ridghill, the widow of Rev. J. Ridghill of Welbourne Church, England. As the boy had become his grandfather's ward when his father died, John Peyton Dulany was obliged to go to England to settle the estate, which was in litigation for a number of years.

In 1841 Richard joined his father in England. His letters home include his impressions of the Tower of London, the zoological gardens and museum.

In 1847 young Richard followed the Dulany tradition of marrying well. Rebecca Ann Dulany (1828-1858) was the daughter of Colonel Henry Rozier Dulany of Shuter's Hill and Frances Addison Carter of Sabine Hall, making Richard and Rebecca first cousins once removed. Richard would have met Rebecca during family visits to Shuter's Hill. They were married on October 7, 1847, in a ceremony performed by the Rev. J. Merriken of the Methodist Episcopal Church in Alexandria.

Rebecca, at age six, had inherited an immense fortune from Rebecca, Lady Hunter, who was part of the branch of the family that had returned to England after the Revolution. Lady Hunter, the daughter of Ann Dulany and the adventurer de la Serre, had been adopted by her uncle, Daniel Dulany III, when her mother and father were divorced. It has been estimated that her estate exceeded 500,000 pounds, not counting personal property that included more than 5,000 ounces of silver and a diamond ring that had belonged to either the elder or younger Daniel. Her estate was worth $19.5 million in 1995 dollars.

A unique term of the will stipulated that in order to inherit, a female inheritor's husband must take the name of Dulany. Lady Hunter would have been pleased that her heir had actually married a Dulany.

Richard and Rebecca honeymooned in the south, including New Orleans, then travelled north to Philadelphia and as far west as St. Louis. Their first child, Mary Carter Dulany, was born on June 8, 1849. The Dulanys then spent a few years in Europe, living in England, France and Italy. Their second daughter, Frances Addison Carter Dulany, called Fanny, was born on May 15, 1851, in Paris.

Richard's interest in horses and livestock appears in a letter written to his father from England in 1851:

> On Wednesday we shall leave for Windsor and Oxford after which take in the Duke of Richmonds park wh[ich] are said to be the best conducted in England. After the races I shall travel about the country until it is time to go home.

His account books show that he purchased livestock in 1851 and 1852 and shipped them to Welbourne. In an undated letter to his father he wrote:

> The great yearly Cattle, sheep and pig fair is now open here. Upton and I visited it on Thursday. I was much gratified and astonished at the condition and beauty of the stock. I am determined if possible to bring some home with me and would willingly pay Mr. Armistead's expenses for a few weeks in England for the benefit of his judgment, you will please tell him this if he intends coming this summer to the fair.

Dulany and his neighbors formed The Upperville Union Club, with Dulany elected president and his cousin, Richard Welby Carter, the secretary. Interest in the first show, advertised in *The Southern Planter* in 1857, was keen, and there were many entries. The magazine stated, "We have several times urged the farmers of Virginia to form just such a club for the improvement of their various breeds of horses, but so far as we know, this is the first successful attempt at the kind. The object, which the title of this Association sufficiently expresses, is a very laudable one, and no locality offers a fairer field for its accomplishment than the counties of Loudoun and Fauquier." Dulany went to New York to purchase a silver cup from Tiffany's for the trophy, but when Tiffany heard the reason for it, he donated the prize without cost. The Upperville Colt and Horse Show is the oldest continuous horse show in America.

As part of his breeding program, Dulany imported a stallion named Black Hawk in 1856. Scrivington, a four-year-old Cleveland bay with black legs, was bought the same year and advertised at stud the next year in *The Southern Planter*.

In 1858, on August 30th, there occurred the greatest tragedy of Richard Dulany's life, the loss of his wife Rebecca at age thirty, probably from tuberculosis. She had always been delicate, and in his letters from Europe Richard had expressed great concern for her health. Despite this delicacy, she had borne three more children: John Peyton Dulany (Johnny or Jonny) in 1853, Henry Grafton Dulany (Hal) in 1854 and Richard Hunter Dulany (Dick) in 1856. Her obituary was written by her husband:

> She moved in her family circle not only devotedly loved, but admired and respected by all. Loved for her amenity of manner, loved for the Christian charity of her character, and loved for all social excellencies; admired for every external grace, and every female virtue. Nor will the bitter tears of anguish, grief, and loss, be confined to those alone to whom she was by consanguinity united. Hers was a wide field of charity and love. The poor receive her munificence, the orphan found in her a mother, and in her the afflicted ever met one to provide for their temporal comfort, and to direct them in tones of eloquence and love to Him who alone giveth spiritual consolation. Her family mourn, and are not to be comforted, but it should be a consolation (sweet to dwell upon,) that her soul is at peace in the bosom of her Father and her God.

Crushed with grief, he wrote to his brother-in-law, Carlyle Whiting on October 12, 1858:

> I thank you for your kind offer to take charge of one of my children. In regard to my children, until the last few weeks or years ... I had scarcely thought of my responsibility for them;

their mother having so entirely devoted her health and at last
her life to their education and comfort. I feel now when it is too
late, how completely Rebecca was the slave to her children and
what she considered her duties as wife and mistress. Would to
God it were possible for me to live over again the last ten years
of my life. How short sighted, and selfish, the best of us and
never know what we have to enjoy until the time is past never,
never to be recalled. I feel now that my life is of some
importance to my children to watch over them and educate
until they are sufficiently fledged to leave their nest, and then
I pray God I may close my eyes never to open them in this world
again.

Although only thirty-eight years old when his wife died, Richard never
remarried.

The Coming War

$\mathcal{T}$he next two years were momentous ones for the nation, with unfolding
events that included John Brown's raid at Harper's Ferry with his trial
and subsequent execution, the divisive presidential campaign of 1860 and the
election of Abraham Lincoln with the smallest popular vote on record. For more
than forty years the North and South had managed to compromise their political
and social differences. Compromise ended when South Carolina seceded from
the Union on December 20, 1860.

The Dulanys, like many Virginians, were conservative and Unionist in their
sympathies. They had close family connections in Baltimore and Annapolis, and
business ties in England, New York and Boston. Their children went to school
in the North. They were well-traveled and wealthy. Yet above all else they were
Virginians, and her call would determine their fate.

Despite the dilemma posed by his conservative views coupled with his loyalty
to Virginia, Richard Henry Dulany's unfailing determination to fight for the
South's cause was an inspiration to others. He thought it impossible that a united
people whose love of their state brought them home from every quarter could
be defeated. Years after the war, on August 7, 1896, General William H. Payne
penned a letter to Colonel Dulany:

I do not exaggerate when I say that there is no man in the State of Virginia whose splendid generosity and loyal patriotism and gallantry as a soldier I have more respect than I have for you. I well remember when the war began that although you did not think then that it was necessary or inevitable, you plunged instantly into the melee, staking fortune, home and everything upon the result; and you fought to a finish. I recollect very well how you placed your private means at the disposition of your poorer neighbors, mounting, arming and equipping them from your pockets. You have become to me something of an ideal man.

I was always struck not only with your gallantry but with the fact that wound after wound was never used by you as a means of retiring from the conflict, but as soon as you could crawl from a sick bed you were in the saddle again. I have often spoken of you as one who had won and had a right to wear the wreath of a general, and have spoken frequently to Rosser and spoken of him for not having seen that you had the command and title of a brigadier general. I think it doubtful, Colonel, whether you are aware of the high admiration I have for you, but we are both getting old now, and I want you to know it before we cross over the river.

In April 1861, as the national tragedy unfolded, there lived at Welbourne a close-knit but extended family: the patriarch, John Peyton Dulany, age 73; his widowed son, Richard Henry Dulany, age 40; Richard's children: Mary, age 11; Fanny, age 9; John, age 7; Hal, age 6; and Dick, age 4; the Swiss tutor, Mr. C.E. Weidmayer, age 38; the Irish nurse, Miss Margaret Moriarty, age 28; and assorted other relatives: John Peyton Dulany's nieces, Mary Ann Evans, age 60, and Elizabeth "Mittie" D. Herbert, age 37; and his granddaughter, Julia B. Whiting, age 21.

Other family members, servants, neighbors, business acquaintances and military personnel are identified when they appear in the letters. Several genealogical charts in an appendix are provided so the reader may recognize the relationships among the Dulany, deButts, Carter, Whiting and other families who populate these writings. Some family photographs will be found near the middle of this book.

"The ... farmers brought us corn and large buckets of milk and tubs of icewater. These acts of kindness warm our hearts very much toward our people and make us the more anxious to prepare ourselves as soldiers to drive back to their own country the Yankees who wish to oppress us."

Richard H. Dulany, August 1861

1861

he Dulanys were strong Unionists, as were many Virginians. William H. Dulany of Fairfax County was elected as one of two delegates to the state convention on a platform that was moderately Unionist, defeating the secessionist candidate, Alfred Moss.

Along with Loudoun County delegate John Armistead Carter of Crednal, Dulany voted against secession but did, however, declare that he would never consent to purchase peace "at the price of the honor and the interest of Virginia."[1]

Virginia passed an Ordinance of Secession on April 17, 1861, five days after the fall of Fort Sumter. Six weeks later Richard Henry Dulany of Welbourne, ready to protect his home from Northern aggression, wrote to his sister Mary Whiting, who was at Richland, her home in Stafford County, of his military ambition:

William was the son of Daniel French Dulany and a cousin to Richard Dulany of Welbourne.

May 31, 1861, Welbourne

My dear Sister,

John F. Thompson, an overseer
(1860 U.S. Census).

Mary's husband, George William
Carlyle Whiting.

Possibly Alfred B. Anderson (1860
U.S. Census). An A. Anderson
residence is noted near Welbourne
on a Civil War-era map.[2]

His nephew, John Peyton deButts.
Richard Welby Carter, called
Welby, a cousin of Dulany's late
wife, lived at Crednal, across the
road from Welbourne. He was
captain of a militia company
organized prior to November 1859
that became Co. H, 1st Virginia
Cavalry, on detached service with
the legendary Turner Ashby.[3]

Point of Rocks is on the Potomac
River north of Leesburg.

Elizabeth D. "Mittie" Herbert,
Dulany's cousin, lived at
Welbourne. Mr. Weidmayer was
the Swiss tutor. Vaucluse was the
Fairfax County home of
Constance Cary, Mittie's cousin.[4]
Jeffrey Moriarty, age 70, was the
coachman at Welbourne.

Mary's 16-year-old son, Clarence
Carlyle Whiting.

Mr. Thompson leaves in the morning, so I have an opportunity of sending you a few lines.

I received your letter yesterday and was truly glad to hear that you were all well. I hope that as the weather gets warmer Carlyle will improve in health. Mr. Anderson will make no [wheat] cradles and for fear Carlyle may be disappointed I send two of mine and Mr. Thompson thinks he can get one from his brother.

We are all well and are in good spirits as the state of our country admits. All the young men in the neighborhood have joined the army. All the young Carters and John deButts are in Welby Carter's Co. I spent a day and night with them and Ashby's Co. at the Point of Rocks [Maryland] a few days since. The boys had rather hard fare, straw and a blanket being their only bed, but they all seemed to be willing to put up with any thing if they could only get a fair fight with Lincoln's men.

John deButts has the hardest time of any of them as one Sergeant is sick and he does the work of two; he is up all night every other night in the week as he has to post all the sentinels which is done every two hours. He has but little fear if he can get within pistol shot as he is the best shot at the Point.

All our friends are well. Mittie took Mr. Weidmayer to drive her to Vaucluse this morning. A willful woman can be turned when water is taught to run uphill. I am very sorry now that I did not send her down by Jeffries [sic] but really was so surprised at her going that I did not think of it until she had gone.

Clarence is well but very serious to join the army. I do not know what his intentions are as he seems to confide only in himself. I have volunteered to prove to him that the State did not need his services in the ranks and that he stood the same chance of a commission that I did of General Lee's place. I think his idea [was] that by offering himself at [Manassas] Junction he could get a commission.

Tell Carlyle that the military ambition that he saw in me so long ago has at last broken out. I have written permission to raise a company of mounted riflemen which shall equip itself and after being thoroughly trained fight when they can't help it. I want the comp'y to act as a mounted police until the state requires more volunteers. I think we being well mounted stand but little chance of being shot as we shall follow the precedent set by Stafford [County]. I am truly glad to hear that eighteen of her armed men had too much magnanimity to fight six of the Yankees who had come ashore and ran away rather than hurt them.

Give my love to Carlyle, cousin Ellen, Julia, Nina, et al.

Ellen Marr Whiting (1817-1903), sister of G. W. Carlyle Whiting. Julia and Nina are two of Carlyle and Mary's six daughters.

Ever your attached brother
R H Dulany

A few days later Mary Whiting received a second letter from Welbourne, this one from her father, John Peyton Dulany:

3 June '61

My Dear Mary

I would have written by Thompson, but as your Bro. wrote to you I thought it would be better for me to write at some other time.

I sincerely regret to inform you that Clarence has joined Richard Carter's Company. I did every thing that I could to prevent [him] but

Richard Welby Carter of Glen Welby.

without success. He certainly is the most willful Boy I ever met with. Perhaps after all it is best, so [he] will at least learn one lesson, to learn to obey. Richard Carter I am sure will take every care of him.

Richard Henry has applied for a commission and expects to raise a Company of Cavalry. He intends to go today to the Point of Rocks to commence learning to drill. There will be hardly a young man left in this neighbourhood.

I think from the present appearances Genl. Lee intends to move on Washington. If he does not, I fear that the Yankees will take Richmond. If they should, it would be most disastrous to the Southern States, both as to our foreign relations and on the yet undetermined [states] with respect to the course they intend to pursue.

John Quincy Marr, captain of the Warrenton Rifles, was killed in a skirmish at Fairfax Court House June 1, 1861.[5]

There has been a brush near Fairfax above Hearn[don, Virginia] between one Troop of Yankees and one Troop belonging to Prince William County, and by a Company commanded by Capt. Marr who was killed. Our men as usual ran away from a much inferior force. I find they are much better at boasting than fighting.

Rebecca Rogers deButts Pinkney, wife of Capt. Robert F. Pinkney of the U.S. Navy, was a distant relative.

Captain Pinkney and Rebecca left us nearly two weeks ago. I do not think Rebecca can possibly live much longer. She is so much reduced that you would hardly know her.

Mitty Herbert & Mr. Weidmayer started for the District (Alexandria) on Tuesday last. I tried to prevail upon her not to subject herself and Weidmayer to the probability of perhaps insult and indignity, but it was useless, go she would, and I am now anxiously waiting to hear from them.

I heard from your Sister a few days since. She made affectionate inquiries after you. She says she has written frequently to you without receiving an answer. John deButts is very highly spoken of, I have no doubt if he has an opportunity he will distinguish himself. Love to all. When I can visit you without danger of losing my horses, I shall see you, love to all, you are too numerous to mention by name.

The Northern Army have taken possession of Shuter's Hill and have nearly ruined it.

[unsigned]

Mary's sister, Julia Dulany deButts Roszell lived at Wheatland, a farm near Hillsboro, about fifteen miles north of Welbourne.

Shuter's Hill was occupied by John Peyton Dulany's nephew, Henry Rozier Dulany. Once the site of Fort Ellsworth, it is now the Masonic Memorial to George Washington.[6]

Richard Dulany received permission to raise a troop on July 1, 1861. Men from Loudoun and Fauquier counties enlisted at the small hamlet of Union (now Unison), Virginia, on July 24th. Like many Southern units, this one took the name of its commander, although the Dulany Troop was also known as the Loudoun Rangers.

These young men were the sons of Dulany's neighbors; if he did not know them personally, he was well known to them. Amanda Virginia Edmonds of Belle Grove in Fauquier County, when she learned that her brother Sid had joined the Dulany Troop, wrote:

He has a good Captain and an able one. His men will not suffer for want of anything that he can procure. He is a kind hearted and a very moral man. As long as Sid is going I am glad he is a member of his company.[7]

Dulany kept a meticulous record of his company, listing the names alphabetically in a register and recording the exact cost of everything: horses, blankets, pots and pans—even a quid of tobacco for each man.

On Thursday, July 25, 1861, the Dulany Troop began its march to Ashland, Virginia, about fifteen miles north of Richmond, where a camp of instruction had been established. It took four and a half days for the new recruits to march the 125 miles, and near Fredericksburg, Dulany became temporarily separated from his command. His men joked about "Dulany's lost company."[8]

In a letter to his daughter Fanny, postmarked August 5, 1861, Dulany gives some details of the company's first march, but there is no mention of the mishap:

Cavalry Camp, Ashland, Va.

My dear Fanny

I received your most welcome and well written letter on Friday evening, I had been so constantly occupied since that time, that I have been unable to write to you until this morning—this being the only day (Sunday) in the week in which we have no drill.

After I left on Thursday we marched within two miles of Warrenton and encamped for the night. I had then to see that all the men cleaned and fastened and fed their horses properly, after which we took our supper, some of the men sitting on a log others on the grass and officers at a table.

At nine o'clock Mr. Gibson, our first Sergeant, placed a guard of two men over the horses to see that none of them got loose or were taken away. The guard was composed of two men, each having a loaded gun, and after they had walked for two hours up and down the long line of horses they were relieved by two other men who performed the same duty until they were relieved after having been on guard for two hours. In this way our horses and

Bruce Gibson, from Upperville, would be promoted captain in the 6th Virginia Cavalry and captured at the battle of Yellow Tavern on May 11, 1864. He was one of the "Immortal Six Hundred," Confederate prisoners used by the Union as a human shield in their defense of Morris Island, in Charleston Harbor, S.C.[9]

wagons were kept safely every night during our march.

We got here in four and a half days. On the way we were treated very kindly by the people. Some of them would give us food night and morning for all our horses (79) and supper and breakfast for all the men and then refuse to take any pay.

The first day we halted for dinner near Salem. The farmers brought us corn and large buckets of milk and tubs of ice water. These acts of kindness warm our hearts very much toward our people and make us the more anxious to prepare ourselves as soldiers to drive back to their own country the Yankees who wish to oppress us.

Salem is now called Marshall, Virginia.

Take your map and ask Mr. Weidmayer to show you which are the Northern and which [are] the Southern States and to point out to you the place where the battle was fought two weeks ago and where our Merciful and Kind Father in Heaven gave us the victory over our enemies. It is now said by the Northern papers that their loss was ten thousand. Ask Cousin Mittie to show you the short accounts of the battles in the newspapers and try and recollect the names of the principal officers and the battle fields.

First Manassas (Bull Run), July 21, 1861.

When we arrived here the officers gave me a large shed for our quarters; the men have a blanket each and some straw to lay upon. Your Uncle Hal sleeps in his hammock and your Cousin Robert and I have a place about as large as two stalls in Grand Pa's stable boarded off from the other quarters, with a dirt floor with a few planks for our bedstead and straw for our bed and one blanket to cover us. I gave my blanket to one of the boys who had none.

Uncle Hal is Henry Grafton Dulany of Oakley, near Upperville, Dulany's late wife's brother. Cousin Robert Carter, a lieutenant of Co. A, 6th Virginia Cavalry, would later be promoted to captain and serve as quartermaster.[10]

I must now close my letter as I wish to go

Mary, Jonny, Hal and Dick were Dulany's other children. His elderly, widowed cousin, Mary Ann Evans, lived at Welbourne.

to church. Give much love to Grand Papa to Mary, Jonny, Hal, Dick and Mr. Weidmayer, Cousin Mittie and Cousin Mary. Also to the servants. Try my darling child to be obedient to Cousin Mittie and your Grand Papa, as well as to Mr. Weidmayer. Be careful about your dress, your teeth and nails and never forget to read your Bible and to pray earnestly for your father as well as yourself, for unless we are *sincere Christians* and *strive* to do duty, every blessing that we receive in this life will but render us the more miserable in the next. That a good God may bless and keep you is the sincere prayer of your devoted father

R.H. Dulany

Richard H. Dulany to his daughter, Mary:

Ashland Cavalry Camp. Aug. 10th 1861

My darling Child

I received your very welcome letter yesterday and was truly glad to learn that you were all well at Welbourne. Fanny wrote me that you had holiday for this month. Let me know how you spend your time, do you often go to see your Aunt Ida, or Cousin Eliza or Cousin Sue? Let me know where Mr. Weidmayer is, and if you ever ride together on horseback? I want you to ride on Kate at least three times a week and if a long ride tires you, take short ones. I hope you take great care of your teeth and practice your music regularly. If your Aunt Ida or your Grandfather comes to Ashland I want Fan and you to come too, and bring your side saddle and riding dress with you. Your saddle could be fastened to your trunk.

Aunt Ida is Mary Eliza (Powell) Dulany of Oakley, Uncle Hal's wife. Cousin Eliza is the wife of Robert Carter. Cousin Sue is Sue (Grayson) Hall, wife of Henry Arthur Hall, the son of Edward Hall and Louisa French Dulany.

I saw from a letter from your Aunt Ida that there had been some foolish report about my horse having thrown and hurt me. You must never believe anything you hear about me unless I write to you myself. I have never had better health in my life; my time is fully occupied and I eat three hearty meals every day. We still board at the Hotel as I have not been able to commence housekeeping in the little tent I have put up. I went to Richmond the other day and bought six pretty white cups and saucers, as many knives and forks and plates, some dishes, a coffee and tea pot, but have no coffee yet to put in my pot, and no tea kettle to boil the water for my tea, but by the time you come to see me I will have everything ready, and you shall make my tea for me as you did at home. Mr. Ingram the tavern keeper says he hopes we will soon commence house keeping as your Uncle Hal and cousin eat up all his profits.

There are a good many ladies here from Richmond but I have no time to make acquaintances. If I could have your Grand Papa and my little ones tonight I would not care to know another person.

I am sitting on a camp stool, with a piece of plank on my knees for a desk and by me is my bed of straw upon which your Cousin Robert has been sleeping soundly for the last two hours.

I cannot go to bed until two o'clock as I shall have to take a guard of three men after or about one o'clock and see that all the sentinels are at their posts and know their duty. One young man was caught asleep the other night at his post, and the next day he was tried and condemned to be placed in the guard house or jail for thirty days and not to go out except to do some hard work. On yesterday two of my men were tried for drunkenness and were condemned to twenty

Charles W. Field, colonel of the 6th Virginia Cavalry. He would rise to major general and have command of John Bell Hood's old division when it surrendered at Appomattox.[11]

Nancy Jackson was the children's nurse or "mammy," and John was her husband. They were slaves. [12] Dulany consistently spells his son's name Jonny.

John Haley, age fifty, was an overseer (1860 U.S. Census). Garner Peters was a slave. One of Dulany's prize horses, Scrivington, was sent north in the care of Peters when the war began. He brought the horse safely back to Welbourne in 1865.

days imprisonment and hard labour. The other men give me but little trouble.

Col. Field came to see us this evening and said that I had the best drilled men that had ever been here, for the time they had been taught. He then took them to drill them himself. Being behind the company, he ordered them to gallop, when they all went so fast that the Col. could not keep up with them and the horses' feet made so much noise that they (the men) could not hear the command to halt. The Col. then ordered me to take command myself as the Company had run away from him.

Tell your Grandpapa that watermelons are now in season. There are two large ones lying by me now, I wish your Grandpapa had [them].

Tell Nancy that John is well. Give a good deal of love to your Grandfather and ask him to write to me. Tell Jonny, Hal and Richard that if they love their father they will be good and obedient boys for my sake.

Fan and you will I know try hard and do what you think to be right, and what I would have you to do if I were at home. Remember me to Cousin Mittie and Cousin William [Herbert] and cousin Mary also to Mr. Weidmayer, Mr. Haley, and all the servants. Have you heard anything of Garner?

I must now stop or you will get tired of reading, so good night my dear child and never forget to pray for your devoted father

R.H. Dulany

P.S. Bring me two pair of white pants and my new white coat if you come.

While Captain Dulany was with his company at Ashland, he was visited by his daughters Mary and Fanny. They were accompanied by their Aunt Ida, who reported that they came by rail, arriving on August 24th. They stayed at the hotel for a week, where they played the piano for the enjoyment of the guests and soldiers. They also went on long rides with their father and watched the company drill.

On September 12, 1861, Special Order No. 276 was issued, officially designating the Dulany Troop as Company A, 6th Virginia Cavalry, under the command of Charles W. Field. Hal Dulany was a lieutenant in Company A. The unit was ordered to Manassas almost immediately.[13]

Richard H. Dulany to his father:

Richmond, 12 Sept. 1861

My dear Father

I have some wheat at the Rectortown Station [on the Manassas Gap Railroad] which I would like to have sent to Clifton to be ground as it is being destroyed by the rats. The sooner it is moved the better.

Please ask William to have as many sheep brought from the mountain as can be grazed at Millsville. I have just been attached to the 6th Regt. Col. Field commanding. I suppose we shall go to Manassas next week.

I sent the check to Donaldson to pay [for] the rams he purchased.

When you write please let me know how everything looks on the farm. I would get a letter at Ashland written in the next four days.

The men seem much gratified at the prospect of going to Manassas.

As ever your devoted son
R.H. Dulany

Clifton, on modern Va. 623, was owned by Elizabeth Grayson Lewis Carter and farmed by her step-nephew, Joseph Lewis. A mill was located there on Pantherskin Creek.

Dulany had land at Millsville, a settlement on Goose Creek about two miles east of Welbourne. It no longer exists.

Andrew Donaldson is listed as an agent for Dulany on a number of requisitions for supplies and fodder.[14]

Nine days later Richard wrote to his sister, Mary Whiting, who was at home in Stafford County:

Ashland, Sep 21st 1861

My dear Sister

I am ordered to leave here on Tuesday the 24th for Fairfax Court House. We have eighty-five revolvers, the same number of carbines and some twenty swords. I have been drilling my compy. here since the 27th of July and find the men, having learned about as much as I can teach them, begin to lose interest in their drill and require more excitement.

The only trouble I have had has been caused by whiskey, but I find that prompt and severe punishment has a happy effect on all the men. I confined two men for drunkenness a few days after my arrival here and although one of them had been half drunk for six mo. before he joined our company, he has been perfectly sober for two weeks and says he shall drink no more. I hope the poor fellow will have the firmness to keep his resolve. He came to me some days ago to get a pr. of gloves as his hands had been very much blistered, he never having done as much work before in all his life.

Cassius and Bladen are with me and give me more anxiety than all the rest of my Company. They are both very fond of drink, and I have had Cassius confined for the last week. I find it hard to punish him; he is so perfectly amiable and unselfish in all other respects. Several of the men have asked for his release and I even find it hard to keep the surgeon from giving him drink when he suffers for it, he has made himself so popular by his good nature. I ordered the surgeon this morning to send Cassius from the hospital to

Brothers Cassius C. and Bladen T. Dulany, Richard's cousins, joined his troop on July 24, 1861. Cassius provided J.R.H. Deakins as a substitute that fall. Applying for amnesty after the war, he wrote, "Since [1861] I have remained quietly upon my farms & have had no participation either directly or indirectly in the rebellion." Bladen provided William Nightingale as a substitute.15

the guard house as he was not sick enough to remain in hospital. When he wished to carry out the order the sick sent me word please not to take him away as he was the only one who cared to nurse them. Is it not a pity that such a man should be willing to throw himself away? Make your young sons obey you cost what it may or you may have, as we all may, something of the same in our families. Entire indulgence has ruined more than this cruel war will destroy for Virginia.

I suppose you have heard of the death of Robert Armistead who was shot at Springfield, Mo., and yesterday the body of poor Augustine Washington was brought to Richmond from western Va. I have tried to feel no hatred or revenge towards the Northern people and really do not at this time, but it must be because I can not realize the death of my best friends by their murderous hands. God help me to do my duty and not let me mistake mere apathy for the desire to do no murder. I sometimes think that every northern soldier who puts his foot on our soil justly forfeits his life, but then to be one of the instruments of their destruction is far from being a pleasant thought.

I would like to write you a full sheet this evening but the drill bugle will soon sound and beside my Company's duties I have the entire charge of this Post, Col. Field having gone to take command of his regmt.

If I can possibly call on Wednesday for an hour, I shall do so on my way to Fairfax. With much love to all I am as ever your devoted brother

R.H. Dulany

[P.S.] The bugle has sounded.

The battle of Wilson's Creek, also known as Springfield, Missouri, August 10, 1861.

Lt. Col. John Augustine Washington, assistant adjutant general on Gen. Robert E. Lee's staff, was killed near Cheat Mountain, W.Va., September 13, 1861.[16] His home, Waveland, was in Fauquier County, near Salem.

Letter of Capt. Dulany to his daughter Mary:

Near Centreville, named for
Virginia's wartime governor, John
Letcher.

Camp Letcher, Oct. 24, 1861

My dear Mary,

This letter must answer both yours and my dear little Fan's as I have not time to write to both of you. Give a great deal of love to John, Hal, and Dick. Encourage them to talk of me every day, expecially when they get into a bad humor as we are all liable to do sometimes. Tell them how very anxious I am that they should love each other tenderly and never quarrel or tease each other.

I hope both Fan and you practice your music at regular hours. It is better to practice every day one hour, say from eight to nine o'clock, than two hours if done just as you may happen to feel like it. John must practice a half hour daily with you and you must not get out of patience if he does not learn as fast as you think he ought. I would rather he should not learn at all unless you teach him at the same hour every day.

Give my love to Cousin Mittie and thank her for the clothes she sent me. Tell her that I should like to have a pair of pants made of the cloth purchased for the servants as I have often to sleep in my clothes on the ground. Let them be "reinforced," that is lined on the legs next to the saddle. Mr. Weidmayer knows how it should be done.

Remember me kindly to Mr. Weidmayer and try hard to learn as he wishes to teach you. I want you all to speak French at the table. Tell your cousin Julia she must help you to remember this. Give her my love and say that I should like to have a long letter from her after your taking a ride together all over the farm and seeing every horse, colt, calf, and pig on the place.

I have been in camp for two days and my turn comes in the morning to take my company out, to what is called our outer lines, to watch that the enemy may not march upon our army at night or any other time without our Generals knowing it and taking our army unawares.

One of my men shot himself the other day through his foot. His father came after him today and took him home. He was one of my best men and I am very sorry to lose him. He said when he was leaving that I must not take his name off my roll as he hoped soon to be well and back again to join me.

The accident victim was Thomas Arthur Carter, who enlisted in the Dulany Troop on July 24, 1861. The incident occurred on October 21, 1861.[17]

When we go on picket I place from two to four men on every hill that overlooks the roads leading from the enemy. One of these men sits on his horse for two hours and one watches by his horse but on the ground because he can hear any noise better standing on the ground. The other two rest for two hours and then relieve the two who have been watching. At night I visit them and then post them below the hill because they can then see better if anyone comes over the hills. They stop every man, and unless they can give our signals they are kept until we are relieved by another company, when we take them to be tried by our Colonel. Almost every night we catch someone.

We were all very glad to hear of the victory of our forces at or near Leesburg. The prisoners, some six hundred, were brought to Mancira [?] on their way south. Were any of our friends killed or wounded? We have sent large reinforcemenets to Genl. Evans, who commands our army near Leesburg.

The battle of Balls Bluff, October 21, 1861.

General Nathan "Shanks" Evans

We have some beautiful views of the army near our camp. When I am looking where the beautiful white tents covering hill and valley and the many regiments parading with their glistening arms, I wish that your cousin Julia and you could be with me, as I know how much you would enjoy it.

I fear I have written too much, so will close with the hope that you attend to all your duties both in regard to your person and mind, that I would have you do if with you, never forgetting to pray for your father night and morning that he may soon be returned to you in health and happiness.

With much love to my dear Father and all our household, I am your fondly attached father,

R.H. Dulany

[P.S.] Go see your cousin Ellen and pay her what attention you can.

Due to illness, Captain Dulany received a furlough from the camp at Centreville dated December 24, 1861, and spent the Christmas holidays with his family at Welbourne.[18]

"Lamented Ashby was our Bayard—His mantle is said to have fallen upon you, both of character and position. May Heaven bless and protect you is the prayer of a ~~little~~*
                              Little Rebel"*

Written upon Richard H. Dulany's
appointment to the 7th Virginia Cavalry,
C.S.A., in 1862, by one of his daughters

1862

As the winds of war blew across the South that winter, domestic activities continued, for the moment, almost as usual.

Letter of Julia B. Whiting, who was staying at Welbourne, to her mother, Mary Whiting at their home, Richland, in Stafford County:

Saturday Jan. 18th. [1862]

Dear Mama,

I have just received your letter and am glad to hear that Father and the children are well. I have had a very bad cold for some time and for a few days was confined to my room. I am getting over its effects now and hope that I shall start to school quite well. You could not think that I should go to school without seeing you all at home. Uncle Richard dismissed old Jeffrey and the new driver has not yet arrived; as soon as he makes his appearance I shall set out that I may spend a week with you. The

Merino is a woven or knitted fabric that takes its name from the merino sheep, noted for its fine wool.

Mr. Lefebore ran a school in Richmond.

Two Walker Armisteads joined Co. A, 6th Virginia Cavalry: Gen. Lewis A. Armistead's brother, Walker K., Jr., enlisted on September 15, 1861; the general's son, Walker K., enlisted on May 1, 1862.[1]

The elder Walker's niece, Frances Addison Carter, married Henry Rozier Dulany. Their daughter, Rebecca Ann, was Richard Dulany's late wife.

great difficulty we have in procuring every thing has delayed me a good deal with my work.

I have not been able to get sewing silk to make up my dress. I have just finished my night gown and have put my clothes in good repair. I am much obliged to you for the merino dress and also for your kindness about money for my expenses. Grandpapa insists upon paying my expenses himself at school and the $60 you sent will I am sure be quite sufficient for my wardrobe this year, and my other expenses.

Mr. Wiedmayer wishes to purchase Alice Gray. If Father has not sold her I should prefer his having her to any one else, as he always takes excellent care of his horse. He mentioned $150 as her value and Grandpapa says that at the rate horses are selling here, she is worth it. I have just had a letter from Mr. Lefebore; the expenses for the half session amount to $195.

Walker Armistead came from camp this week bring a letter from Uncle R. who was quite well. He had not yet gone into his cabin as the tent was still comfortable. As we have no one to attend to the horses we can go neither in the carriage nor on horseback, and I can give you no news. I should think it would be very unsafe for you to remain at Richland while the Yankees continue to make such attacks. It is a wonder you have all escaped so well. Clarence rode out this morning to find a wagon for the overseer. He was here a few days since and seemed very anxious to get rid of his bargain.

The children are all well, and have grown a good deal, particularly John. I do not think the girls have grown as much as Mary & Alice [Whiting]. As for their studies, there is a great difference between them and the advantage is

on the boys' side. John and Hal write very well
for little fellows they are obliged to write every
week to their papa which is a great advantage
to them. They both read remarkably well
French as well as English, and translate with
ease. Of course Mr. Wiedmayer accustoms
them to speak it. John is also coming on very
well with his music. The children are all
obliged to read every night from the time the
candles are brought in. Mary reads history, the
boys and Fan story books. I think this would
be a good plan for the children at home. Mary
has read history with me ever since I came up.
She has just completed Tyler's ... [End of letter
missing.]

Portion of another letter of Julia's:

The other day John was reading about
David and when he came to the part about
killing Goliath he stopped and asked how it
was possible for David to do it when he had
never been drilled. Wasn't that a funny idea.
I send a list of the lessons the children here
learn as you may like to see them; the first are
the girl's lessons.

Mon. & Wed.: Fasquelle's Gram. & exer.,
French reading, Spelling, Arithmetic,
Drawing, Grammar; Tues. & Thurs.:
Surennes French Manual, French Poetry,
Geography, Italian, History, Dictation; Friday:
Composition, Writing & Drawing, Reading.

The boys—Mon. & Wed., Surennes
Manual, French reading, Writing & Spelling,
English reading; Tues. & Thurs.: Surennes
manual, French reading, geography,
Arithmetic, Writing; Friday: Composition,
French, Reading, Spelling.

I should like to know what lessons the girls

are learning.

Richard Dulany Whiting is Julia's
brother.

Kiss Richard and the boys for me and give my love to all. Ask Mama to send you up soon.

Your affectionate
Sister

In the winter of 1861-62, Joseph E. Johnston's army settled into winter quarters near Centreville, Virginia, where Captain Dulany wrote the following letter to his father.

Named for Maj. Gen. Gustavus
W. Smith.

Camp Smith, Feb. 4th. 1862

My dear Father,

Michael Moriarty (17), a hostler, may have been the son of the retired coachman. Margaret Moriaty was the children's nurse. (1860 U.S. Census)

I have your letter by John. I gave Michl. permission to spend one day in camp on account of the rain. I settled the accounts of his father, Margaret and himself.

The account of sales of my cattle I do not understand. The cattle sold for upwards of $90 each which would bring $8820. Darby accounts for but $7550. After you deduct the amount due to yourself please send Haley to

There were three Pancoasts in Loudoun County at the time; a J. Pancoast lived near Welbourne.[2]

Pancoast for Carter's two notes which are secured by a deed of trust on Millsville. I want the notes paid and the trust raised from the land. I think the notes are for some fifteen hundred dollars. Tell Haley if Pancoast refuses to take the money that I will have it placed to his credit in one of the banks and sue for the notes.

I am very glad to hear the children and you continue in such good health and the servants are recovering. A large number of my men are sick with severe colds. We had a very cold ride of some thirty miles yesterday with the snow and sleet driving in our faces from 1/2 past 8 o'clock until about 10 after one o'clock.

General [Jeb] Stuart had asked the Captains of our Regiment frequently to try and find out if the enemy were building a bridge across the Accotink but would give them no order to go and see for themselves. The report would come in by one captain that the Yankee pickets were on this side of the bridge and that the cars were running it, the next company out would inform the General that they had learned from the Irish neighbourhood that the bridge was not being rebuilt although pickets or videttes were placed there.

Accotink Creek in Fairfax County.

On Sunday morning the General asked me again if I could find anything about the bridge, evidently expecting it to be rebuilt. I told him that if he would give the order I would go and see, so on Monday I went with twenty five of my men. We went by Mr. George Burke's and getting below the bridge came up to it along the railroad. As I had expected, the storm had driven all the Yankees to the shelter of their huts and we did not even find a lonely vidette.

George Burke, brother of Silas Burke for whom Burke's Station on the Orange and Alexandria Railroad was named.[3]

The bridge had been burnt at one end some fifteen feet and about five on the other and some of [the] large timbers sawn in two. I tried to burn the remaining portion but it snowed too fast. The men were much disappointed in having seen no Yankees after five hours ride with mud from ten to fifteen inches deep, those with bearded faces looking like old Father Winter and his oldest sons.

I got to Centreville just at dark and found the General at dinner—he would receive no report from me until I had dined and as his dinner put us both in a very good humour I enjoyed an hour, with good cheer and a warm fire very much.

The Grigsby House at
Centreville.[4]

Gen. P.G.T. Beauregard
commanded the right wing at the
battle of First Manassas, July 21,
1861.[5]

Lt. George E. Plaster, Co. A, 6th
Virginia Cavalry.

I find Generals Johnston (who lives in the
same house) and Stuart much alike in one
particular: when at leisure very pleasant
gentlemen but on duty as short and snappish
as possible. I suppose you have Johnston's and
Beauregard's reports. I much prefer the
former. He writes like a soldier and gives us
confidence in reading his words. The more I
see of him the more I appreciate him. Lieut.
Plaster lost a very valuable horse last
night—some one struck him with a spear just
behind the right foreleg and killed him almost
immediately; the horse was one of the best in
the regiment.

With much love to all at home, I am very
sincerely

Your devoted son
R.H. Dulany

P.S. I do not recollect the exact amount due
Sister Julia, but please pay her $500 on
account of coupons.

R.H.D.

Richard H. Dulany to his sister, Mary Whiting:

Camp Smith Feb 11th 1862

My dear Sister

You can hardly imagine how much
pleasure it would give to see Carlyle since he
is upon his feet again. I hope he can with his
returning health get rid entirely of that little
imp "discontent." I do not know what would
delight me as much as to be with you for a week
or two and listening to his plans of
improvement [and] to see them being carried
out each day of my visit. If ever I saw a man
who was born farmer, it is Carlyle. He has my
fervent prayers for his speedy and entire

restoration in health and happiness.

When I was with you did I give you a statement of the amount I hold for you? Let me know immediately as I am anxious to settle all my business affairs, so that should our Master shorten my life, there may be but little trouble in arranging my papers. Ask Carlyle to send me a statement of our accounts. I will send him a check on [R.H.] Maury in Richmond in full of our settlement. How would you like the amount due you invested? I send you a check for one hundred and fifty dollars. Do you want more? I will write again shortly as soon as I get a letter from you. With much love to Carlyle, Cousin Ellen, Nina and the children, I am as ever your devoted brother

R.H. Dulany

Maury is a banker.

Mary McIntyre Eliason Mason sent the following letter to Mary Whiting, in part to assure her that her son, Clarence, had been seen recently and was well:

Fredericksburg, March 26th [1862]

My dear Mrs. Whiting

I promised Clarence this morning when he left us, that I would certainly try to send you a letter by a safe hand to tell you how well and bright he looked after his fortnight's campaign (I believe it has been that long since he left Welbourne—perhaps longer). Rutty and himself came down on Monday as an escort to Col. Harrison, the Lt. Col. of their Regiment. I am afraid to tell you *where* they came from, as I may after all have to trust this to the Mail, and there may be Yankees dodging about in Stafford yet.

Both the boys looked the picture of health and did not seem to feel the slightest fatigue

Rutledge "Rutty" Eliason, Mary's brother, enlisted in the Dulany Troop, July 24, 1861. He later was on detached service with Stuart.

Lt. Col. Julien Harrison (1827-77) would be promoted to colonel of the 6th Virginia Cavalry. He resigned briefly for medical reasons, returned to his regiment and was wounded at Brandy Station on October 11, 1863.[6]

from their long ride. Clarence was evidently
very anxious to push on into Stafford but his
leave did not give him time and I tried to
console him by telling him you would not want
him to come if it was at any personal risk.
Neither of them had much to repay them for
the trip, though Clarence was highly delighted
at the acquisition of a pair of handsome boots.

Clarence presented altogether a highly
respectable appearance, but Rutty was very
much annoyed at having to meet ladies after
having been separated from his baggage and
sleeping without a tent for three weeks.

Clarence reported all well at Welbourne
and his Uncle [Richard Dulany] safe and
sound in Camp—& went off better satisfied
himself after seeing Mrs. Ned Waller & Dr.
Spence, who gave him much later news from
you than I could.

I have always regretted not seeing more of
you since you have been at Richland. Now
that Mr. Whiting's health is so much better,
can't you both come & make us a visit? And
also Miss Ellen [Whiting]. I would give
something pretty to see her. I think you are all
the bravest people I ever knew, to stand there
as a mark for the enemy's shot & shell!

We have bad news from Winchester
today—but hope the "silver lining to the
cloud" may peep out tomorrow. Mother is still
in Upperville so you may know I am not in the
very best of spirits in the world. I am afraid the
Federals will find that neighborhood more
attractive than Stafford.

Mr. Collins says he always told them if they
would invite *Gen. Sickles* over to take a look at
the country about Evansport, he wouldn't
want to go any farther. It was quite a pleasant
surprise to us to hear that they had withdrawn

On March 11, 1862, Stonewall
Jackson evacuated Winchester,
marching southward.[7]

Her mother, Mary Carter Eliason,
aunt of Rebecca Ann Dulany, was
the younger sister of John
Armistead Carter.

Brig. Gen. Daniel E. Sickles, U.S.A.

Evansport was on the Potomac,
where the Quantico Marine Base
is today.

into our own lines.

The last three days have brought more than one pleasant surprise. Yesterday Web made his appearance as Aide to General Smith—& then came Hal [Dulany] on recruiting service—But I must not gossip any more for fear saying anything I ought not to say. I am terribly patriotic—& would be very loath to us this dangerous weapon of ones (the tongue) to the injury of my Country or of those I love so dearly.

Mr. Whiting had better change his mind & bring you all within our lines while he can. My kindest regards to Miss Ellen & himself. If I can ever oblige you by shopping for you, sending any thing to Julia or in any way, you must let me know, & believe me very affectionately yours

Mary M.M.

Richard Welby "Web" Carter's company acted as escort to General Gustavus W. Smith.[8]

In March 1862, nine companies of the 28th Pennsylvania Infantry under Colonel John W. Geary occupied Loudoun County. They reached Upperville on March 15th and, in scouting the area, captured an officer and a number of privates of the 6th Virginia Cavalry.[9]

John Peyton Dulany, in the following statement, which survives only in part, gives a vivid description of the actions of the federal troops who paid several visits to Welbourne. Dulany consistently misspelled the colonel's name as Gary; the spelling has been corrected below.

Statement

I, John Peyton Dulany of the county of Loudoun in the State of Virginia, make the following statement which I wish to be considered as if made upon oath. I am upwards of seventy years of age, and have lived in the county of Loudoun for the last forty years. My family now consists of five grandchildren, the oldest twelve years old, their teacher, Mr. Weidmayer, a citizen of Switzerland, two nieces, Miss Herbert and Mrs. Evans, and the servants.

I have an only son, Richard Henry Dulany, who is forty years old and is now with the Confederate Army. I have never in any way taken part in the present war, never in any way approved of secession and did not vote for the secession of the State of Virginia.

About the last of March, Col. Geary of the United States army occupied the town of Upperville with his command (about four miles from my residence).

A short time after my house was surrounded about twelve o'clock at night by a body of armed soldiers. I suppose some thirty or forty. I got out of bed, went to the door and asked what was wanted; one of the persons spoke and announced himself as Captain Gallier of Col. Geary's command, sent to search my home for my son Richard H. Dulany. I assured him my son was not in the house or so far as I had any reason to believe in the neighbourhood. He expressed his regret notwithstanding my assurance at having to search the house, but he must obey orders. I told him certainly, I knew that.

Captain Gallier then came in, and went through the house. I am glad to state that throughout Capt. Gallier behaved like a gentleman and an officer. I offered to have some supper prepared for him and his men, he said the men would like something to eat, which was accordingly prepared for them.

On or about the sixteenth of April, Col. Geary having removed his camp as I am told to Rectortown about seven or eight miles from my house, another armed party of soldiers came to my house with two officers, who announced themselves as Capt. McCabe [and] Lieutenant Laws, that they were acting under the orders of Col. Geary, and came to take horses. I asked to see their authority; they would not show any but said if I chose I could go and see Col. Geary and ask him.

They then went to the stables, took my riding mare, a very valuable animal and my two carriage horses that cost me seven hundred dollars; returned to the house and talked a good deal. On their leaving I told them I protested against their taking my property and that I considered it robbery. On leaving the farm the carriages horses got away from the men and returned.

On or about the twenty fourth of April Capt. McCabe and Lieut. Laws with another officer, who I was told was a Major in Col. Geary's command (but whose name I have forgotten) came again to my house with an armed force. Capt. McCabe, however, seemed to act as if in command, stationed a guard around the house, commanding that no one should leave it. He and the Lieutenant and Major went to the stables and servants' house and again took my two carriage horses and carriage harness. As Captain McCabe rode off he said he would visit me again.

On or about the twenty eighth of April Capt. McCabe and Lieut. Laws came to my house with an armed body of soldiers, stationed a guard around the house, placed me and the teacher, Mr. Wiedmayer, the only two white male adults about the house, under

Capt. George F. McCabe was mustered into service August 17, 1861, and commanded Co. O, 28th Pennsylvania Infantry. He was transferred to Co. B, 147th Pennsylvania Infantry, on October 28, 1862. Lt. Peter F. Laws, Co. C, 28th Pennsylvania Infantry, was mustered into service July 3, 1861, in Philadelphia. He was promoted to captain July 1, 1862, and was killed at Sharpsburg, September 17, 1862.[10]

The nameless major most likely is Ario Pardee, Jr., enlisted on June 28, 1861, and promoted to major on November 1, 1861, before becoming lieutenant colonel of the 147th Pennsylvania Infantry, October 9, 1862.[11]

arrest; went to my store room, broke open the lock, took out nearly all the tea, coffee, sugar, wine, whiskey, etc., that I had for my family's use, and when approached by my niece, Miss Herbert, and told that the key for the store room would be sent for if wanted, Capt. McCabe in a most insolent manner told her he would not wait for the key and broke the lock.

Capt. McCabe and Lieut. Laws then went upstairs and as I am informed by Miss Herbert and Mrs. Evans and verily believe, searched the rooms upstairs to the garret, opening trunks and wardrobes, where there was nothing but clothes and ladies dresses, and when requested by Miss Herbert not to open a particular trunk, she telling them it contained nothing but some articles and clothes, which had belonged to Mrs. Dulany before her death, they refused her request, opened the trunk and scattered the contents about.

During the whole of this scene, I am assured by my niece Miss Herbert, Capt. McCabe's language and gestures were most insolent and threatening to her; at one time telling her she should be arrested and sent to Washington, at another time crying out to the man below to fire the house, etc.

Capt. McCabe went to my gardener (who is a white man), and I am told by him and verily believe, cursed and abused him with my servants, drew his sword, threatening if he did not tell him where I had put my bacon he would cut his head off. He then had the house where I had put the bacon broken open, took what he wanted, I do not know how much, but a large quantity, not leaving me enough for my family's use, and then ordered dinner for his men.

He called them into my dining room where the men dined, after which they left, Capt.

McCabe taking with them in a wagon and horsecart my bacon, four of five demi-johns of whiskey, a trunk with the clothes of one of my granddaughters, a gold snuff box, a silver tumbler and the keys of the wardrobes and rooms up stairs. During this scene Lieutenant Laws commanded me to give up my letters and private correspondence, I told him that I had none, but if I had I would not give them.

Julia B. Whiting later noted: "This is all of my Grandfather's statement that I have found among my Mother's papers."

Attached is the following list of items, apparently stolen, written in pencil on the statement:

Madeira wine
1/2 barrel of whiskey
1/2 barrel of brown sugar
6 loaves white sugar
2 chests of tea
3 saddles
2 bridles
1 silver spoon
3 silver handled knives
2 guns
3 horses

With the Confederates under Stonewall Jackson becoming active in the Shenandoah Valley, Geary's command left Loudoun County.

On April 29th Amanda Edmonds received a letter from her brother Sid, who was with the Dulany Troop, wherein he repeated a rumor that Dulany had been offered the rank of lieutenant colonel in Ashby's command. Dulany's company, attached to Ashby's command, was at Flint Hill in Rappahannock County. On May 18, 1862,

Markham and Linden are in western Fauquier County, along modern I-66.

Miss Edmonds wrote in her diary:

Several [of the Yankees] were near there killing Dulany's sheep (commissary stock) when he surprised them and took fifteen and an officer with two trunks containing six hundred dollars in gold, captured two wagons and killed two Yanks. Those that were left were double quicked down the railroad. For revenge they have arrested every man between Markham and Linden and say they are going to drive off the women and children. O! What cruelty! Bravo to the gallant Dulany troop. It is said there were five hundred of them but we can only rely on say so.[12]

On May 15th, several companies of the 6th Virginia Cavalry, including Dulany's, set a trap for troops of Company O, 28th Pennsylvania Infantry, at Linden Station on the Manassas Gap Railroad. The Official Records contain a report from General Geary to Edward M. Stanton, Secretary of War, written at Rectortown on May 16.[13] In part it says:

... A company of infantry of my command was yesterday ordered to Linden, to remain stationed there. A detachment of 17 men, guarding the company wagon, reached there a short time before the main body of the company, which was on the train. They were attacked by a body of cavalry, variously estimated from 300 to 600, coming upon them from four directions. Our men resisted them keeping up a sharp fire under shelter of the depot, which was riddled with bullets. My men were overpowered; 1 was killed and 14 taken prisoners, 3 of whom were wounded. When the balance of the company came up the enemy hastily retired under fire, and with some loss.

*Lieutenant Joseph A. Moore of the 28th
Pennsylvania Infantry reported on May 16th that
among the captives was Charles Murphy, the
Negro servant of the Capt. George McCabe in
John Peyton Dulany's complaint.*

He reports that the rebel cavalry numbered

500 or 600 armed with Minié rifles and
carbines—the lowest estimate made was
300—under command of Lieutenant-Colonel
[Thomas] Munford, consisting of Captains
Dulany's, Green's, White's and other
companies, of Colonel Stuart's cavalry; they
came into the place in three divisions, the right
on the main road leading south, the center off
the mountain in front of the depot, the left by
a mountain road about a quarter of a mile west
of the depot and coming to the rear of the
depot. So well concerted was the plan, that
they supposed them to be thousands. ... The
inhabitants condemned the rebels very much
for the barbarous and treacherous manner
they shot and wounded our men after having
surrendered their arms.[14]

*Richard Dulany's name was now known by the
enemy, and soldiers of the 28th Pennsylvania who
came past Oakley and Welbourne in the next few
weeks always inquired as to whether it was the
home of the rebel captain.*

*On May 23rd, Jackson continued his rapid
march up the Luray Valley toward Front Royal in
pursuit of General Nathaniel P. Banks. He sent
the 6th Virginia Cavalry and the 2nd Virginia
Cavalry under Colonel Thomas T. Munford to
cut the railroad and telegraph communications
between Strasburg and Front Royal. The army
engaged the Federals at Front Royal, and Jackson
was victorious; but the Federals burnt the bridge*

over the North Fork of the Shenandoah River in an effort to delay the pursuit. Jackson ordered the four companies of the 6th Virginia Cavalry to cross the barely passable bridge. Captain C.E. Flournoy, commanding the 6th, obeyed, moving down the Valley pike toward Winchester with a force not exceeding 200 men. In command of the Federals was Colonel John R. Kenly with about 1,000 men.

Jackson ordered Captain George A. Baxter of Company K and Company A under Dulany to charge on the right of the turnpike; Company E under Captain C.E. Flournoy on the left; and Company B under Captain Daniel Grimsley to charge up the center. The enemy was driven from his position but reformed at Cedarville, about three miles down the turnpike, in an orchard at Fairview, the home of Thomas McKay. The 6th Virginia again charged, putting the enemy to complete rout. General Jackson reported that in all his experience, this was the most gallant and effective cavalry charge he had ever seen. Two pieces of artillery were captured; the federal commander, Kenly, was wounded and captured. Dulany's company lost one man killed and one man wounded.[15]

Amanda Edmonds wrote of the fight in a diary entry on May 28, 1862:

George F. Sheetz, captain of Co. F, 7th Virginia Cavalry, was described: "Bold as a lion, his courage was tempered by prudence; impetuous in battle as a thunderbolt, he was as quiet and modest as a woman when in camp."[16]

Joe Gibson and Bruce came down this morning leaving Dulany's command at Darkesville, are scouting every day into Martinsburg. Dulany had one killed and three wounded. Ashby lost three Captains. Dulany saw Sheetz shot, turned and fired over his shoulder killing the Yankee. Ashby saw that he [Sheetz] had fallen and said, "I had rather lost any other man than him."[17]

Jackson pursued Banks and defeated him at Winchester on May 25th without the help of Ashby's cavalry.

On June 1st, near Strasburg, Richard Dulany received his first wound in the war, a gunshot in the upper right thigh that shattered the bone. The wound would prove to be very painful, and it would keep him from his command for almost three months.

Colonel Thomas T. Munford reported what happened:

We marched from Charles Town to Kernstown on the 30th; had no feed for our horses; on the morning of June 1 we started at early dawn to cover our retreat to Strasburg, at which place we were kept in line of battle nearly the whole day, watching for the approach of both Shields and Frémont. Then we got about a third of a ration of corn for our horses.

Generals James Shields and John C. Frémont.

That night we were halted in rear of General Taylor's brigade, who were cooking rations about two and one-half hours. The Sixth Regiment (cavalry) was in the rear, and our men were completely worn down and most of them sleeping on their horses.

General Richard Taylor's Louisiana brigade.

Captain Dulany ... was in command of the rear guard, and was approached by the Yankee cavalry. It was dark, and when challenged they replied, "Ashby's cavalry." Having been previously informed that General Ashby had one company out, he allowed them to approach very near, and suddenly they fired a volley and shot him. The Sixth Cavalry was surprised and dashed through the Second [Virginia Cavalry] who were sleeping and relying upon the Sixth to guard the rear, as we had alternated each day with that regiment.

Captain Dulany was badly shot in the leg and several of his men captured. To add to the confusion thus created, a part of the Seventh Louisiana fired into our ranks.

This was our first surprise. Many of our men were nearly exhausted from hunger and loss of sleep. We had been in the saddle and had had no regular rations for three days. My command was soon formed and we drove them back, capturing three or four, who in the dark mistook us for their friends.[18]

Hal had several glass eyes made after his mishap—one was clear and others had varying degrees of bloodshot.

Hal Dulany was wounded in the eye in the same skirmish. This wound and the fear that if he stayed in the army he would lose sight in his good eye led to his resignation.[19]

On June 6th, Turner Ashby was killed near Harrisonburg. Family tradition says that Richard Dulany was considered as his successor. The family back at Welbourne apparently thought it was so. One of his daughters wrote:

The lamented Ashby was our Bayard—
His mantle is said to have fallen upon
you, both of character and position.
May Heaven bless and protect you is
the prayer of a ~~little~~

Little Rebel

Two days after Dulany's wounding, Mittie Herbert, who apparently had not yet heard of the tragedy, wrote to Julia Whiting, who was then in Richmond:

Saturday, June 7th, 1862

My dear Julia:

What numberless things have happened since we parted. We and your own family thrown into Yankee lines to be pillaged and insulted—every one around here has been tormented with their visits.

Your Grandpapa's carriage horses, grey mare, John deButt's grey, Celeste, mule and cart have all gone from here—at Oakley no horse is left for them to go anywhere—they also took from here Clarence's whiskey, Richard's wine, tea, white sugar, brown sugar, two or three wagon loads of meat, besides numberless other things too numerous to mention.

We have been uneasy about your whereabouts—have you been able to study during this wearing out time of anxiety? Have you been able to hear from your parents? We have not heard a word from there.

Mary and Carlyle Whiting were at home in Stafford County.

I hope you have seen Clarence; he is courier to General Stuart, he did not enter this time with as much enthusiasm as before. I hope he continues well.

At the battle of Williamsburg, May 5, 1862, Stuart praised Clarence Whiting for his "signal zeal and intelligence."[20]

Your Grandpapa is well now though he has suffered from great debility this spring. I think, however, the last visit of the Yankees acted as a tonic and cured him—everything goes on as usual.

Seven men servants have gone from here. Regie, George, Frank, Henry [Jackson], Clifford [Hoe], Billy [Gillison] and Armistead [Corbin], and all of Ida's but two, in fact, they are going every day—one of the best parts of the war I *think*, except some disagreeable ones who remain.

Slaves. Mary D.L. White noted that Jackson, Hoe, Gillison and Corbin "all came back (the others I do not know anything about) when they found the Yankees would not give what they had promised."

Your friends are well but Miss Margaret, I do not think she can live more than a few weeks—but I know it will be a blessed change for her—certainly this world is very dark now. Mrs. Kinsolving died last week, leaving a little baby two weeks old.

Lucy Kinsolving, wife of Rev. O.A. Kinsolving, Episcopal minister at Upperville.

Rocky Ford is on Goose Creek at Welbourne.

Anna was the daughter of Robert Bolling of Bollingbrook, about ten miles SW of Welbourne.

Weidmayer, a Swiss citizen, was able to cross the Union lines. Rebecca Winn, sister of John Peyton Dulany, wife of Timothy Winn, U.S.N. Aurelia Fairfax Irwin, daughter of Margaret (Herbert) and Thomas, 9th Lord Fairfax.

Sophie deButts, sister of Rebecca Rogers deButts Pinkney, was married to Charles Morton Stewart. They lived in Baltimore.

If you can hear of an opportunity, do write us a few lines saying how you get along. Tomorrow is Mary's birthday so they have gone to Rocky Ford to fish to-day. Anna Bolling is here for a day or two. (Richard is over the [Blue] Ridge with Jackson.)

Mr. Weidmayer came from Alexandria ten days ago—he went to New York, Philadelphia and Baltimore saw Aunt Winn and Aurelia —all well.

If you hear of Mrs. Pinkney let her know Mr. Weidmayer saw Sophie and Mr. Stewart—they are all well, but Sophie had been sick. Mr. Weidmayer said he never should have known it she looked so well. This letter is to go by quite a nice man, be *very* civil to him.

Your attached cousin
E.D. Herbert

From the writings of Ida Dulany of Oakley:

June 11. Mamma returned from Leesburg this morning and brought the sad news that Brother Richard [Dulany] was wounded badly in the thigh. It was a great, great shock to me, making their constant danger seem so real and making me anxious for him. Poor fellow!

Went to Welbourne this afternoon to see Uncle John [Peyton Dulany] but found that he had heard only a rumor, which he did not credit. He seemed mightily distressed but seemed to take comfort in the thought that it was not a severe wound. I am anxious to go to Brother Richard at once and if I do Mr. Weidmeyer will go with me. I will take two chances—try if I can to get a pass from the authorities, and if not, will start secretly and attempt to cross the lines between the pickets.

I long to go, we will be so anxious here, and then I shall be near Hal without being either useless or burdensome.

June 13. Yesterday morning directly after breakfast Mr. Ayre called to tell me he had been to examine the lines and see if I could get out. He reports it an entire impossibility. I am troubled very much to hear it but still hope I may get a pass.

George Ayre lived at Ayreshire on the Trappe Road north of Upperville.

Mr. Weidmayer has given up all idea of going and Uncle John has sent Edward Carr, thinking he has a better chance of getting through the lines than I would have. Our anxiety will be almost insupportable until he returns.

Today Mr. Ayre came again bringing a Richmond *Dispatch* in which I was *terribly shocked* to see an advertisement for the body of "Clarence Whiting, supposed to have been killed in Saturday's battle before Richmond," with an exact description of his person. Poor fellow, it seems but yesterday that I saw his bright handsome face—his mother's idol. As each fresh shock comes I wonder if that will not be the last to us, and yet every one makes me realize more fully the danger to all.[22]

Reports of Clarence Whiting's death were false. He was captured at the battle of Seven Pines, May 31, 1862, held at Fort Delaware Prison and exchanged on August 5, 1862.[21]

Richard H. Dulany wrote to his niece, Julia Whiting from the home of James Hall, a cousin who lived near Buffalo Springs Spa in Amherst County. Dulany had gone there to recuperate from his leg wound.

June 27th 1862
James Hall near Amherst C.H.

My dear Julia,

I have been thinking a great deal about you and sympathize most deeply with you in this, your first great affliction. It is not for me to point you the way to the only source of

Probably referring to her brother Clarence's capture.

comfort. I am very anxious to get you to Welbourne and if you can find Cousin Rebecca Pinkney in Richmond she would be glad to accompany you. She wrote me some time ago that she wishes to go to Welbourne. If Hare [illegible—paper smudged] is out of employment he had better come with you, otherwise I will send Walker Armistead for you.

Sarah and Richard deButts lived near Linden in Fauquier County, Virginia.

I wish you to come first and stay a day or two with me, I will then send you to Charlottesville in the cars and hire some kind of carriage there to take you first to Sarah deButts and then home. It is reported that the Yankees have withdrawn their troops from the neighbourhood of Linden—if true you will go directly home only stopping one night at Sarah's.

Remember me kindly to Dr. —— [?].

As ever, your devoted Uncle
R.H. Dulany

P.S. On the 1st of the month I was shot through the upper part of my right leg and although I am in no danger I fear it will be a long time before I shall be able to get into my saddle again. Eliza Carter is with me, she desires [to send] much love to you.

While recuperating, Dulany received a letter from his nine-year-old son, John Peyton Dulany.

June 1862

My dear Papa,

How is your leg and cousin Robert and all my relations. Is cousin Eliza with you yet? The Yankees have taken all our hams, but we got some more, and I don't know where they came from. I think that the last letter you wrote is the best letter you have written. How far are you from here? I want to [see] you very much indeed. Cousin Mary sends her [love] to you and she says she wishes she could make you some nice tea and toast. She said she hopes you[r] leg will soon get well. And I have got a great many musics to play for you.

Your affectionate son,
John

Richard Dulany to his children:

July 27th 1862

My dear Children

Look on the map and see if you can find Buffalo Springs. They are some sixty miles south of Charlottesville. Buffalo Springs is very much like that of the White Sulphur [Springs] but the grounds & buildings are far from beautiful, being hemmed in all sides by high hills or mountains. The spring is at the bottom of quite a steep hill and on the top of the hill is a house [that] was once the tavern and on each side of the walk toward the spring is a row of very poor cabins.

In one of these cabins there is now lying on a stretcher a poor wounded soldier who this morning was able to get to the stable some hundred yards off for the first time with one crutch. Near the doors sits a young lady of some twenty summers reading the morning service since she can't enjoy a Baptist's preaching.

From an adjoining room a lady "fair fat and forty" with a young girl of fourteen has just gone and is getting to a carriage to go to church or rather to meeting. The carriage is being driven by a young gentleman about five ft. high, with quite a moustache and the faint, very faint, prospect of whiskers which he tries to cultivate having very little else to do. This young gentleman gets quite tipsy sometimes

The Buffalo Springs Spa in Amherst County no longer exists.

but he is very amiable and so funny that it is hard to scold him for it.

The third gentleman of the party is a soldier on the sick list (his back being too weak to ride) he has large whiskers and a long curling moustache, has very bow legs which enables him to carry his back ten or fifteen miles without the slightest trouble to catch trout in the mountain streams. One day he caught with the help of one person one hundred trout and at the other times forty a day by himself. These trout were much enjoyed by the first mentioned person as well as by the ladies of the party.

The owner of the springs not being willing to take boarders, the party had to rent two small cabins and keep house for themselves which they found more pleasant than boarding as they can live as they please. They have three servants, two carriages and five horses so they can live in some style.

The marketing is quite different from that in Loudoun as chickens sell for from thirty to forty cents a pound. The trout cost nothing is quite an addition to the fare.

How much Mr. Weidmayer and Jonny would enjoy rambling through the mountains catching trout with this bow legged soldier who is an old acquaintance of Mr. Weidmayer.

If the Yankees are driven back far enough by the 10th of Aug., this party expect to leave the springs and move toward the Potomac and may call at Welbourne on the way.

I want each of you to answer my letter and I will write first to the one who can guess the names of all the persons referred to in this letter.

As ever your devoted Father
R.H. Dulany

Undated letter of Hal Dulany to his niece, Mary Dulany of Welbourne, probably written in mid-August 1862:

Dear May,

    Your papa has left me a very limited space for my note, but as he has given you all the news I have very little to write. Clarence was exchanged last week and immediately came to see us & procure a horse & saddle, he will return to General Stuart this week. He is very much grown and improved in every way. He was very fortunate in meeting some old acquaintances among the young men imprisoned in F. D., little G. Burwell among them, and as his relations in B[altimore] supplied him with every comfort, he appears to have been more lucky than many others.

    I think you would have enjoyed a visit here the last few days. We have had a very pleasant time, as pleasant as refugees whose hearts and thoughts are at home could have. But it is a great pleasure to have your papa and Clarence with us, both safe & well after all the dangers they were exposed to.

    We leave here this week for Coz. J. Hall's. Where our next move will be I cannot tell, if we beat the Y's, home perhaps. Don't you long for peace once more. Write me a long letter, and tell all about everyone and all that Mr. W. says about Nama [?], Father, the children. ...

The end of this letter is missing. A note on the top reads "Love to Fannie & the boys. Tell Dick I have heard nothing of apple dumplings."

Richard H. Dulany to his daughter Mary:

Buffalo Springs 17 Aug 1862

May is Mary's nickname

George Harrison Burwell, Jr., (1848-1926) would have been fourteen years old during his imprisonment at Fort Delaware in 1862.

James Dulany Hall of Amherst County.

My dear Mary

I received your second letter by your Uncle Hal, who joined me at yr. cousin James Hall's on Sunday last. I had started to Richmond but meeting Clarence and not being very well, I left Lynchburg on my return to this place, early Sunday morning and went as far as your cousin's to breakfast. In the evening your uncle arrived and the second day after James drove us over in his wagon accompanied by his son Willy. Willy is the age of John. He is a very fine boy and attached me very much to him by his kind attentions when I first came to his father's.

Louisa is James Hall's daughter.

Louisa Hall has been with us all the time and says her French lessons to yr. Cousin Julia every day and is improving quite fast. She is going to boarding school in October. Your Cousin Rosa and the other children are all well. Uncle Hal stayed with us several days. He entertained me very pleasantly by his conversation.

Rosa Gunnell Hall, wife of James D. Hall.

Moses, who has taken poor John's place (but cannot fill it), seems very much afraid of Uncle's talking too much. He passed Uncle and myself where we were sitting in the grove the other day and went to your Eliza and said, "Missis, Master Hal is the finest conversation gentleman I ever saw, if she don't cure Master pretty soon I'm afraid he will kill him." Uncle enjoyed the speech as much as any of us. Moses is very attentive and would make a good servant if he was not so fond of whiskey.

I have never seen any servant white or black that I could trust as I did John and Nancy. Julia is also I think a servant of good principle and I have every reason to believe perfectly honest. Remember me both to her and Nancy and to Priscilla, who you should go see often. She was yr. Grandmother's favorite servant.

Servants John & Nancy Jackson, Julia Peters, a chambermaid, and Priscilla, the cook, according to Mary D. L. White, a grand-daughter of Richard Dulany.

Tell Pris. that Alfred is well and desires me to send his love to her and to Charley and his respects to his Master and Miss Mary. He is my cook and does well. He is very anxious that I should make a visit home before I return to my Regmt.

We shall have been here a month on Tuesday next, on which day I expect to leave via Lynchburg and James Hall's to report to Col. Jones of the 7th Va. Cava. formerly commanded by the gallant Turner Ashby. General Jackson was kind enough to have me promoted by the President to Lieut. Col. of this Regmt. This place I much prefer to the command (entire) of the Regmt as it is without the least discipline. Col. Jones being an old army officer I hope it will not be long in getting the men in good training.

It is very pleasant to hear my old company spoken of frequently as the best in the 6th. I rode about a half mile on horseback two days since and felt no inconvenience for it, so I hope that by the time I get to my Regmt. which will be in some eight or nine days, to be able to report "fit for duty." It will then have been nearly three months since I left the army.

Genl. Jackson met the Yankees near Mitchell's Station on last Saturday (9th) and won another glorious but bloody victory. The Enemy were driven back three miles with the loss of one General and twenty eight other officers and nearly 500 men prisoners about 600 killed and upwards of 1200 wounded and missing. We lost Genl. Winder, Col. Cunningham and 100 men killed and 600 wounded and missing. Some of the missing have come in.

We are expecting a general engagement every day. If we are victorious, which may God

Alfred Hoe was Dulany's body servant. Charley may be Charlie Ford, a Whiting servant.

Col. William E. Jones, whose nickname, "Grumble," revealed much about his personality.

Dulany was appointed lieutenant colonel of the 7th Virginia Cavalry, although not elected by the men to that position. The appointment of Jones and Dulany caused some resentment among the men of Ashby's old command.[23]

The battle of Cedar Mountain: Union 314 killed, 1,445 wounded, 594 missing; Confederate 231 killed, 1,107 wounded.[24] Among the Confederate losses were Gen. Charles S. Winder of Maryland, and Richard H. Cunningham, Jr., lieutenant colonel of the 21st Virginia Infantry.[25]

grant, I think it will not be long before we drive the rogues out of our dear old State.

The package with letters from your brothers and sister and Mr. W's report gave me much pleasure. Your reports were not quite as good the last month as I would have liked, but I can make some excuses for the warm weather and the excitement of the times. Your letter by your Uncle was not near so well written as the first. Try and write a larger hand. You can make it as small as you please after you learn to write well. Your first letter was very well written.

I hope you take *regular* exercise and are careful about your teeth. Before going to bed use your brush or pass something between all your teeth and wash your mouth with cool water. If you forget this you will regret it all your afterlife.

I hope Fan and you are learning some new music, I expect to enjoy your playing very much when I get home. How does Jonny come on with his music? Tell him with much love that I do not wish to lose his reputation of *perseverance*, for with perseverance he may accomplish almost anything he may wish.

Give my love to Hal. Tell him I received his letter too. The only objection I have to any of your letters is that they are rather short. Is Fan as strong and fat as ever? How I should like to see her in a romp now. God bless you all, how much I do want to see you.

Tell Dick that there are few things I prize so highly as *true courage*, if he has it he will always speak the *truth* and hurrah for Jeff. Davis when he sees the Yankees.

I am glad that Julia [Peters] has too much sense to leave Dick. If she could see the servants [in] the coming winter who have gone off, she will never regret it. Already in

Family legend says that the children sat on the fence and cheered for Jefferson Davis when the Yankees came by.

New York, Pennsylvania & in Indiana the lower classes of white men are driving them from their houses and burning them because the negroes are reducing the price of labour.

Remember me kindly to Mr. Haley and all the servants that remain. How is Miss Margaret? Go to see her as soon as you receive this and tell her how sorry I am to hear that she is sick and although I was well taken care of while sick by yr. Cousin Eliza I frequently missed her soft hand and kind cheerful words; I have been so accustomed to them in sickness. Remember me in kind terms to Mr. Weidmayer and tell him that I should be much pleased to hear from him sometimes. How is Cousin Armistead? Does he ever leave home? I suppose he gets as far as Welbourne sometimes to look over the pages of Walter Scott and have his hair brushed.

John Armistead Carter of Crednal, uncle of Rebecca Ann Dulany.

Next to your Grand Father there is no one you should be so attentive to as your Uncle Armistead; he was your mother's nearest and best friend and if he could have been my worst enemy this would make him always dear, very dear, to me and should make him so to all my children. Thank your cousin Mittie for her note enclosed with the children's. Tell her she must keep up her courage and be ready to fight with the children as we have pledged to the Yanks that should we all fall, the women and children will still resist until not one be left in the whole South. As for myself I have always been confident of our success in the end although we have and we will lose many, very many of our best and bravest men.

Rebecca Dulany had been John Armistead Carter's ward after her father's death.

How I pity those men who have been obliged to stay home during the war. To receive the insults and threats of the worst brutes that ever curst [sic] a land or people and

Rev. Stephen Samuel Roszell
(1812-82), a prominent
Methodist minister, married Julia
Dulany on August 5, 1845, her
second husband. During the war,
they lived at Wheatland, near
Hillsboro, Va.

George F. McCabe.

Henry Arthur Hall and his wife,
Susan Grayson Hall.

without the power of resistance must be far more bitter than death itself. How to speak of those who should have been in the Army or those who have sneaked back inside the enemy lines to avoid the hardships of camp life or the fear of a soldier's death, I can find no words to express my utter detestation of them. They are more contemptible than the Yankees themselves and more bitter enemies to our Government.

Have you heard lately from your Aunt Julia or Uncle Roszell? If you have let me know how they are when you write. If you have opportunity, write to her and tell her that I am nearly well again and hope to soon be in my saddle (the one that McCabe stole) again and to assist in ridding our state of pests worse than Egyptian locusts and, bro. Sam would say, more loathsome than her toads. If I find that there is not a chaplain in our Regmt, I will try and get the refusal of it for bro. Sam if he thinks he can stand it.

Your cousin Julia [Whiting] is with me and is looking better than I ever saw her. She has fattened very much since she came from Richmond. Her appetite for young chickens would break a poor soldier. Your cousin Eliza is also looking well—if she should continue to improve in "condition" for many weeks more, your Cousin Robert [Carter] will have to have his legs strengthened to be able to hold her on his knees. Give my love to your Cousin Henry Arthur and his wife when you see them. Tell Father I wrote him a few days since, not having ink I have to use a pencil.

Let your next be a long letter. Write a letter every day in form of a journal.

Ever your affectionate Father
R.H. Dulany

Evidently Dulany did not return to duty as soon
as he anticipated. "Grumble" Jones had assumed
command of the 7th Virginia Cavalry on July 18th
at Gordonsville. On the morning of August 2nd,
near Orange Court House, during a severe
skirmish, Jones was wounded and Maj. Thomas
Marshall was captured. During the battles of
Second Manassas and Sharpsburg, the 7th
Virginia Cavalry was commanded by Captain
Samuel B. Myers.[26]

On September 1st, Dulany's sister-in-law, Ida,
mentioned in her diary that she saw him at Cousin
Burr Harrison's. Apparently he was near his
home, probably still recuperating from his wound.

Jones was promoted to brigadier general on
October 3rd. Dulany was promoted to colonel of
the 7th Virginia Cavalry on October 30th;
Thomas Marshall was promoted to lieutenant
colonel, and Samuel Myers to major.[27]

In late October 1862 General Stuart's cavalry
moved into Loudoun County in an effort to screen
Lee's movement of his army from Winchester to
Culpeper. As the federal cavalry under Gen.
Alfred Pleasonton crossed the Potomac at Berlin
(now Brunswick), Maryland, Stuart aggressively
moved to meet him. On October 30th, he arrived
at the hamlet of Bloomfield, a few miles from
Welbourne.

A series of cavalry battles began at Mountville,
about five miles northeast of Welbourne, on
October 31st. They again clashed near Union
(now called Unison), about three miles northwest
of Welbourne, on November 2nd. In the following
letter, only part of which survives, Julia Whiting
describes the exciting events that occurred at
Welbourne during this time.

Julia Whiting to her mother, Mary D. Whiting:

Welbourne, Nov 21st [1862]

Dear Mamma,

I can hardly tell you with what delight I welcomed your letter, the first I had received from home since the 20th of March, nearly eight months. You can imagine the relief it was to me to hear that you were all well, I had been so anxious about Father & my dear little Guy, and in addition to this was the pleasure of seeing Clarence return in safety; the change in the position of our own and the Yankee forces and the unsettled conditions of the country had made [us] very uneasy about him, we all feared that he might encounter the Yankees unexpectedly.

But I must go back now and give you a sketch of the stirring events of the first two weeks of this month, in the order in which they occurred. The day after Clarence left Welbourne on his visit to you we were kept in a constant state of excitement. Scouts coming in reported the Yankees advancing. The pickets of Uncle Richard's old company, the Dulany Troop as it is called, were drawn in from their advanced position and stationed at Crednal and on the road just about the chapel.

All here was in motion in the house [with] arrangements for Uncle's departure. At the stable all hands [were] employed in leading the wagons with the hogs killed that morning, which were to be taken to the army, and mounted on horse back, only waiting for the wagons they were to guard, were Uncle Richard and Lieut. Plaster with several soldiers. At length the word was given and about an hour before sunset, the pickets were all withdrawn from their

Guy Fairfax Whiting, her brother.

The chapel was built at Welbourne for the slaves. Now called the Church House, it is a residence on Welbourne Road.

outposts and the party started.

A few moments after, Mr. Weidmayer, the girls and myself set off through Seaton's woods to guide a little soldier by the shortest route to Upperville. After leaving him in sight of Clifton, we returned by the old road.

Just after passing Quaker lane we heard the sound of horses' feet and the clank of sabres, and looking back perceived a large party of cavalry; the gathering twilight and the shadow of the trees beneath which they were moving did not permit us to perceive their uniform, but as our own men had just retreated we knew they must be Yankees. Nothing was left for it but to quicken our pace as much as was consistent with our dignity, (for upon no consideration should they have the pleasure of supposing that they had frightened us) and by arriving a few moments before conceal everything of value; as soon as we reached the first gate the little girls started at full speed for the house.

When Mr. Weidmayer and I reached it one would have imagined that an attack was expected, such fastening of windows, locking of doors, hurry and confusion. Passing through the frightened servants I entered Grandpapa's room and in a few seconds here came the Yankees—but much to our surprise in a steady trot instead of their usual furious gallop. The officer left his men and riding up to Grandpapa who stood at his door, bowed and began "I was sent here Sir by Col. Dulany. General Stuart and his cavalry are a short distance behind me." Just fancy what a revolution of feeling these words caused, to find instead of the Yankees whom we had been anathematising, our own gallant men & above all to learn that instead of being left to Yankee rule we were to

The "old road" may be the road from the stone bridge over Goose Creek to the Little River Turnpike, connecting Quaker Lane and the Willisville Road.

have our dashing Stuart with us.

Uncle Richard had invited the whole company to supper at Welbourne, never were more welcome guests. Uncle Richard joined us by supper time and our whole party assembled with very different feelings to those in which they had separated at sunset.

On Friday Stuart was to pass through Union so at twelve o'clock, mounted on Kate, I rode there with Grandpapa and had the pleasure of seeing the General pass. He is a fine looking fellow with hair and beard the color of Dr. Eliason's, whom indeed he resembles a little, and is a splendid rider.

I had a still better opportunity the same day of seeing my favorite general. Soon after supper he came to Welbourne with Dr. Eliason, they were just from a skirmish with the Yankees and were very tired and very hungry. Supper was ordered for them at once in Grandpapa's room and I had the pleasure of making Gen. Stuart's coffee.

Wouldn't Nina and Alice have been charmed to have been in my place. He spoke of Clarence in the highest terms and ended by saying that he really loved him. I wish he had proved it by giving him a commission. However, leaving my disappointment in this out of the question, as well as a few doubts as to the General's sincerity, for those who wish to please universally are not always quite sincere; I like Stuart exceedingly.

Saturday evening we had visitors again— Capt. Farley, one of Stuart's aides and the best scout, it is said, in the army. Major Pelham of the artillery, attached to Stuart's command and our old acquaintance Mr. Landstreet. Captain Farley is a South Carolinian with a very pleasant manner but with a touch of

Dr. Talcott Eliason of Upperville, a surgeon on Stuart's staff,[28] was a first cousin of Rebecca Dulany.

Nina and Alice are two of her sisters.

Capt. William D. Farley.[29]
Major John Pelham.
Rev. John Landstreet, a Methodist minister, whose circuit included Loudoun County, served briefly on Stuart's staff as an aide-de-camp. He had been the chaplain of the 1st Virginia Cavalry.[30]

conceit which is not quite becoming. I dislike conceited men; it is quite bad enough for a woman, but the Lord of Creation should be above such petty weakness. However, the Captain was very agreeable, though rather too often the hero of his own stories; the stories themselves [were] very amusing.

Major Pelham (does not that name remind you of Bulwer's hero?) is an Alabamian about twenty one or two, a graduate of West Point, and so bright and intelligent, you could hardly believe in looking at his youthful face & figure that he ranked as major. What a pleasant evening that was. I wonder if I shall ever see my two acquaintances again.

Lord Edward Bulwer-Lytton's novel, *Pelham, Or Adventures of a Gentleman*.

The young major was known as the "Gallant" Pelham.

On a visit to Welbourne, Maj. Pelham scratched on the parlor window: "G.C. Walker Oct 28 1862 J." Walker was Pelham's aide-de-camp. When Mary Dulany called the young officer to breakfast, she saw him hastily pull his hand down from the parlor window, where he was evidently about to etch his own name. Later, she saw the inscription.[31]

Julia's letter continues:

This Sunday was to be a memorable day to all the inmates at Welbourne. While at the breakfast table the distant report of a cannon was heard followed by another and another. "There go your guns, Pelham," said Capt. Farley, and as the steady firing continued they requested Uncle Richard to order their horses and we all left the table and went into the porch to discover the direction from which the sound proceeded.

We had a merry chat with the officers while waiting for the horses. Capt. Farley showed us the canteen and sabre he wore marked with the name of a Yankee Capt., trophies of the fight on Friday, when he had shot their former owner and one of his men had afterwards brought them to him. He jested with us upon his banditti appearance and laughingly declared that it was not worthwhile to dress well to fight Yankees. I fancy that the gallant Captain was aware that his picturesque dress, plumed hat &c., was more becoming than a more elegant costume and arranged it accordingly. When they rode off I charged them to let me know if the fight was near enough to be seen from the hills around as we were all anxious to see the Yankees whipped. I little fancied what a close view of it, we should have before the close of the day.

Hardly had the two officers disappeared over the hill on their way to Union than the head of the long wagon train disappeared by Cousin Armistead's [Crednal]. Here was a new subject for speculation—was Stuart falling back or was this only precautionary measure. In any case, some hours must elapse before the cavalry would pass, so giving orders to have everything ready for departure, Uncle Richard started to church with Cousin Mit, leaving me to give breakfast to the soldiers who accompanied the wagons and who from lame horses or other causes could not enter the fight.

It would take me too long to relate all the incidents of that busy morning, how Mary, Fanny and I divided our time between the gate in the grove where we dispensed sundry glasses of milk or water to the thirsty soldiers and the dining room where we distributed breakfast to the poor hungry fellows. After the last wagon and soldiers had disappeared Uncle Richard returned, not having been able to reach church on account of the wagons. Still the firing approached nearer and nearer, about two o'clock a regiment descended the hill and took up its position in the lower part of Cousin Armistead's field, while on every hill around videttes were stationed. Uncle Richard, who had left from Upperville at one o'clock, had given us all directions to prepare as much bread and meat and an injunction to keep out of the way of the shells [as] he rode off.

Grandpapa and I now went to the hill above the house from which we had a fine view of Venus Hill. Cousin Mit joined us there and we stood for some time watching the Yankee shells which whistled through the air and fell in and beyond Seaton's wood where some of our men were sheltered. Cousin Mit left us to procure some dinner for the soldier who was stationed on the hill, who could not leave his post. Hardly had she left us before a shell came whistling by struck the ground within a few feet of Grandpapa and myself, making the vidette's horse dodge, I assure you, and rebounding flew across the road and fell in the orchard. Grandpapa insisted upon our leaving the hill as the Yankees had found the range and the shells flew fast over our heads, we came down therefore by the wire fence by the grove just in time to meet Capt. Farley as he cantered up.

Of course we supplied him with dinner then and there and listened to his account of the fight, while the officers with him were supplied in the dining room. At length all our troops had retired from the Hill with the exception of some 14 or so sharpshooters who still maintained their position. The Yankees

Venus Hill was west of Crednal.

The Seaton place adjoined Welbourne to the west.

were now all around the stables and behind
the house while our gallant little band were in
front keeping up so rapid and deadly a fire that
as few as they were the Yankees were afraid to
leave cover; a Yankee Capt. advancing to lead
his men, a sharpshooter shot him down and
the first man that followed was felled by a ball
from the same pistol. From the front porch we
had a full view of the whole fight; every few
moments a rider would dash ... [rest of the
letter missing]

*Ida Dulany viewed the fighting from Oakley.
She recorded in her journal:*

D.H. Hill's division formed a line
of battle on Vineyard Hill, near
her home, but were not engaged.

Gen. Stuart's cavalry fell back slowly before
the enemy, disputing every inch of the way,
the enemy occupying the ground as he
retreated. I sat on the balcony of my room and
watched the battle which became very distinct
from the flashes of the artillery as night came
on. With the aid of a spy-glass we could see
many movements of our men, the enemy being
entirely concealed by the woods. It is strange
for us in our sheltered, quiet country, to hear
the roar and see the flash of artillery, to watch
the movements of an army and feed at night
dozens of soldiers wearied with a hard day's
fight.[32]

*Fanny Dulany also left an account of the
cavalry fighting near Welbourne and the visit of
General Stuart and his staff:*

Early November, 1862

Major Pelham, Captain Farley, and Mr.

Landstreet, were here Saturday evening. They spent the night. The next morning when we arose, we heard the shells from Pelham's battery exploding very rapidly. As soon as they had breakfasted the three gentlemen rode off to Union which is only 2–1/2 miles from here, where our men were. About two or perhaps three after they left, we heard a rumbling confused noise which sounded something like distant thunder; in about a quarter of an hour afterwards the advance guard of our troops appeared.

We immediately set to work, to have all the flour and meal which was in the house, made into bread for the soldiers who soon appeared, led by our gallant Stuart. The firing still continued. We were very busy all that day running backwards and forwards, feeding the men, distributing the meat and bread among them, & dipping and handing the milk from the buckets & tubs, to those who were on horseback.

In the course of the day Gen. Stuart rode up. We asked him if he would not dismount, so as to eat his dinner more comfortably; Thank you ladies said he, but I have not the time. Cousin Julia then handed him a plate with some dinner on it, and then offered him a knife & fork, which however he refused, saying that he was more accustomed to use his fingers, and therefore could eat better with more expedition with them. So Cousin Julia held the plate for him, & he seemed to enjoy his dinner very much. We then filled his knapsack with apples, after which he rode off.

About an hour afterwards we saw Captain Farley and his horse both dodge beautifully as a cannon ball whizzed near them.

Will Farley was mortally wounded at the battle of Brandy Station, June 9, 1863; a shell took off his foot.

The Yankees came nearer, and the bullets ticked on the tin roof like hail. At about five in the evening the whole place was crowded with the horrid Yankees.

During the day, we had had two tubs, one of water, the other of milk, placed on the gate posts, & by one we had left a large silver goblet; hundreds after hundreds of *Southern* soldiers passed, & drank out of the cup, and it was brought back to the house, by one of the last of our soldiers. In the evening it was by the carelessness of the servants left on the dumb-waiter, which communicates between the kitchen, & the dining room. Of course the former is the first place a soldier thinks of, & when the Yankees came, it was crowded with them; one of them happened to look up the waiter, and seeing the goblet, took it, & this was the last we ever heard of it.

At Welbourne today there is a silver tumbler that Fanny Dulany Lemmon had inscribed: "Made to replace one taken by a Yankee officer in 1863." She may have meant 1862.

In December 1862, Jones's brigade was detached from Stuart and began operating in the Shenandoah Valley. In the collection of letters at Welbourne is one from Stonewall Jackson to Colonel Dulany:

Dec. 5th, 1862

Colonel:

I am much obliged to you for the excellent pair of pants you sent. Please give my thanks to the maker of them. I would do it myself if I knew the name.

Sincerely yr. friend
T.J. Jackson

On the letter the colonel wrote,
Note: I send this letter for Mary. We have just camped near Luray. May God's best blessings rest with all the inmates of my dear home. RHD.

The next letter, from Fanny Dulany to her father, is not dated:

Dear Papa,

I hope you will get leave of absence, on Christmas, so that you can come home, as you did last Christmas.

Mr. Weidmayer says that he is quite sure that the war will be over before next spring, and that you will be a General and Cousin Clarence Colonel under your command, which, I hope will be the case.

We go out to walk, nearly every evening except when it is too cold. Dick says his lessons every morning to Cousin Mit.

We get along very well in our lessons with Cousin Julia. I hope you and your men will pay us a visit.

Mrs. Rutter was here yesterday morning, she said that while the Yankees were about they asked her when she had seen the "Rebel" army, and she told them that she saw the "devil" army then.

J. Eliza Rutter, age fifty-three. (1860 U.S. Census)

Grand Papa went out hunting yesterday but did not see a single bird. Mr. White came here Tuesday from Richmond, he brought us a great deal of news but I have not time to tell you what he said. I will not have time to do anything except to sign my name.

> Your affectionate daughter
> Fanny Dulany.

Letter of Julia B. Whiting to her uncle, Richard H. Dulany:

December 7th [1862]

Dear Uncle,

We are all delighted to hear of your late good fortune, the news comes in good time to

Sir Percy Wyndham, colonel of
the 1st New Jersey Cavalry.

rally Grandpapa's spirits which were rather depressed by the account of Sir Percy Windham's [sic] success in surprising our men. I hope you will soon have the pleasure of sending this adventurous knight with an escort to share the hospitabilities [sic] of Richmond.

Clarence Whiting.

You will be amused by Mr. Weidmayer's prediction. I don't see much chance of poor C's promotion.

The girls are coming on very well with some of their studies. Fanny is improving very much in writing and composition. Mr. Haley and three of his daughters have been very ill with typhoid fever, it will probably be more than a month before he will be able to go about. Henry has not appeared yet. No one is permitted now to pass the Yankee lines, Grandpa is afraid that they are preparing another expedition against us.

Your affectionate niece,
Julia B. Whiting

Letter of Colonel Dulany to Fanny:

Named for Gen. William E.
"Grumble" Jones.

Camp Jones [Clarke County], Dec. 8th, 1862

My dear Fanny,

I received your very welcome and well written letter some ten days since. I should be much pleased to hear from both Mary and yourself more frequently. You need not care to write very long letters, so that you inform me how you are getting along with your studies and as to your health and any other news in regard to the family, or flowers, or farm, or neighborhood.

Nancy Seaton, age 71, and
probably a widow, is identified as a
farmer in the 1860 U.S. Census.

I was sorry to hear that my old neighbor Mrs. Seaton had been so badly treated by the Yankees.

When Clarence goes to Welbourne I will send you some money for Christmas. I think that the best use you could make of it would be to buy yarn and get Mrs. Haley or Mrs. Rutter to help you and Mary knit some two or three dozen pairs of thick socks for our bare-footed soldiers. If you have fifty pr. made and will send them to Genl. Jackson I will forward them in your name. Get Mr. Triplett and Mr. Haley to give you all the wool they can find on the farm. There are many skins lying about from which wool can be had. The servant women could knit a great deal before Christmas.

Triplett was the overseer for Col. Dulany's farm at Millsville

Ask your grandfather to show you Col. Imboden's letter to the people of Augusta [County]. If you and Mary exert yourselves with the assistance of Cousin Mittie and Cousin Mary, you can accomplish much in two weeks. Mrs. Rutter would card and spin wool for you as fast, I expect, as you can have it knit. Let the socks be a little longer than usual.

Col. John D. Imboden

Let me hear from you by Clarence.

With much love to Father, Mary and the boys, and every other member of the household. I am very sincerely

> your attached father
> R.H. Dulany

The following letter was written to Colonel Dulany by an unidentified woman, possibly a relative, who simply signed herself as "A." It is included here for her Northern perspective.

December 18th, 1862

Dear Richard,

I do not remember having experienced so genuine a sensation of pleasure as I did when in opening your letter received two days ago, I recognized your handwriting. It was so long since I was enabled to obtain any tiding of your and yours that I fairly devoured its contents, and then too you seemed to know how every detail would gratify me. There are so few sincere friendships in this world that those I know to be true are clung to by me as the drowning sailor clings to a straw.

Since I have seen you, my dear friend, I have met with some very severe trials, none more severe I assure you than the *entire* separation from my Sister's children. And when you consider that that separation is owing to the misconduct of their Father you will readily appreciate the pain I suffer. I had nursed those little ones so faithfully and loved them so tenderly that when they were snatched away from me in so ungentlemanly and unkind a manner I need not say that it nearly broke my heart. When we meet, which God grant may be soon I will tell you much that I cannot write in connection with this affair. Suffice it to say, that Willie is pretty well ruined morally speaking.

I am now living with my Father. This affair has been a great blow to him for he also is deprived of the visits of his grandchildren.

Some time ago I sent a letter to your Father which may have reached him. I hope it did as I should like him to know how often you are all in my thoughts. Your little darlings too will, I fear, forget their attached Aunt on this side of the lines.

Richard, dear, how relieved I feel when I think of our darling R. being spared all these hardships. God was merciful when he took her from this vale of tears. She was not strong enough to bear all this, nerves and health were so shattered to be so exposed. I know you must often reflect as I do and that you are too

Rebecca Dulany, the colonel's late wife.

unselfish to wish her back now. Just so with me
as regards my Sister, I feel happy to think that
before her husband's real character was
unmasked she was taken away to a better world.

You enquire after Mrs. M——. When I last
heard of her she was enjoying good health. You
know that she does not live here now. Some
months since we received a letter from Julia W
enquiring after her brother. We made every
possible enquiry but to no avail and concluded
that he had rejoined his friends. Should you
write again, which by the way I hope you will do,
let me know whether our surmises were correct.

Then Hal and Ida too are subjects of
uneasiness with me. I enclose a letter from my
sister to your niece Julia. Will you forward it.

It is easy to see, dear Richard, that you are
heart and soul in this war. I am of a very pacific
nature and deeply regret that present state of
affairs. My interests and sympathies are very
much exercised for you know the home of all
my Mother's relations. Men who are
surrounded as you are by the excitement and
interests naturally attending your undertaking
can scarcely, I suppose, understand the quiet
view I take of all this and the earnest desire to
see it terminated, but we read of the thousands
that are sacrificed to the rapacity of our
politicians and feel that nothing is done to tend
to a pacification. How and when will it end.

Of course we in these cities do not feel the
inconveniences of all this excepting as regards
the increase in our expense as well as the
decrease of our means. So far I have been so
fortunate not to have suffered much, for my
wants are not above my means. But there are
those around me whose prosperity is situated
in the Southern states and who consequently
are very much straitened by this state of

Julia Whiting was looking for
information about Clarence, then
a prisoner of war. He had been
exchanged by the time this letter
was written.

affairs. I have heard of no one yet who has been so seriously affected as you seem to have been judging from the nature of your letter, but your consolation must be that it is all in a good cause.

You threatened me that if I did not soon answer your letter to write again very shortly. I hope my answering it will not alter your intentions, for now you know how your thoughts gratify me. When you write home, give my love to all and tell your Father I long to see him and that I know he would not give me the greeting he gave the general, but if I quite understand how that was.

Battle of Fredericksburg,
December 13, 1862.

You must have been engaged in the recent battle. Very bloody there were, at least the numbers of killed & wounded is reported as very considerable. They tell me that Genl. McClellan was called to Washington yesterday. It may be that he will again be tendered the command. We were great admirers of his talents but I trust he may have the spunk to refuse to yield to Mr. Lincoln's tears, for he certainly deserved better treatment than he received. The Democratic party is rapidly on the increase now. It is stated that McClellan is a favorite with the party so that a great deal of the sympathy he now receives is a party feeling. No one, however, can refuse him a great deal of admiration for his forebearance & now farewell my dear friend. May God protect you and spare you to your children is the wish and prayers of

Yours affectionately

A.

Letter of Colonel Richard H. Dulany to his father, John Peyton Dulany:

Camp near Luray 21 Dec [1862]

My dear father

I have an opportunity of sending you a few lines by Robert Carter. I got to this camp last night and was just making myself comfortable when I received a dispatch from Genl. Jones that as the enemy had taken possession of Strasburg with between 3500 and 5000 men, I must move to New Market by daybreak tomorrow. The Genl. I think will make a stand if we are pressed although the Yankees have too much Artillery for us. The Cavalry of the enemy gives us no chance to try our strength with them as they seldom move without being backed by Artillery.

I should like so much to be with you at Christmas but it is impossible under present circumstances. Nothing could induce me to be absent from my command while there is any probability of a fight. My own impression is that Milroy will go from Strasburg to Winchester and that we shall follow his footsteps. He now numbers about two to our one.

Do you know if the Yanks took my colts from the Laucks? It is well that I did not send my cows to the Valley as I had intended as the Valley is now more exposed than our own [county]. I hope that Mr. Haley and his family have recovered. Give my kind regards to Mr. Haley and tell him how sorry I was to hear of his sickness.

I was much shocked to hear of the horrible accident to Dr. Leith's son. Please let me know how he is when you write and tell the Dr. I sympathize most deeply with him. As God is most merciful, our afflictions only prove how much chastening we require to win us from our idols. Do you ever hear from Sister Julia? Let me hear how she is and as to bro. Sam and the children.

Union general Robert Huston Milroy

Isaac H. Lauck, age forty-four, lived near Bloomfield (1860 Census). The Lauck farm was on Quaker Lane, according to a note by Mary Dulany Lemmon White.

Dr. Theoderick Leith, age fifty-four, lived near Union (1860 U.S. Census).

Give much love to my dear children, I hope they do not give you much uneasiness. Remember me in kindest terms to Cousin Armistead, Julia, Mittie, and cousin Mary and also Mr. Weidmayer. I send him five hundred dollars in interest bearing notes with which he will please credit my account. If Mr. W. should go to Washington during the holidays I should be glad for him to get me exchange on England for the Peora bonds if sold. We have just started another fine Steamer from England. A gentleman who came across our lines three days since got me to telegraph the Navy department that the vessel had been purchased and fitted as Sec. of War had desired.

I should be glad if Cousin Armistead or Mr. Weidmayer could go to New York and draw the amount due John and buy Exchange on England with it, I send a check for the trial. If obtained it will pay better now than hereafter. Charles Stewart might do better than either of the others—so I send the check in his name.

Send Alfred back on Monday with Robert Carter,

As ever your devoted son
R.H. Dulany

Probably his nephew, John Peyton deButts, heir to the fortune from Welbourne of England.

The following letter is undated, but Stuart passed near Middleburg after his raid on Union supplies at Dumfries in late December 1862.

Letter of John Peyton Dulany to his son, Richard H. Dulany:

My dear Richard,

I will try to write you a few lines, my hand is so tremulous that I can with difficulty make a letter. Two of your colts that were with Lauck are safe. I, or rather Edward, found one

Edward was John Peyton Dulany's body servant.

of your bay colts on the day before yesterday in Fauquier. I have sent him today to try and find the rest of them that were driven off by the Yankees.

I am now in hourly expectation of a visit from General Stuart and his staff—they sent me word by one of his officers that they would pay me a visit.

You have no doubt heard of his daring exploit in rear of the Yankees, capturing 300 men, horses, etc. I should not be surprised if they intended staying some time in this part of Virginia. I think it is the impression that the Yankees intend to fall back nearly to Washington. Haley is still confined to the house; he will not, I fear, be able to attend to any business this winter. His daughters are getting better.

I have had the icehouse filled.

I have waited until six o'clock and the General has not made his appearance so I will try and give you some account of his successful raid as I have heard from one of his staff. Stuart on Saturday with portion of Hampton and Lee's brigades left the Rappahannock supported by flying artillery under Pelham, crossed the river at Kelly's ford, attacked the enemy at Dumfries, finding it very strongly garrisoned with infantry and artillery, moved around towards Occoquan—attacked the Yankees (they having a large force) captured two hundred Yankees with their horses.

Took the camp, etc., had to burn fifty wagons that he could not get off—sent back thirteen wagons containing everything (or as far as it went) that our Army was in want of—then crossed the Occoquan to Burke's station, burnt the railroad bridge across Accotink eight miles from Alexandria.

Brig. Gen. Wade Hampton of South Carolina and Brig. Gen. W.H.F. "Rooney" Lee each commanded a brigade of cavalry.

Peter Gooding's tavern near Annandale. Maj. Gen. Henry W. Slocum commanded the Union XII Corps.

Stuart wired a message to the Union quartermaster general, Montgomery Meigs, complaining of the poor quality of the mules he had just captured.

He went to Peter Gooding's at dark [and] found 6000 Yankees under Slocum's command; built camp fires as a blind and drew off his men during the night.

From what the officer told me the Yankees must have burnt a very large amount of their stores. Stuart, having got possession of the wires, communicated with [the federal] Government, informing them that General Stuart was marching on Washington in force. It must have created great excitement. Stuart is certainly a very dashing officer.

I forgot say that while they were at Burke's they received an order from Washington to burn all stores at Fairfax station, fearing they might fall into the hands of our army.

You will receive some letters from the children—all are well. As Alfred is spending his honeymoon, I think I will send this letter by Rector. Always send me papers when you have an opportunity. Farewell, my beloved boy believe me ever

Your devoted Father
J.P.D.

"It is an awful thing to be obligated to take another's life, but it is our duty nevertheless and the more that are killed in each engagement the sooner the war will close."

Richard H. Dulany, March 3, 1863

1863

The beginning of 1863 found Dulany and the 7th Virginia Cavalry in camp near New Market. In this undated letter to his daughter, probably written during this period, Richard Dulany relates the concerns of a father, not a colonel.

Head Quarters 7th Va. Cav.
near New Market

My dear Fanny

I have just come in from drill and feeling somewhat homesick I have determined to have a little chat with you although I have to do all the talking myself.

Last night was very cold, indeed one of the coldest of the winter but as I have a new English blanket I slept quite soundly and only waked twice by Alfred making up the fire. I believe I fear the cold much more on account of the flowers than for myself. I hope that not many of them have died. Nothing would give me so much pleasure as to beautify my home that I might the more certainly attach my dear children to it. There are few pleasures so innocent or so lasting as those we receive in trying to give pleasure and in cultivating kindly feelings toward those among whom Providence has placed us. One deserves but little credit for being good tempered while with those who treat her or him with kindness or forbearance. When the temper is tried by harshness or rebuke not deserved, then it [is] for [us] to show that the religious principles we are taught in reading our Bibles have had their proper effect, and we forgive the unkindness and feel no desire for revenge.

Do you recollect two lines your dear Mother said her Mother taught your Uncle and her when they were little children

"When you think upon your Mother
Mind, be kind to one another."

I wish my children to remember this as being taught by one who loved them dearer than life itself, and not only remember but act upon it.

I fear I think too much about the future of my children for my own happiness. If I could see you all sincere Christians I should have little else to wish for. God has blessed you all with health and with many more friends and comforts that falls to the lot of most children, for all of which He will hold you accountable. Try my dear Child to make the most of your present advantages. Study hard and practice your music regularly. You can not tell when your teachers may leave you and if they should you will regret it when too late if you do not now make the best of your time.

I want both your sister and yourself to be very particular in regard to your teeth and nails. I hope Dr. Williams did not forget his promise to attend to your teeth.

When you write give me an exact account of the manner in which you spend your time, from the moment you get up until you go to bed at night. Write as if I did not know that you ever read, washed your face or eat. Tell Mary to do likewise.

How does Pauline come on? Does she keep house and the garden in better order than the one in which she lived before? I do not wish you to play with her children unless she keeps them clean. I hope the boys are learning to speak French very fast. Mary and you must speak no English to them after dinner each day. Your Cousin Julia will assist you in doing as I request.

Pauline was the wife of Henry Erskine, the gardener.

Mary and you can give any clothes too small for you away when ever your Cousin Mittie will consent to it. I am perfectly willing to leave every thing of this kind to her judgment. Give my love to her and tell her not to let Dick remain in my debt. I could still write much more to you but Mr. Osbourne is waiting to take my letters to Upperville. I send some papers by him for your Uncle Armistead and Grandpa.

Mary and you must read to the boys of our success in Texas and Charleston.

Give much love to your Grand Pa, Cousin Julia (who might write to me and send the letters from the La Roches), Cousin Mary and the children.

Remember me also in kind terms to Julia, Nancy, and the cook and any of the other servants who inquire for me. Write to me and send your letter to the care of Mr. Hunter in Upperville who will forward it by Mr.

Gen. John B. Magruder recaptured Galveston, Texas, on January 1st. On January 21st, at Sabine Pass, two Confederate steamers attacked the Union blockade, capturing 13 guns, 109 prisoners and causing a million dollars worth in damage.[1] On January 30th, two steamboats, the *Chicora* and the *Palmetto State*, sank most of the Union blockading fleet off Charleston.[2]

Osbourne who will leave Upperville Tuesday next. Ask Grandpa to write if he has heard from Mr. Weidmayer.

As ever your devoted father
R.H. Dulany

Letter of Fanny Dulany to her father, Richard H. Dulany:

January 23rd. [1863]

Dear Papa,

I am very glad to have this opportunity to write to you. Mr. Weidmayer has gone to Oakley this morning to see if Aunt Ida is ready to go with him to Baltimore, as he is going tomorrow morning.

Mr. Francis came here yesterday after dinner I think that we ought to be very thankful to our Almighty Father, for giving us the victory over the Yankees, at Vicksburg.

We have never gotten the yarn to knit our poor soldiers the socks.

We are very much obliged to you for the money which you sent us by Cousin Clarence.

I am going to give Mr. Weidmayer some money to get me a book to give to Mary on her birthday, as I expect it will be the only opportunity I will have.

Grand-Pa told us that when General Van Dorn entered Holly Springs, all the citizens came out to meet the soldiers, and one of the ladies went and told some of them that there was a Yankee officer in her house, and that they must come and take him; they went and looked all about for him, but could not find him, at last they look[ed] under the bed, and saw him with nothing on but his shirt and

Grant's campaign at Vicksburg was thwarted by Gen. Earl Van Dorn's raid on his supply base and Forrest's destruction of sixty miles of railroad.[3]

General Van Dorn's raid on Grant's supplies at Holly Springs, Mississippi, December 20-25, 1862.[4]

pulled him out.

Grand-Pa sent Gus to Mr. Addison Carter's to see if he could get some cider and as he was going through the woods he found a Yankee's portfolio; he brought it home. It had some writing paper and some envelopes in it, the envelopes had the Union flag in one corner of them and two others had a Yankee Suave [sic] holding the Yankee flag up and stepping on ours. There were two or three letters, from a father and a brother, to a son, in the father's letter was that the North was a wicked Nation and that they were a great deal nearer being victorious last year, than they were this.

Pauline was very glad that you had not paid Henry all his money.

All send their love. Please write soon.

> Your affectionate daughter
> Fanny Dulany

Gus is the butler.

Addison Carter of Willisville is a distant cousin of Rebecca Dulany, the colonel's late wife.

Zouave soldiers wore exotic, colorful uniforms topped with a fez. They were popular in both the North and South.[5]

Henry had a drinking problem.

Dispatch of General William E. Jones to Richard H. Dulany, who was near Petersburg and Moorefield, West Virginia, where his unit had participated in a raid on January 3-5 that netted fifty-one horses, five wagons and a large, portable bakery oven:[6]

Hd Qrs V.D. [Valley District]
Newmarket, Va.
Jan. the 28th 1863.

Colonel

As soon as the safety of the train will admit of it you will return with your troops to their respective camps. It is probably your wagons are or will all be loaded before this reaches you and if so you can commence your return at once. It was my intention to have joined you on a scout to the lower Valley but I have postponed it for the present.

Very Respectfully
Your Obt. Svt.
W.E.Jones
Brig. Genl. Cmdg.

Letter of Richard H. Dulany to his daughter,
Mary:

Camp New Market
Feb. 7th 1863

My dear Mary

I was much astonished and pleased at the appearance of Mr. Weidmayer and Mike in camp today. Mr. Weidmayer seems to be suffering somewhat from cold but is looking better than I ever saw him. Jonny's letter was a real treat. There is a freshness about it that brings my dear boy almost into my very presence. While I am anxious for you as well as your sister to be fine musicians still I do not want you to practice enough to injure your health or take you from your other studies, one and a half hours for practice and a half hour for playing for your friends I think sufficient. It is not the length of time, as much as the close attention paid while studying, that gives good results. When you can not get out take as much exercise as possible in the house. Are you paying any attention to your flowers?

I want to see you all very much—the more because we are all weather bound. The snow keeps us all in the camp except for two hours a day which we spend drilling. We can not advance upon our enemies until the cross roads become better. As soon as the snow clears away and the roads dry a little I trust we shall be able to prove that we can fight as well as drill.

My men do not give much trouble although they have been subjected to but little discipline until now. I had to buck one man a few days since because he refused to work, this soon brought him to terms. It was the most severe punishment I have ever inflicted.

"Bucking" a soldier is tying his hands together at the wrists and slipping them down over his knees, then running a stick under the knees and over the arms.[7]

I wish you could see the portable bakery I captured at Petersburg—it bakes fifty loaves at a time and enough, by using it fourteen hours a day, for five hundred men. By its use I save one third the flour, which makes just fourteen dollars a day. This I have placed in the hands of one of the officers and when the fund becomes large enough I will have it distributed for the benefit of the Regmt. The men are allowed one pound of flour each a day. In baking this will make a pound and a third of bread by the water used in making. I shall show the oven to Mr. Weidmayer and he will explain it to you.

I hope you keep yourself informed upon all the engagements between our troops and the Yankees. You will see in the papers I send by Mr. Weidmayer an account of our success at Charleston. I am glad to hear Mr. W. brought your Grand Pa some groceries. So far we have been living on those we captured. Bacon is getting scarce in the army and the rations have been reduced 1/4 pound and the men receive 1/5 pound of sugar instead. While we are using beef we get full rations. I never hear a complaint from the men although they have often to pay one fifth of a whole year's wage for a pair of boots. Some of the men who get twelve dollars a month pay forty five dollars for one pr. of boots. It is getting too late for me to write much more.

Major Elijah V. White of the 35th
Battalion Virginia Cavalry.

Tell Cousin Mittie I have sent her a copy
of a Yankee girl's letter which I think the best
I have seen. It was captured by Major White.
With much love to each and every member of
our household I am your devoted father
R.H. Dulany

[P.S.] There are several old Ledgers in the
garret in a box, I want you to get me two of the
largest and send them to me by Mr. Kinchloe
who will be at Welbourne next week. Tell
Cousin Mittie please to get the butter if it is
first rate. I will try and send you some apples by
a wagon that I send for the bellows and anvil
at the shop below the stable.

*Letter of Richard H. Dulany to his father, John
Peyton Dulany:*

Camp New Market, 9th Feb.

Dear Father,
You will think that I intend to establish a
daily mail between us if I bother you with many
more letters. I send for the bellow and anvil as
we have no use for it at Welbourne and we are
much in want of it here. If the servants have
any dried apples please send all they can spare.

Did you get a letter from me enclosing a
hundred dollar interest-bearing note a week or
two since? If you have any of the first issue of
Confederate notes you had better keep until
you get an opportunity to invest them as the
Gov. will sell no more eight percent bonds
after the 1st of April and only now in the
redemption of the first issued notes.

Do you think it would be a good plan to sell
your Missouri bonds and invest in Confederate
notes in Loudoun. Mike tells me that they can
be bought at fifty cents on the dollar. I do not

think Missouri bonds as good as Va's.

Mr. Weidmayer says that John Burke can
sell your Missouri bonds of $1000 for $2000 in
the Va. notes. If he can, you can make fifty
percent in the sale of the notes and purchase
Va. bonds, that is with the whole transaction.
Va. notes sell at a premium in Richmond of 25
to 35 percent to the runners of the Blockade.
This would make nearly sixty percent. I do not
know what risk you run in the bonds crossing
the lines, but from Mr. Wiedmayer's former
success I think there is little or no risk.

Ask Cousin Armistead what he thinks of
the following quotations from the New York
Herald:

Reg. Bonds	Jan. 3	10th	17th	24th	31st
US 6's	98	97	95	95	92-3/4
Va.	62	64	64-1/2	69	71
Missouri	61-1/2	65	64-3/4	66-3/4	65-3/4

You must recollect that these quotations
are from Northern papers and the stocks are
purchased by our enemies, even although we
have refused to pay the Yankees with principal
or interest in our bonds. The English demand
I suppose really regulates the price of the Va's.
If you could exchange even you would do well.
Va. 6's now worth in Richmond 106. If you act
at all, I think you can not do so too soon.

I enclose a note to Mr. Weidmayer, if he
has not started, please give it to him. I have
asked him to purchase for me a cavalry horse.
I dislike the idea of even the chance of losing
Black Hawk when I may get another at one
fourth his value that will answer every
purpose. The horses Mr. W. purchased are too
delicate and the best riding horse will not
jump. The Yanks could have caught me easily
if they had had the courage to follow as I could
not get him over a fence three feet high when

John Burke of the banking firm of
Burke & Herbert in Alexandria

Black Hawk was a prize horse.

within short range of their guns at Berryville.

Please send by Mr. Kinchloe two old blank account books which I have written Mary for.

As ever your devoted son
R.H. Dulany

On February 26, Dulany was involved in actions near Strasburg and Middletown. His report to Capt. Walter K. Martin, Asst. Adj. Gen., was published in the Official Records and is quoted here in full:

Camp Myers was near New Market

Thomas Marshall, grandson of Chief Justice John Marshall, was born at Oak Hill, Fauquier County, Virginia, in 1826. He was a volunteer aide-de-camp to Stonewall Jackson before becoming captain, then lieutenant colonel of the 7th Virginia Cavalry on October 30, 1862; he often commanded the regiment in Col. Dulany's absence. Col. Dulany and his men maintained the highest opinion of him.[8]

Oliver Ridgeway Funsten, Clarke County doctor and farmer, enlisted in Co. D, 6th Virginia Cavalry, and transferred on November 1, 1863, to the 11th Virginia.[9]

Camp Myers, Va., March 16, 1863.

Captain: On returning to my camp from Edinburg, on February 26, I found my regiment had been ordered to mount and move down the Valley turnpike to meet the enemy, who were said to be near Woodstock in considerable force and coming up the pike. Lieutenant-Colonel Marshall had taken command, and had left, with 220 men, about fifteen or twenty minutes before I returned. I immediately started to overtake the regiment, and, after a gallop of 12 miles, reached the head of the column, 4 miles below Woodstock. Here I met a courier from General Jones, ordering me to press forward, as he, with Colonel Funsten, had attacked the enemy, routed him, and was driving him toward Strasburg.

After a forced march of 19 miles, we came up with General Jones and Colonel Funsten at Strasburg, where the Eleventh, or rather what remained of it—the larger portion of it having gone back with prisoners as they were captured—had halted from sheer exhaustion. General Jones here ordered me to move forward rapidly, as the Yankees had halted and reformed on the hill beyond the town. When we reached the high ground beyond Strasburg, we found the enemy had retired, and again formed about 300 yards south of Cedar Creek. About 130 had crossed the creek, and, as near as I could estimate, about 250 had formed to meet us. As we came in sight of each other, they seemed to advance slowly toward us, but when we got within 200 yards, our sabers drawn, and the charge ordered, their hearts failed them, and, wheeling in beautiful order, they went at full speed to the bridge, crossed, and again formed to receive us. As but 2 men could cross the bridge abreast, they could easily have prevented our crossing with their long-range guns, as their position was very strong and higher than the bridge.

Changing the direction of our column, we crossed the creek at the ford, some 200 yards below the bridge. As soon as a portion of my command had crossed, the enemy again broke, not waiting for us to close with them. Having rested their horses some ten minutes, and the advantage of a start of a long and steep hill, we could not overtake them until near Middletown.

The race now became truly exciting. It was a helter-skelter chase, the fastest horses in our column taking the lead. As we came up with the rear, not a man that I saw offered to surrender until driven back by the sabers of my men or shot. Some, finding we were overtaking them, slipped from their horses and sought refuge in the houses along the road, and many had thrown their pistols away when captured. We captured about 70 prisoners—5 of them were too nearly dead to move or parole, and 2 others were left on the roadside, being broken down and unable to travel—53 horses, and a large number of arms.

At 1-1/2 miles beyond Middletown I had reluctantly to order a halt, as by far the large number of our horses were nearly, and many completely, broken down, after a race of 26 miles.

Respectfully,
R.H. Dulany,
Colonel Seventh Virginia Cavalry[10]

Jones in his own report stated, "The willingness of the men and the strength of the horses are a whole volume in praise of the sound judgment and untiring industry, during the past rigorous winter, of Colonels Funsten and Dulany, and on this occasion both gallantly led what they had so well prepared."[11]

An undated letter of John Peyton Dulany to Richard H. Dulany contains the first reference to the partisan ranger John Singleton Mosby, who had begun operations in Loudoun County in January of 1863. On June 10, 1863, at Rector's Crossroads [now Atoka], Mosby's command would officially become Company A, 43rd Battalion Virginia Cavalry.

Welbourne

My Dear Son,

I have to congratulate you upon the safe arrival of Mr. Weidmayer, who will write you an account of his adventures. He has had a most unpleasant trip of it in which he has displayed a great deal of tact and judgment. He has been very fortunate in succeeding in his mission. Charles Stewart has shown himself in this instance as in every other truly your friend. Mr. Wiedmayer has purchased the horse that Hal Dulany once owned. I fear he is too thin in flesh to be of much service for some time. Mr. Weidmayer had to leave the mare and horse at the river, as they put him under arrest, and sent him back to Baltimore, and from thence to Washington, and during the time that he was absent, the miserable wretches rode the horse almost to death. I do not think the horse is safe here as the Yankees have made a raid coming up as far as Middleburg.

Capt. Moseby [sic] (I think is his name) with about twenty men made a charge on them two nights since—John deButts took one prisoner and a horse. These attacks on them generally result in their making their reprisals on us. Unless our men could remain and protect our property, it would be better for us if they staid away.

I feel great anxiety about Vicksburg and Charleston, if we can only beat them off from those points, I shall be much more sanguine than I am at present. England & France I think have plainly showed that they have no intention of interference.

I send you some late Northern papers. I wrote you a long letter intending to send it by Moses, but he went off without it. I sent it yesterday by Rutty Eliason. I do not think you will feel disposed to find fault with the shortness of my letters in future. If you have an opportunity of having your horses attended to, do you not think it would be better to send and get the horse Mr. Weidmayer purchased for you, as I think he is very unsafe where he is. I am afraid you will be very much disappointed in his appearance. I am glad to say that Haley is sometimes well enough to ride over to Welbourne tho' still very weak & emaciated. Farewell my beloved son. May God protect you.

J.P.D.

John Peyton deButts had joined Mosby's Rangers.

Partial letter of Richard H. Dulany to his father, John Peyton Dulany, describing his recent

engagement in words more emotionally charged
than those used in his official report:

March 3rd 1863.
Camp Myers near New Market.

My dear Father,
    Your letter written since Moses made you
a visit was handed to me last night. We have
had quite a stirring time since I last wrote. On
the morning of the 26th I left camp with
Clarence to take a fencing lesson in Edinburg
about two miles from Camp. When we
returned we found the Regiment had been
ordered to advance and meet the Enemy who
were advancing in force up the Valley pike.
The 11th Cav., Col. Funsten being nearest the
pike, got the start of the 7th by some fifteen
minutes. As soon as Clarence and I could get
our arms we started at a rapid gait to overtake
Col. Marshall, who in my absence had taken
command of my regiment.
    After a gallop of five or six miles we came
in with our regiment and on reaching the head
of the column Col. Marshall informed me that
the 11th were but a half mile in advance and
that the Yankee Cavalry numbering five
hundred were four miles this side of Strasburg.
Before we could overtake the 11th we received
a dispatch from Genl Jones telling us to hurry
on as they were in sight of the Yanks. The
Genl. found the rear guard dismounted and
charged and cut them off from the main body.
He then charged the main body. Four of the
11th were shot and I fear they will all die. After
a very slight resistance the enemy retreated at
full speed, having men from their rear
captured or shot at every stop. The men of the
11th returning with their prisoners impeded us
somewhat, but we overtook Col. Funsten at

Strasburg with a portion of his command. The Yankees had made a stand and had driven his advance back to this point.

Genl. Jones here met me and ordered me to advance and attack the enemy who had ralleyed and formed on the hill above the town. Passing Col. Funsten, who had captured about one hundred men and horses besides having killed and wounded a number, we went at a brisk gallop to the top of the hill and found the Yanks had left. I then ordered Lieut. Smith with fifteen men from Hatcher's company forward as an advance guard. Coming to the top of the next hill, I found my advance falling back and galloping to the top of the hill I saw about two hundred Cav. had formed in the low land, about three hundred yards this side Cedar Creek bridge. They were in a very compact body and I was certain would give us a hard fight as they had about the same number on the other side of the creek.

As soon as my men closed up a little (one column being very much scattered from our long and hard ride) I ordered the sabers drawn and the charge. The Yanks commenced a slow march toward us, but when the boys gave one yell, their hearts failed them and wheeling in beautiful order they started for the bridge, crossed and reformed on the other side of the creek. As we could only cross the bridge by twos and at a walk, it would have been easy matter for them to prevent our crossing, so I ordered the head of the column to the right and crossed at a ford a hundred yards below. As we cleared the creek they broke again and then we had a helter skelter race for three miles. Their horses having had rest for two or three minutes and a start of two hundred yards over a steep hill, we had hard work to catch up

Granville T. Smith, 1st lieutenant, Co. A, 7th Virginia Cavalry, was cited by Gen. Jones for personally wounding four of the enemy with his saber.[12]

Dan Hatcher led the company. The Hatcher family owned a mill on Cromwell's Run, west of Middleburg.

with them, but by dint of cruel spurring we came up with the rear of their column at Middletown ten miles from Winchester. Then we commenced using our sabers and pistols in good earnest and before we had ridden with them two miles we had captured sixty-odd men, fifty-three horses, and killed or wounded ten or fifteen. Black Hawk proved his worth and speed. I had sometimes to fall back to urge the men forward and then with a blow with the flat side of my saber, he would soon regain the head of the column.

When I got into their rear I returned my saber and drew my pistol as I could hardly miss a man when I could touch him with the barrel. Scarcely a man asked for quarter until entirely cut off by my men. In passing one man I shot him directly above the hip and as he did not surrender I again shot him through the neck when he fell from his horse. Passing another I shot him through the back when he threw both hands [up] and fell backwards from his horse. I did not wish to shoot again at such close quarters and the next man I came up with I struck him a back hand lick with my pistol across the nose which tumbled him over as if he had been shot.

Capt. John H. Magruder, Co. B., 7th Virginia Cavalry.

Lieut. Smith and Capt. Magruder kept at the head of our men and used their sabers with rapidity but with too little force. They seemed more anxious to merely punish their adversaries than to kill them. If they had used their pistols we should have punished the enemy much more severely. It is an awful thing to be obliged to take another's life, but it is our duty never the less, and the more that are killed in each engagement the sooner the war will close and life will be saved in the end.

The Yanks fired a few shots after we closed with [them] but [they] seemed to know nothing of defending themselves with the saber. After running our horses twenty seven [miles] and leaving all my men behind except fifteen I ordered a halt that they might close up, as they were now scattered over two miles. Lieut. Ashby seemed to regret the order very much, as he said he had just come up with a Yankee and was in the act of trying [to find out] how hard a blow a Yankee could take over the head without falling. The Yanks paid little attention to my halting, keeping the gait they had been running for many miles. An hour after we fell back, two hundred and eighty cavalry came out from Winchester and came as far as Strasburg.

3rd Lt. Luther R. Ashby, Co. A, 7th Virginia Cavalry.

A citizen has come out from Middletown who says that they (Yanks) said [they] were fired into by infantry and pursued by Jackson for four miles with artillery and that they had lost two hundred and sixty men. We claim but two hundred and thirty. We all (the 7th) got back to our camp at 11 o'clock at night after a ride of fifty-odd miles in some ten hours. We returned in a very slow walk as our horses were much jaded. I did not lose a man.

The day after our return I sold the captured horses for about ten thousand dollars after selecting of the best for our transportation. Clarence seemed much mortified that he did not get with the head of our column until just as I halted; his mare had attempted to run away with him, and while he was trying to shorten his curb we passed him. He has been taking fencing lessons and was very anxious to put his lessons into practice. If I had gone twenty yards farther he would have had an opportunity.

Henry H. "Harry" Hatcher
resigned from the 7th Virginia
Cavalry to join Mosby's Rangers.

Cousin A. is probably Arthur
deButts since the reference is to
John deButts's investment.

You could not have received one of my
letters in which I gave you reason why I could
not get a commission for Clarence. Genls. Lee
or Stuart are the only persons who can give
commissions. Ninety-nine out of a hundred
commissions are elective and are obtained by
men who have raised Companies or have been
elected by the men. I have just given Clarence
the place of Sergeant Major, which has become
vacant by the resignation of Harry Hatcher, one
of the most daring men of the army.

I hope Mr. Weidmayer has returned. I feel
quite anxious about him. Please ask cousin A.
if he objects to investing John's funds in Va.
registered stock. I should be glad to receive an
answer to [my] letter to him. I will try and get
you a few condemned horses if I can. All horses
sell high here, being very scarce. Could not
Mike purchase them in Loudoun? or in Md? I
told Mike he might put the small field by Mrs.
Rutter's in corn for one half. Could you not
put one hundred acres of good land at such
terms. Mike wanted me to give him two thirds
but I would keep every acre in sod rather than
let such land at less. It is certain of ten blls. if a
good season, which at $5 per bll. would pay $25
for the cultivation. I suppose you can run two
plows, which ought to break seventy-five to ninety
acres, which would ... [rest of letter missing]

*Union depredations did not occur only at
Welbourne. From Richland in Stafford County
Mary Ann Dulany Whiting, Col. Dulany's sister,
wrote to General Marsena R. Patrick,
Provost-Marshal of the Army of the Potomac,
requesting compensation for goods confiscated by
Union troops:*

March 5, 63
General Patrick

Sir

I have heard from many of your
benevolence, and that you were willing to
compensate those who had lost by your
division of the Army. I hope that I have not
been misinformed, for if I should not be
renumerated at least for some of the property
taken from our estate I know not what I shall
do for a subsistence.

When your Army first invaded our portion
of Virginia, we were surrounded by plenty, our
farm well stocked and the crops of two years
upon it. Now all that is left us is the wheat and
even that has not entirely escaped, as the
cavalrymen frequently feed their horses upon
them. They have taken the last ear of corn out
of the corn house, which was full, and a shock
of hay, and for that I received $200. The same
quantity of hay this year bring [illegible]. The
hay alone brought $200 last year.

The evening before the Army advanced
upon Fredericksburg a party of Soldiers came
into my yard and took from it the only two
horses I had left for the cultivation of the farm.
The Captain of the party gave his receipt for
the horses and said that he had orders from the
Provost to take them. The next morning I
went to headquarters to endeavor to have the
horses returned.

I saw them both in camp, one was attached
to a baggage wagon, the other was in
possession of a young man attached to General   Gen. Albion P. Howe
Howe's staff.

I applied to General Pratt, who was then in   Gen. Calvin E. Pratt
command of the Regiments. He promised me
in the presence of his staff, for he was at the

head of the Army and just about to advance, that he would return the horses the next day, but he has not kept his word.

If it should be in your power to have me paid for the horses, I would be very grateful to you. I have eight children to support and but fifteen dollars in current funds to meet all expenses, and there is no one to provide for them but myself.

Very respectfully
Mary D. Whiting

P.S. The horses are worth $300. I could not purchase such for $500. I have written to General Pratt, but have received no answer. If it should not be in your power to pay for the horses, please enclose this letter to General Pratt.

References to Mosby's raids indicate that the following undated letter was written by John Peyton Dulany to his son on Wednesday, March 18, or Wednesday, March 25, 1863:

Wednesday
Welbourne

My dear Richard,

I have just received your note requesting me to send you a hat and some collars—I sent the hat but you carried off all the collars you had. I regret very much that you should have lost the services of Black Hawk at the very time you stood most in need of them. Will the bay supply his loss? We are well, thank God. I send two letters from the girls who will no doubt give you all the gossip of the neighborhood.

Capt. Mosby sent out five of his men the day before yesterday. They returned with five Yankees and their horses, etc. two lieutenants & three privates. He started on yesterday on a

Black Hawk was not hurt in battle; he had foundered.

Mosby conducted a raid at Herndon Station on March 17 and one on March 23 to capture federal outposts at Chantilly and Frying Pan.

scout with about a hundred men.

I feel very anxious about John deButts as I have no doubt but they will meet a large force. They have gone into the neighborhood of Lovettsville where it is said the Yankees have from four or five hundred cavalry. Mosby's success has made him very reckless. He told me he had captured from the enemy from four to five hundred men and an equal number of horses.

Lovettsville is twenty miles NNE of Welbourne, about two miles south of Berlin (Brunswick), Md.

I was very sorry to hear that you will be on the Court Martial to try R. Carter but I suppose there is no help for it.

This number is likely a cumulative figure of men captured during all the raids since January 1863.[13]

Possibly Richard Welby Carter of Crednal; records incomplete.

From private appearances I think that Gen. Hooker intends making a move—it is reported that they intend to make a stand somewhere near Centreville, near a place that has always been so fatal to them. The papers of the 17th records so many victories that I can hardly give them credence, but I presume you are much better posted on what is going on in the world than I am who so seldom see a paper. The weather has been so unfavourable that very little has been done on the farm or garden.

Dulany suspects that Maj. Gen. Joseph Hooker, then commander of the Army of the Potomac, will take a stand near Manassas.

I think the man you have employed is very industrious so far. I hope it will continue. Let me hear from you by every opportunity. You know how much anxiety I feel about you. May our gracious merciful God watch over and preserve you from all danger is the prayer of your

fond Father
J.P.D.

Letter of Richard H. Dulany to his daughter Fanny:

Camp near Front Royal 26 March [1863]

My dear Fan

I have to thank you for another very

acceptable letter. Both Mary and you are improving in your writing as well as in your composition. Continue to take pains and you will find but little trouble in writing a good hand. Your Cousin Julia in her last note informed me that you were studying well. If you knew the pleasure such information gives me you would not regret your application to your books but try still more each hour of your school days. I look forward with much pleasure, if God spares my life to the end of this war, to the enjoyment of my dear children's society, and the more they improve themselves the more we shall each to have to enjoy.

We moved to this place two days since. The weather was very unpleasant during our march and our wagon horses suffered great fatigue from the bad condition of the roads.

At dawn on March 17, 1863, Brig. Gen. Averell crossed the Rappahannock River at Kelly's Ford, surprising Brig. Gen. Fitzhugh Lee. Pelham charged with the 3rd Virginia Cavalry and was wounded by shell fragments. He died early the next day.[14]

I suppose you heard of the fight between a portion of our cavalry under General Stuart and a large force of the Enemy near Kelly's Ford. Poor Pelham was killed and we lost many men before Genl. Stuart succeeded in driving the Yankees across the river. One hundred and fifty Yankee cavalry came as far as one of my picket posts this morning but returned as soon as they perceived our videttes. I suppose they merely desired to know where we were.

Tell your Grandfather that I caught Stewart who deserted from my Company last March, who offered to lead the Yankees to Welbourne. I have charged him with desertion, and I think the Court will either sentence him to work with ball and chain, during the war, upon public works or he will be shot, which he richly deserves. It was a hard struggle between feeling and duty before I could make up my mind to take him from his wife and children, but many better men may be kept from the crime of desertion by Stewart's punishment as an example.

Our commissary stores were so low some time since that Genl. Jones had to send one of my companies and one from the 11th to north western Virginia to get cattle. One of the men has returned with some prisoners and informs me that they had secured five hundred.

When we fail to get beef, we give the men only one fourth of a pound of bacon a day. While this is not more than a third as much as they really require, I have never seen one man grumble. Once a number of the men came to my tent to show me the allowance and asked if they could not have more as one man could eat more than four received. I told them that I was sorry that I could not increase the allowance as we had so large an army to feed. They looked a little disappointed but without a complaint turned laughingly away, saying that they would live on bread on that day so that they might have a half pound of meat the next. Ask your Grand Pa if he thinks such men can be subdued?

We are waiting anxiously to hear something from Vicksburg and Charleston as the enemy are making every effort to capture these cities. We see almost every week Northern papers of victories won over our troops and of steamboats captured, but we have not to wait long before the same paper confesses that they were misinformed.

How are the boys getting on with their studies? Does John improve in his music? Tell him that I shall expect to find him much improved when I return. I have applied for a short leave of absence that I may make you a visit before the spring campaign commences.

Our Brigade will have active work and

William N. Stewart of Co. A, 6th Virginia Cavalry, was taken prisoner of war in March 1862 (or may have deserted) and exchanged in August 1862 from Fort Delaware. He was detailed to public works in the provost marshal's office or as a detective on the Virginia Central Railroad from December 2, 1863, to March 27, 1865.[15]

The deButts home, Grassland, was in Warren County.

Capt. Daniel C. Hatcher of Co. A, 7th Virginia Cavalry, who would later be promoted to major and command the remnants of the Seventh at the surrender at Appomattox.[16]

plenty of it as soon as the grass grows.

I am very sorry to hear that Mr. Weidmayer is sick, I hope it is only from the excitement of his trip.

If I do not get a leave of absence in two weeks I will write him to try and make some arrangements to bring you all to your Cousin Richard deButts that I may see you there. I am not more than (12) twelve miles from his house.

Say to your Grand Pa that I received his letter and Mr. Weidmayer's and some newspapers by Capt. Hatcher. Remember me in kindest terms to Mr. Weidmayer and tell him how much I am indebted to him for his kind attention to my business in New York. I received his letter which interested me very much—I have just received Northern papers which show that they are not at all sanguine of taking Vicksburg. If we can only be successful in our next two great battles, we may then look for peace.

Our scouts inform us this morning that the Yankees are leaving Winchester. I hope this may be so.

Say to your Cousin Julia that as I hope to be at Welbourne before long I shall not answer her letter.

With much love to Cousin Mittie, Cousin Mary, Julia, May and the boys, I am as ever your devotedly attached father

R.H. Dulany

[P.S.] Remember me in kind terms to the servants.

On April 20th, Jones and Imboden began an expedition to destroy the Baltimore & Ohio Railroad between Oakland, Maryland, and Rowlesburg, West Virginia. Their route lay

*through Greenland Gap, where the enemy made
a stand around a log church.*

*On April 25, Dulany and Lieutenant Colonel
Marshall were ordered to charge the works.
Which of the colonels should lead the charge was
a matter of military etiquette, settled when
Marshall took the head of the column over some
demur from Dulany. Dulany was wounded,
falling within easy range of federal marksmen. His
horse was killed in the fray, for which he was later
compensated. Afterward Marshall joked that it
looked as if he wished to leave the dangerous place
to Col. Dulany.*

*The Federals were finally driven from the
church by burning it, but the Confederates had
suffered appalling casualties, and Jones had some
trouble in calming his men, some of whom wanted
to shoot the prisoners.*

*George Neese, of the horse artillery, saw
Dulany at Moorefield the next day. He may have
recuperated in a private home or temporary
hospital for some time.*[17]

Fanny Dulany to her father:

April 25th

Dear Papa,

   We have missed you very much since you
went away. We are very sorry to hear that
Black Hawk was foundered. Cousin Mit, Mr.
Weidmayer and myself, walked to Church in
Upperville last Sunday. I was very warm but
not at all tired when we got there, we had
Communion.

   After church was over, we saw Aunt Ida,
and cousin Sophy Carter, who is staying at
Oakley. She, and Cousin Fanny are coming
here next week.

   Then we went to see Aunt Mary Eliason,

Louisa deButts was the daughter of Richard and Sarah deButts of Grassland.

Mr. Reardon was the gardener at Welbourne.

Nancy Jackson, the mammy; Julia Peters, a chambermaid; and "Aunt" Emily, a cook.

she was looking very well. After we had stayed with her a little while, we went to cousin Eliza's and ate dinner and stayed until five o'clock; she and Lou deButts came with us as far as the bridge below Mr. Glasscock's, on our way back home.

When we came to the creek Cousin Mit, said she could not go across the log, and insisted on going up the side of the creek to see if she could not find a place to get over; but the water was too deep everywhere but just as she had made up her mind to come over the log Mr. Reardon came by on horseback and Uncle Armistead called to him and asked him if "he would not take that lady across the creek" not knowing who it was.

But of course Cousin Mit would not get up behind Mr. Reardon, so she told Uncle Armistead if he would come across and get on the horse then she would get up behind him, and come over. So Uncle Armistead came over and got on the horse, and Cousin Mit got behind him. But just as the horse got in the middle of the creek, Cousin Mit got in such a fit of laughter she nearly fell in but they got over safely.

Mr. Reardon seems to be a very industrious man.

We have had a great deal of rain for the last two or three days, Grandpa says that it will put back the work in the garden for nearly a week, but it seems to be clearing up now.

We are all well; all the children send their love, as well as mammy, Julia and Aunt Emily.

Your affectionate daughter
Fanny C. Dulany

Letter of Mary Dulany to her father:

May 4th. [1863]

My Dear Papa,

We received your letter last night, I am very sorry that you have been wounded, and wish very much that I could come to see you; last night when I read your letter to the boys Johnnie suddenly commenced sobbing violently, and when I asked him what was the matter, (thinking that he would say because you were wounded) he answered because Papa can't fight any more.

Major Mosby went three miles the other side of Warrenton yesterday and captured a whole regiment but a brigade coming up recaptured all but forty, Major Mosby lost ten men, two killed and eight either wounded or captured poor Capt. Du Chene [sic] was so badly wounded that he was left on the field.

> Mosby captured forty from the 1st (West) Virginia Cavalry, U.S.A., but lost them to the 5th New York & 1st Vermont cavalries at Warrenton Junction (now Calverton).[18] Samuel P. Ducheane was taken to Old Capitol Prison, exchanged, and later served in the Confederate Signal Corps.[19]

I have told you everything in my journal, except that Cousin Mitty and Cousin Julia met us at church yesterday, and that we spent the day at Aunt Mary's and came home in the evening.

Your affectionate daughter
Mary Dulany.

Grandpapa saw Cousin Johnny an hour or two ago in Upperville.

> John Peyton deButts

A second letter, enclosed with the above, from Julia Whiting to Richard H. Dulany, added some details:

Private Richard Y. (Dick) Moran,
Co. A., was among the wounded.
Born in 1814 in Loudoun County,
he was said to be the oldest man
to serve with Mosby.[20]
Madison Monroe Templeton,[21]
who had been commended by
Gen. John Hood for gallantry and
valuable service as a courier at the
battle of Sharpsburg.

The Major arrived here about 10 o'clock last night alone, bringing us the news of his discomfiture. He lost ten men killed wounded & prisoners that he knew of, there might be more. Moran of Middleburg and a scout named Templeman [sic] were killed, our acquaintance Capt. Ducheane was shot through the body and left with the Yankees. These were the only names he mentioned. Mosby came through Warrenton yesterday. The Yankees had been there just before and asked for a surgeon to attend to our men as theirs had their hands full.

Grandpapa has gone to Upperville this morning with Mosby. His men were to meet him there, on his return I suppose we shall hear more fully of our loss in the fight.

I wish you could come home and remain with us until you can rejoin your regiment. As your wound does not prevent you from riding you could always reach the mountains before the Yankees came, should they inflict themselves upon us again, and I am sure it would be much pleasanter for you to be at home.

Things are not very bright at present, no one doubts our final success, but there must be many a hard fought field first; and every one seems shadowed by gloomy foreboding of the sorrows that this campaign may bring upon us.

Poor Mama, what she must suffer now, she who has never been hopeful from the beginning and who has had so much to depress her since.

Grandpapa desires me to tell you that he thinks it would be imprudent for you to come home as the Yankees might come upon us at any time.

Your affectionate niece
J.B.W.

*John Peyton Dulany to his son Richard, an
undated letter probably written on May 6th:*

Welbourne
[May 6, 1863]

My dear Richard,

I was from home when your boys called or
I would [have] written to you, but as the
children have anticipated any information
that I could have given you, it is of less
importance.

You have no doubt heard of the daring raid
Major Mosby made three days since. He
attacked the first Va. regiment—captured
three hundred men and horses. Before he
could get them off they were strongly
re-inforced by two other regiments, who were
within half a mile of the first Va. Major
Mosby's force consisted of only from one
hundred to one hundred and twenty men—he
had of course to relinquish his prize very much
to his mortification. I fear that Mosby is too
reckless—he makes himself very conspicuous
in his dress and accoutrements. He has lost
several very brave men, but it has not yet been
ascertained how many.

We are all very anxious to hear from Lee's
army, the general impression is that there has
been a very severe fight. May our merciful
Father give us victory.

I only regret that I can not be grateful
enough for your miraculous escape. I sincerely
hope, my dear son, that you will not think of
coming home. The Yankees are all around us.
Between forty and fifty were here looking for
horses. The captain told his men to take
anything they wanted—they were in too great
a hurry to avail themselves of his permission.

1st (West) Virginia Cavalry, USA.

5th New York Cavalry and the 1st
Vermont Cavalry.

The battle of Chancellorsville,
May 1-3, 1863, considered by
many to be Lee's greatest tactical
victory.

George Hooper's blacksmith shop at Mt. Defiance, on the SW corner of Zulla Road and the Little River Turnpike (now U.S. 50), was a favorite meeting place for Mosby's men.

Their army consisting of 3,000 men came as far as the blacksmith's on the little turnpike. We could distinguish the flash of their guns very plainly from the Hill, above the house. They carried off with them about forty old men and boys and some horses. I see their papers give them credit for taking off that number of Mosby's men.

The farmers are very backward in planting. I fear that we shall not be able to begin planting for two or three weeks. We have continual rain; I do not think I ever knew so much rainfall as fell yesterday. Unfortunately, I had the lambs cut in the morning. The shepherd has been very ill for the last two weeks, is now getting better. I will know what has become of the sacks that the wool was in. It is impossible to get cotton in this country under five dollars a yard. If you could send some lint, they would do perhaps to put wool, &tc., [word effaced]

As I have filled up my paper and no doubt exhausted your patience, I bid you, my beloved boy, farewell

J.P.D.

[P.S.] If you would like Mr. Weidmayer to pay you a visit I am sure it would give him pleasure. I sincerely wish that the infirmity of age did not admonish me that it was too late for me to leave home.

Letter of Fanny Dulany to her father:

May 14th, 1863.

Dear Papa,

We were very sorry to hear of poor general Jackson's death, but were very glad of our great victory; which convinces me more, and more,

Stonewall Jackson died of pneumonia on May 10, 1863; he had been wounded by his own men.

that God is on our side.

Yesterday about twelve o'clock a company of Yankees, (at least I do not suppose there was more) passed by the front gate, but only two of them came to the house. They only stopped a few minutes, and then they rode away very rapidly; I suppose they were afraid of being left behind.

That same evening while I was practicing I thought I heard words, and on looking out the window, saw a few Yankees coming down the new road. I went in Grand Pa's room to tell him, and then went upstairs.

After a little while we thought of the silver, which was in the dining room; Cousin Mit told me to go in and get it, and when I went downstairs I saw Grand Pa talking to Captain Powell, who had followed the Yankees from Leesburg.

Captain or rather Major Mosby and Cousin Johnnie were chased by the Yankees, from Mr. Glascock's hill nearly to Mr. Bolling's.

Tomorrow is my birthday; I will be 12 years old; we are going to have a picnic, at rocky ford, or at a very pretty place in Mr. Glascock's woods.

I hope you do not suffer much from your wound.

Mary's and my vegetable gardens are all fixed, and I have planted beans, pop-corn, and cucumbers in mine. Mary has not planted anything in hers yet except pop-corn and beans; mine are seven inches tall, and my corn is almost all up.

The boys have not spaded theirs yet, but Johnnie has a good many strawberries in his.

May 15, 1863—This morning when I came in the parlor, I saw a fan, a book, and a little box, on the center table, and after having been there a little while, Dick came in bringing a basket full of flowers, which looked perfectly beautiful, and a wreath of lilies of the valley,

Capt. Edward B. Powell, Co. F, 6th Virginia Cavalry, enrolling officer for Loudoun, Fauquier, Prince William and Fairfax counties.[22]

On May 14, 1863, a detachment under Capt. William F. Boyd, 1st New York Cavalry, chased about forty of Mosby's men from Upperville to the mountains.[23]

Aquilla Glascock of Rockburn; Robert Bolling of Bollingbrook.

and gave them to me. Hal gave me the fan,
Mary the book, and Johnnie, six very pretty
Sunday-school cards.

Letter of John Peyton Dulany to his son:

Welbourne, Saturday, 16 May 1863.

My Dear Son,

As Mr. Weidmayer intends starting on
Monday morning to pay you a visit I do not
feel disposed to let him go without a few lines
altho' all I can say will be anticipated by the
many letters you will get by him. I send you a
horse that I purchased from John
deButts—left him to be valued by Armistead
and Henry Arthur Hall. Armistead put him
[at] $700, Hall $450, which will make him cost
you $575. It is almost impossible to buy a horse
at any price here.

Since I last wrote to you a few days since
the Yankees have paid us two visits. It really
appears that our men and the Yankees must
have some understanding. The Yankees are
sure to be here the day after Mosby's raid—on
yesterday the Yankees were here with 210
men—they went the whole circuit of the
county. They met with very little opposition
from our men, altho' there was Capt. Mosby,
Capt. Powell and a captain from Maryland
whose name I have forgotten, in the county,
but whose men could not be collected.

All appears to be in confusion. I hear this
morning that Capt. [Dan] Hatcher is in the
neighbourhood. Alas, he is a day too late. A
part of the Yankee cavalry passed up the road
by the house—about forty, evidently very
much alarmed, but there were none to make
them afraid. If Mosby does not try to organize
the few men he has with him he had better

return to the army, I know you will think it presumptive to find fault when if I were placed in their situation I could not do as well—perhaps so.

Mr. Weidmayer has this moment come in to inform me that Capt. Hatcher has captured 60 Yankees, I hope it is so. We are still hoping that Gen. Lee will take pity on us and deliver us at least for a few weeks from the tender mercies of the Yankees.

The weather has been so very unfavorable that we have not been able to begin planting corn—the potatoes have been planted. In consequence of the shepherd's illness the sheep have not been sheared, and it has been fortunate as we had a hail storm a day or two since. What do you wish to do with the wool? Will you make some enquiries about the sacks—I do not see how I can do without them.

I have had the satisfaction of hearing cheering news that you are rapidly improving. I have only left myself room to pray that our God may bless and protect my dear Boy

J.P.D.

Jones left the Valley on June 1st, arriving at Madison Court House on the 3rd. Dulany probably accompanied the march. On June 5th, he was admitted to the Charlottesville General Hospital and was placed on Jones's list of casualties. According to his service record, he was treated for "vulnus sclopeticum. Character and location: slight of left arm." The Latin phrase identifies a gunshot wound.

Clarence Whiting was wounded at the battle of Brandy Station on June 9th and was cited for his gallantry by General Jones. He was admitted to Charlottesville General Hospital on June 17, 1863. This partial letter to his grandfather, John

Peyton Dulany, was probably written between June 17 and June 30:

My Dear Grandfather,

Uncle Richard requests me to thank you, Cousin Armistead and children for the letters sent by Mr. Weidmayer, and regrets that he can not answer them. He is at present suffering a good deal from his wound but seems cheerful. The Doctor thinks he is now doing very well and that he will be able to ride in a few days. He is to come here today and Mr. Weidmayer will tell you what he says of the state of the wound. Uncle R. wants you to make Triplett have a place made near the creek in the woods to feed the horses and keep them there all the time, so that they will be less exposed to the Yankees.

He wants you to send the Black Hawk colt and the young Cleveland mare down to some of the Quakers. He thinks that it will be well to send the cattle from Millsville to Grassland and put part of those at Welbourne at Millsville, so that there will be as few as possible at each place.

Uncle Richard expects to be able to ride without giving any injury to his arm by Sunday. What wonderful escapes men have, the ball missing both the elbow and artery, inflecting merely a flesh wound, where a dangerous one could so easily have been given.

Uncle R. has sent for the wool socks and will send them down by Stephen, who has been very sick.

Uncle Richard wishes Alfred Hoe and Reardon to make boxes around the trees that he planted, whenever it is too wet to work in the garden. ... [rest of letter missing.]

Stephen was a servant at Welbourne.

There was a time during the war when Col.
Dulany came behind the Northern lines to see his
family at Welbourne. His horse was hidden in the
cellar, and the colonel was enjoying a visit with his
children when a servant ran in, exclaiming,
"Marse Richard, de Yankees is comin' down de
driveway!" Dulany hurriedly mounted his horse,
galloped toward the stables and raced across the
fields, leaping the high stone fences with ease. The
Federals followed, firing their pistols at the fleeing
figure, but were unable to catch him.

One of the Yankee officers, finding a gauntlet
that Dulany had dropped, decided to have some
fun with the children, who were anxiously waiting
at Welbourne to discover their father's fate. The
Northern lieutenant squeezed the juice of summer
blackberries over the entire glove before taking it
to Mary, Dulany's eldest child at age fourteen.
Explaining that they had not succeeded in
capturing the colonel but had wounded him in his
flight, the Yankee showed her the gauntlet covered
with "blood." Looking closely at the glove, Mary
rather nonchalantly replied, "That's the first time
I ever saw blood with seeds in it."

Undated letter of John Peyton Dulany to his
son, who was still recovering from his wound:

Welbourne

My Dear Richard,

Altho' I have nothing to write about I do
not feel disposed to let Hatcher go without
dropping you a line. I will send by him a bottle
of wine, would have sent you more but do not
like to ask Hatcher to take them as it is
probable he will have a load for himself.

We have not yet finished planting corn,
will shear the sheep this week. It will be hard
to find a safe place to pack it in. It appears

impossible for those not living in the neighbourhood to realize the difficulty of hiding any thing from the Yankees. I have sent several of the colts to the mountains, I hope they will be safe there, but there is no certainty about it.

We all regret very much that you suffer so much from your wound. I only wish you could with safety be here that we might have the pleasure of nursing you. Do, if you can, try to be still for a few weeks.

Clement L. Vallandigham (1820-71) of Ohio, a Southern sympathizer, was imprisoned by Gen. Ambrose E. Burnside for inflammatory speeches. Lincoln banished him to the Confederacy. Horatio Seymour (1810-86), a conservative Democrat and Union loyalist, often found himself at odds with the Lincoln administration.[24]

We are so completely shut out from the world that we seldom know what is going on unless perchance we get hold of a stray newspaper. I think the [Lincoln] administration has made a false move in the case of Vallandigham—it is producing some feeling in New York—the Governor, Seymour, has come out like a man, and denounces the act in no measured terms.

Say to Clarence that he will have to repose on his laurels for a short time. I should suppose of [the] one thousand horses that he captured, [he] might get one that would suit him. Mr. Weidmayer arrived here last evening, very much fatigued.

The horse I sent you I hope will suit you, he was the best that could be procured.

Farewell my beloved Son, as ever your devoted Father,

J.P.D.

[P.S.] Give my love to Clarence, ask him to take a little more pains in writing.

While Dulany was recovering from his wound, the war continued to swirl around Welbourne. At Aldie, on June 17th, was the first clash of cavalry in Lee's march toward Pennsylvania.

On June 21st, after delaying the advance of
Pleasanton's cavalry at Aldie and Middleburg,
Stuart further detained the Federals near
Upperville.

The most effective of these delays was mounted
at Goose Creek bridge, an old stone bridge on
Welbourne land. Col. Strong Vincent's infantry
was ordered to force the crossing, and a charge by
the 83rd Pennsylvania and the 16th Michigan
succeeded in pushing back the defenders. Kilpatrick's
brigade followed the infantry's assault, taking up the
pursuit as the Confederates retreated toward
Upperville.

General John Buford and his troops also passed
through Welbourne in their approach toward the
battlefield.

This engagement on Welbourne land and the
subsequent encampment of federal troops on the
entire farm stripped the family of all provisions and
supplies, to the point that John Peyton Dulany was
forced to petition the provost marshal of the Union
army, General Marsena R. Patrick, for assistance.[25]

Letter of John Peyton Dulany to General
Marsena R. Patrick:

Welbourne Hall
July 22nd 1863.

General Patrick
Provost Ml. Genl. of Army of Potomac.
Head Qrs. Union Loudoun Co. Va.

Sir:

Having been deprived by the federal army
during the several periods of occupation and
passage through this neighbourhood of nearly
all my meat (7000 to 8000 pounds), 200 to 300

sheep, 100 to 180 hogs, many cattle, cows, calves, forage of every kind, my house entered and swept of all supplies of groceries and other conveniences of life—and deprived of all means of renewing my supplies, even of children's wearing apparel, I come to request of you, Sir, a pass and permit to renew such supplies as are necessary for a family's use, which in granting you will confer a great favour on Most respectfully

Yr. Obedt. Servt.

J.P. Dulany

Undated letter of John Peyton Dulany to his son written in mid-July:

Tuesday morn.
Welbourne.

My Dear Son,

As Alfred has just informed me that he intends going back to the army, I embrace the opportunity of writing you a few lines.

You are aware that the Yankee army passed through Welbourne about three weeks since, they encamped on the farm covering almost the whole farm. General Sykes paid me several visits, and General Patrick. They were very courteous and afforded me every protection in their power. General Patrick was very kind to Mary Whiting when he commanded near Richland.

Genl. Sykes gave me a guard of nearly one hundred men, sent an escort with Mr. Weidmayer to General Meade. I found they were anything but Republicans.

We have lost nearly all of our hogs, and I find some difficulty in procuring bacon for the use of the family. Mr. Weidmayer has not yet returned from Baltimore. I am looking for him with some anxiety. I am very anxious to hear

Maj. Gen. George Sykes commanded V Corps, Army of the Potomac.

Gen. George Gordon Meade commanded the Army of the Potomac.

something from the North. I much fear that the peace party have been put down since Genl. Lee's most unfortunate raid to Pennsylvania, I must not however express an opinion on a subject that I do not understand the merits of. I may hope, however, that Lee's next victory may be more decisive than any that he has [word unclear].

You have no doubt heard of Stephen's conduct, it is what I always predicted, as far as I am concerned I would cheerfully send them all to the North. They are only a dead expense to us. The Yankees leave the women and children to be supported until it suits their convenience to take them off.

Clarence left us on yesterday and intends to try and get to the army; it is getting too hot for him here. The Yankees moved in some force on Middleburg yesterday. They carry desolation in their track, taking everything they can find. It is reported they have gone back to The Plains.

Farewell my beloved Son may the God of Love protect you.

As ever your devoted
J.P.D.

Stephen had apparently fled with the Union army as it passed by Welbourne.

The Plains is a village about ten miles south of Welbourne.

A letter from J. Southgate Lemmon of Baltimore to his mother exists among the Dulany papers. Lemmon was in the 1st Maryland Infantry, C.S.A, and married Fanny Dulany after the war. This letter was apparently written aboard a ship, and in it Lemmon describes what seems to be a clandestine excursion into Virginia:

On "St. Shannon"
July 23rd 63

Dear Mother

I had only time in Halifax to drop you a line to assure you of my safety owing to the fact that instead of having to wait there over a week for the "Asia" we found this packet steamer there going to sail the very day of our arrival from Bermuda. I wrote you the outlines of my trip after leaving Geo. D. So will only add that I got through remarkably well & had almost a pleasant trip on the Va. side.

I crossed the river in the afternoon having to swim the canal between the pickets & during the absence of the patrol who passed within a few feet of me on his beat. As soon as he passed, taking off my coat, pants, vest, shoes I plunged in & swam across, carrying my watch & papers in the crown of my hat & my clothes in one hand, swimming with the other. The distance, however, being greater than I supposed, I got my clothes wet. I then swam back & brought over my shoes & some underclothes & then had to make a third trip to get my revolver, which I was of course particularly anxious to keep dry. I now still had a harder task to perform—viz. to carry this heavy bundle to the nearest island, wading through a very strong current & the river so deep in some places as to almost carry me off my feet, my clothes being so heavy with water that it was as much as I could do to lift them out of the stream, so I had to carry them *in it*.

When I reached the nearest island—some 200 yrds—I was screened from view by the bushes. So I stopped, put on my clothes, & wrung the water out of the remainder as best I could & then waded some 30 or 40 yards to the main island where after some difficulty I

George D. Lemmon, South's brother, was an assistant adjutant general on General James Jay Archers's staff at Gettysburg.

Chesapeake and Ohio Canal.

Probably Young's Island in the Dranesville area.

managed to get on my soaking shoes.

This island is quite large, being some five miles long by half a mile wide. I walked up the Virginia side about a mile. Where the Potomac looked shallow I started to wade again some 300 yards & reached the shore safely but thoroughly fagged out with carrying my heavy bundle against the strong current.

As I had been told that I would find myself within 8 miles of Leesburg on reaching the Va. shore & that Mosby's pickets had been seen opposite the day before, I felt safe & walking inland about a mile went up to the first house I saw. An old farmer came to the door & smiling at my wet plight, which was very evident, asked me whence I came. I told him. He hesitated at first, till I convinced him that I was all right & not a spy & then took me into his confidence & told me how the land lay. His story was short & sweet; I was 18 miles from Leesburg—Mosby's lines did not come further down than Leesburg—from there to Washington the whole country was scoured by federal cavalry. His own house had been searched only an hour before by them—not a horse nor conveyance of any sort to be had for love or money—not a guide. That [it] would be madness to strike across country. My only chance would be to go up to Leesburg first.

Being by this time convinced that I was all right, he then told me that his neighbor was going off that night to get a horse through the lines to sell to Mosby & that he might guide me—so we walked over there & when we got near the house, he left me in the bushes & went forward to see that no soldiers nor Yankee neighbors were there. In the meantime I was left to pleasant reflections of my situation & to the happy thought that *he* might be playing me false—so I shifted my position some 20 yards & got my revolver ready for an emergency.

In about twenty minutes he came back with an old farmer & I was again cross-examined to prove innocent of being a spy & then was hastily slipped into the house without being seen by any of his few negroes. Finding we had an hour & a half to spare before starting, he loaned me a suit of rough clothes while mine were drying before the fire. He then gave me some supper & about 9:30 I put on my clothes again only partially dried & we started.

By this time we were joined by a young man with another horse & we started, the old farmer & myself on foot. After walking some three miles the old gent told me he had to go some six miles out of the way to get his horse & told me to walk on to the next crossroad & wait for them by an old school house. I got there & waited accordingly till they would have had time to walk ten miles much less three to walk & three to ride back. I tried to sleep, but mosquitoes, chilliness, the fear of missing them kept me awake. I took my watch from around my neck where I wore it till my clothes dried & at last when quite in despair they galloped up & told me they had lost themselves in a pine forest.

I now mounted behind the young man & trotted off on by no means a *soft* saddle. We rode on till daybreak in by paths to avoid the pike & feds & then thinking ourselves safe at last, slept in the stable loft of a man some 4 miles from Leesburg. About 5 a.m. the man came out of his house & roused us after an hour's nap & gave us the cheering intelligence that Mosby had been driven out [of] that whole country, which from there to Culpeper some 65 miles was in possession of the enemy & again the old story of no horses or guides. He however sent to me a neighbor—an old gentleman who unknowing who I was & where bound stopped his only plow & putting his young son on one & me on the other horse sent me to Middleburg—some twenty-five miles—in time for dinner.

Here I found kind friends & a detachment of Mosby's men trying to get out of the way who carried me to Salem 12 miles. There we fagged out, I spent the night with more kind friends & got a conveyance next day to Culpeper 35 miles—there stayed the night with the Major's sister-in-law & went next day to Richmond by train. In all these journeys we had to take by-roads & narrowly missed the Feds in several places. I crossed the River Sunday, [and] reached Richmond Wednesday —being the only one for some weeks & making the quickest passage for months past. Will write by this mail to Belle. Love to all.

In an undated letter written in August, Nina Whiting, who was at Welbourne with her parents, wrote to her sister Julia, who was at Richland:

August

My dear Sister

When we expected Hanson to go down to Richland I wrote you quite a long letter but do not know what has become of it. I have had a very pleasant visit thus far.

Mary, Fanny & myself have been twice to Oakley, once to Oatlands and Bollingbrook since I have been up here. We spent two days

Willis Hanson, a free black for whom the hamlet of Willisville is named.[26]

Oatlands, near Leesburg, home of George Carter, Jr., whose wife, Katherine Whiting Powell, is Ida (Powell) Dulany's younger sister.

Richard P. Montjoy enlisted in the 7th Louisiana Infantry in 1861, later deserted and joined Mosby in May 1863. Mosby deemed him "one of the bravest of the brave." He was killed at Goresville, north of Leesburg, on November 27, 1864.

The daughters of Henry Tazewell Harrison, a merchant and farmer near Leesburg.

Richard and Clarence were still recuperating in Amherst County.

Possibly Lt. David Humphreys, Co. B, 7th Virginia Cavalry, who had also been wounded at Brandy Station.

Her brothers: Neville (age 9), Guy (age 7) and Richard (age 4).

at each place.

We had a very pleasant time at Bollingbrook. We met Mr. William Bolling, Boyd Smith and Capt. Montjoy of Mosby's Battalion & two Miss Harrisons from Leesburg.

I like the Miss Harrisons very much, but they were very ugly. Anna Bolling brought them over here the day before yesterday to spend the day. Cousin Mary asked Hal what he thought them. He told her, "they were very respectable people but frightfully ugly."

Moses came up yesterday bringing a budget of letters & papers from Uncle Richard & Clarence. Uncle R. says in his letter to Mamma that he is waiting for the arrival of Lieut. Humphries [sic] who was a warm friend of Clarence's who he thought would aid him in getting a Lieutenancy for Clarence. He wrote as he always does, very affectionately, & says Mama must remain perfectly quietly here till he gets a furlough, when he will do all he [has] in his power to aid her in moving to Grassland.

I would give anything if you could send me your riding dress & saddle. Very often I could go out riding with Mr. Weidmayer and Mary if I had it.

Tell Neville that Father has a Shepherd dog's puppy for him and is going to get one for Guy & Richard. Mr. W., Mary & myself take very long walks after supper very often. Last night we walked to the creek & were caught in the rain. I hope you are all well and have escaped the chills.

With love to Aunt Ellen & the children

I remain your affectionate sister

Nina

Colonel Dulany's wound was slowly healing. On August 15, 1863, he was again admitted to the General Hospital in Charlottesville, and on the 30th he was recommended for a 30-day medical furlough. This was approved on September 2nd, and he spent the rest of September and the first week in October at Welbourne.[27]

The colonel's ten-year-old son Johnny died on September 11th of diphtheria or scarlet fever. No mention of this sad happening appears in existing letters.

From the diary of Mary Dulany:

Thursday, Oct. 8th. Papa and Cousin Clarence left yesterday morning. This evening we went with Mr. Weidmayer to gather nuts, and we brought home several baskets full. We have found several small geraniums in the garden which we thought dead, but which are budding from the roots, and have put them in the parlour window.

Friday, Oct. 9th. The weather was very bright and pleasant today. After dinner we went to see Aunt Priscilla and I read to her in the Bible. I am making a blue and white silk basket to give Fanny [for] Christmas. It is rather early to begin Christmas presents, but it takes me a long time because I can only work on them when I am alone.

Saturday, Oct. 10th. This morning Cousin Mit let Dick go to Old Welbourne behind Cousin Welby deButts, but they had not been long gone before she came uneasy for fear the horse would hurt him and went with Fanny to bring him back.

A little while after Aunt Ida and Jenny arrived and as Grandpa and Mr. Weidmayer were out riding there was no one at home but

Old Welbourne was the original Dulany home. Cousin Welby is Samuel Welby deButts II, brother of John Peyton deButts.

Jenny Powell, Ida's sister.

myself. After dinner Mrs. Seaton came to see Cousin Mit but she had not arrived; at last about sunset she returned having after all allowed Dick to ride home.

Sunday [October 11th]. There was no church here today; we read the service upstairs. We had Sunday school as usual at the Chapel this evening.

Monday, October 12th. This morning while we were in school Mr. Carlyle came here to tell us that the Yankees had chased him out of Upperville; and about twelve they were here; they did no harm however, except taking some harness. One of them went into the kitchen and took the bread; he was going to take the ham too, but Aunt Emily refused to let him have it; the Yankee drew his pistol and told her that if she did not let him have it he would shoot her. In reply to this, Aunt Emily took a carving knife in her hand and placed herself before the ham and dared him to touch it. Here an officer interfered, but for this I dare say the affair would have ended in a fight, at least Aunt Emily says "she would have scrumished right long for that ham."

While Dulany was absent because of his wounds, changes had taken place in the cavalry. General Thomas Lafayette Rosser, then colonel of the 5th Virginia Cavalry, assumed command of Jones's brigade on September 23, 1863.[28] Rosser later christened it the "Laurel Brigade." This unit comprised the 7th, 11th and 12th Virginia Cavalry, the 35th Virginia Cavalry Battalion and, at times, the 6th Virginia Cavalry. The men wore sprigs of laurel in their hats. The brigade was in Rappahannock County when Dulany joined it.

*Dispatch from General Thomas L. Rosser to
Colonel Richard H. Dulany:*

Confidential
Culpeper C.H. [Court House]
Nov. 5th 1863

Col:

You will move the Brigade tomorrow
morning, as early as possible, back to our old
Camp near Gaines X Roads, encamping near
the old position, within a mile & a half at
least—command as well together as
possible—Don't fail to send those scouts out,
well in direction of Winchester to discover any
move in direction of *Staunton* by the Enemy.

I will join Comd. tomorrow night if the
Court before which I am witness, can finish
with me—*Certainly* will be up very early the
next morning—

I have some things to go up and I wish you
would send an ambulance in for them
tomorrow. I will want two couriers also.

> I am Col.
> Most respy yours & c
> Thomas L. Rosser
> Brig Gen Comdg

Gaines Crossroads is now the
town of Ben Venue, in
Rappahannock County, Virginia.

*On November 17th Rosser's brigade was
ordered to break its camp near Flint Hill in
Rappahannock County and move to
Chancellorsville. After a brief skirmish at
Stevensburg, the brigade went to Hamilton's
Crossing, near Fredericksburg, to picket the fords.
To the surprise of the Confederates, Meade
crossed the Rappahannock on November 26th,
and the next day his whole army marched up the
Plank Road toward Orange Court House. Rosser
moved his brigade to Todd's Tavern, where he
learned that Meade had failed to picket the Brock*

Road, which crossed his line of march. On November 27th, Rosser attacked Meade's wagon train and captured a number of wagons and mules before he was pushed back.

Mine Run Campaign, November 26-28, 1863.

The next day, Stuart made a reconnaissance around the enemy's left, with Rosser's brigade in the lead. At Parker's Store, the advance guard, Company A of the 7th Virginia Cavalry under Captain Daniel Hatcher, assaulted an enemy camp. The brigade was strung out along a very narrow road, and the lack of formation caused some confusion, but eventually the camp was taken. The cold and hungry Confederates failed to resist the temptation of breakfasts that had been hastily abandoned. The Federals, who had been reinforced, then made a vigorous effort to regain the field in a two-hour fight chiefly among dismounted men. Rosser charged with his whole brigade and took possession of the field, but then slowly withdrew. The losses in his brigade were considerable.

The next day the Confederates expected Meade to attack, but the tempest had passed. Meade and Lee settled down into winter quarters.[29]

From Mary C. Dulany's diary:

Susan Shacklett, daughter of John Shacklett of Salem, Va.

Monday, Nov. 23. Cousin Mit and I walked to Mr. Baldwin's this evening, we met Miss Susan Shacklet, near "the Hill," coming from Berlin. No one, she says, is obliged to take the oath now to get goods from there, because the Yankees are so anxious to get wheat. I think it is very wrong to let them have it. Mr. Baldwin is going to get Fanny and I a new dress.

Lt. William Thomas Turner, Co. A., 43rd Battalion Virginia Cavalry. Mr. Hall is difficult to identify, as there were several Halls in Mosby's command.

Tuesday, Nov. 24th. Lieut. Turner and Mr. Hall were here last night and this morning. Major Mosby had a meet today but did not go on a raid. I suppose not many men assembled in the hard rain. Cousin Mary gave me six geranium slips, I hope they will all live. None of my pet fish have died yet, but Fanny is very tired of hers, so many of them are dead.

Wednesday, Nov. 25th. Grandpa and Mr. Weidmayer rode to Oakley today, they very often ride out together. We went to see Cousin Maria Conway this evening, it was very cold. She told me she had received a letter from Mr. Conway telling her of the death of John Eustace; he did not say whether he was killed or not.

Maria Conway is a distant relative who was apparently staying with the Carters at Crednal. Her husband is Eustace Conway. John Eustace is her nephew.

Thursday [November] 26th. Cousin Mit went to Mr. Ayre today to see Mrs. Graham who is boarding there, but she had gone to Upperville. Cousin Mit received a letter from a Mr. Blackwell this morning saying that as Cousin William had not had time to write himself he had requested him to do so, to let us know that he was well and as he offered to take any letters we might wish to send, I wrote a long one to him.

George Ayre of Ayreshire

William Herbert was Mittie Herbert's brother.

Friday, Nov. 27th. We are going to Cousin Eliza's tomorrow if the weather is good. This evening we went to read to old Uncle Read who is living with his daughter on Violet hill, being too old and weak to attend Aunt Ida's poultry any longer.

Eliza (Hall) Carter

Uncle Read was a servant. Violet Hill is behind the house and stables of Welbourne.

Saturday, 28th. Mr. Richy preached here today; we saw Mr. Boyd Smith in church. Grandpa invited him to dinner but he would not come. We went to see Aunt Priscilla this evening; it was very cold.

Boyd Smith, one of Mosby's Rangers, seemed to spend a good deal of time in the vicinity of Welbourne.

Monday, Nov. 30th. Cousin Mit went to Cousin Eliza's this morning. After school we went too with Mr. Weidmayer who left us at Cousin Eliza's and walked on to Upperville. We had a very cold walk, but we spent a very pleasant day and returned in the evening.

Armistead and Eustace Conway
are Maria Conway's children.
John Armistead Carter was doing
parlor tricks.

The Second Culpeper Raid,
December 1, 1863.

The 1860 census shows several
Bentons in the area.

George Carter of Oatlands

Gertrude was the daughter of
Richard Earle and Sarah (Hall)
deButts.

Uncle Adam was a servant.

Tuesday, Dec. 1st. I hope that all of December will be like today at least for the soldiers' sake, as the boys wish for snow and ice that they may slide. Fanny and I went to see Cousin Maria Conway this evening and Armistead and Eustace returned with us. Uncle Armistead made the table turn for us this evening, to the great amusement of all the boys except Eustace, who was a little frightened.

Wednesday, Dec. 2nd. We did not take a walk today but ran about the yard and garden. Lieut. Turner returned from a raid today, Mosby captured twelve prisoners, their horses and equipment; Lieut. Turner told us of their victories.

Thursday, Dec. 3rd. Having heard that Aunt Mary Eliason had returned to Mrs. Seaton's, we went to see her this evening and took a short walk with her.

Friday, Dec. 4th. This morning while we were at breakfast Mr. Benton came to go netting partridges with Mr. W. so we recited our lessons to Cousin Mit. Aunt Mary Eliason spent the day here and we walked to Mrs. Seaton's with her on her return. Mr. George Carter's gardener was here today, he is going to show Mr. Reardon how to arrange the grapes.

Saturday, Dec. 5th. We walked to Oakley this morning. On our way we stopped at Cousin Eliza's, but there was no one there but Gertrude deButts, Cousin E. having gone to Upperville. Uncle Adam told us to go by the fields to Oakley and showed us what he called a short path. We found it a very long one however, as we had to go over very rough ground through tall weeds and around swamps, but we reached Oakley in spite of all these difficulties.

Sunday, Dec. 6th. We rode to church today

for the first time in months. Mr. Kinsolving preached an excellent sermon, his text was Vanity of vanities, all is vanity. A good many persons spoke to us after church, all of them asked after Papa. Aunt Ida very kindly sent us home in her carriage.

Friday, Dec. 11th. We heard today that Cousin Welby Carter was on his way home, and set up alone in the parlour until nearly eleven, hoping he might come here, but as he did not I suppose he is at home.

Saturday, Dec. 12th. Cousin Welby spent the day with us and there being only one false alarm about the Yankees, we enjoyed his company very much.

Sunday, Dec. 13th. Lieut. Turner and Mr. Smith were here last night and this morning.

We read the service in Grandpa's room to quite a large congregation, our own family, Cousin Maria and her sons, Lieut. Turner and Mr. Smith; Cousin Welby has gone to Glen Welby. Unless he is obliged to go away, Lieut. Turner always goes to church or remains at home, I wish I could say as much for my own cousins.

Wednesday, Dec. 16th. There was a report of the Yankees this evening, which sent Cousin Welby and Lieut. Turner off; we have heard nothing more from them so I suppose it was not true.

Glen Welby, the home of Richard Henry Carter, is in Fauquier County, between Salem and Rectortown.

On December 16th Rosser launched a raid on Sangster's Station on the Orange and Alexandria Railroad. General Lee, hearing that two regiments of federal cavalry were moving up the Valley from Winchester toward Staunton, directed Rosser to cross the Shenandoah behind them and prevent their escape. They reached Fredericksburg and forded the Rappahannock at twilight.

The next few miles led through the old campgrounds of Burnside's army, now a barren waste. Meade's campfires could be seen on the left, and the men were aware they were in enemy territory.

Next day it poured buckets of rain. Rosser, apprehensive that the rising streams would impede his march, speeded up the pace. The 7th Virginia Cavalry was in the van, followed by the 12th Virginia, the 11th Virginia Cavalry and White's 35th Virginia Battalion. At nightfall they reached the Occoquan, and despite the fact that it was rising rapidly, crossed at Wolf Run Shoals.

Rosser followed the road that led directly to Sangster's Station, where he knew the enemy had a force guarding the railroad bridge. He came to a small stream, very deep and rising rapidly. Beyond the stream was a stockaded fort, whose inhabitants had already seen him. With no time to examine the ford, the 7th Virginia under Dulany was ordered to cross and attack, but only Company A, under Captain Daniel Hatcher, responded. The rest of the 7th Virginia, blinded by the storm and the darkness, passed down the stream without crossing it.

The 11th Virginia, under Lt. Col. M. Beale, succeeded in capturing the stockade and the flag of the 164th New York Infantry. A silver bugle was later presented to Captain Hatcher's squadron, and the flag was given to the Virginia Military Institute.

After attending to his wounded and dead, Rosser moved toward Upperville. There could be no rest, as the enemy was in pursuit. The rain turned into sleet, increasing the torture of sleeplessness and fatigue. Horses, hungry and cold, staggered through mud while the men, whose garments were frozen to their skin, exhausted and half-conscious, managed to keep their place in ranks. They reached Upperville at sunrise.

Dulany, close to home, paid a visit to Welbourne just to change clothes on the 18th, and then rejoined his command.

Rosser pressed on through Ashby's Gap and reached the Shenandoah, an angry river that barred their crossing. The weary column had no choice but to continue its march. When they at last reached Front Royal, the men went into camp for the first time in 36 hours, after a march of more than 90 miles.

The next morning Rosser reached Luray; he crossed the river at Conrad's Store and on December 20th reached General Jubal A. Early's army in the Valley, where he learned that the raiding party he was sent to capture had returned to Winchester. The brigade then went into camp, giving their horses an opportunity to regain their strength on the abundant forage thereabouts. They remained there for Christmas.[30]

Meanwhile, back in Loudoun County, Richard Welby Carter found out that it was not safe to be home for the holidays. He was captured on December 17th. Mary Dulany explains what happened in her diary:

Thursday, [December] 17th. This morning Julia rushed upstairs while we were dressing and told us that a horse with a cavalry saddle and bridle had run by the house followed by a party of Yankees; what had become of the rider she could not tell, I dressed as quickly as I could and went down; I was standing near the parlour window talking to Julia when I saw four Yankees go to Grandpa's door, someone in grey was riding between them. I ran to Grandpa's room, and just as I reached the office door, I heard someone say "Good by Uncle John, give my love to May," and I heard someone say just as I opened the door, "Come

He was sent to Camp Chase, in
Ohio, and exchanged on August 3,
1864.

on Col., we will take good care of you."

Even before I saw poor Cousin Welby ride slowly away, I knew the truth. He was captured near his home. His horse fell just as he was running from the Yankees and before he could rise they were at his side.

Friday, [December] 18th. We had an unexpected and very pleasant visit from Papa this morning. We were quite disappointed at not seeing Cousin Clarence; his horse broke down and he had stopped at Charlottesville to recruit it. Papa had ridden all night in a sleet and wind and was tired, dirty and hungry; he had time only to change his clothes and eat his breakfast and then was obliged to go.

"I think, my dear Son, our future never was as dark as now ... the whole world is arrayed against us."

John Peyton Dulany, December 28, 1864

1864

he success of Mosby's guerrilla tactics depended upon the ability of his command to melt into the local population. As the opening entry in Mary Dulany's diary for 1864 indicates, Welbourne frequently provided a safe haven for a number of the rangers.

From the diary of Mary Dulany:

Monday, Jan. 4th, 1864. We have been spending Christmas week at Oakley and returned yesterday evening. Lieut. Turner and Mr. Smith were here last night and are still here; and I played several games of chess. I beat Mr. Smith every game. I have been giving Lieut. Turner both castles and winning always but tonight he won two games. It has been snowing fast all day, how sorry I feel for our poor soldiers.

Tuesday, Jan. 5th. The snow is four or five inches deep. I was determined that neither

Lt. Turner and thirty rangers attacked a 3rd Pennsylvania Cavalry picket near Lee's Ridge, west of Warrenton, and took fifteen prisoners.

Rangers William Watson and John W. Corbin suffered severe frostbite in the sub-zero cold.

William H. Mosby, brother of John S. Mosby, later served as his adjutant.[1]

Daniel French Dulany, in Co. A of Mosby's command, was the son of Daniel F. Dulany, a prominent Unionist in Fairfax County.[2]
Mosby had learned that the camp of the 2nd Maryland Cavalry, U.S.A., under the command of Maj. Henry Cole near Harpers Ferry, was vulnerable to attack.[3]

snow nor cold should keep me in the house, so I put on a pair of old socks and India rubbers and took a nice walk in the snow.

Wednesday, Jan. 6th. We tried in vain to slide on the sleds I gave the boys Christmas this evening, the snow was too dry. Lieut. Turner went to a party this evening; an agreeable preparation for the raid he is going on tomorrow.

Thursday, Jan. 7th. I do not believe that the snow has melted at all since it fell, it has been so bitterly cold. We went to see Cousin Maria. Eustace and Armistead returned with us.

Friday, Jan. 8th. Lieut. Turner gave us a delightful sleigh ride this evening. The last one we had Cousin Welby Carter gave us three years ago. When we were returning, we were speaking of Maj. Mosby. Fanny said she thought his brother must be very proud of him, I said I was sure his sisters must be, sisters always were proud of their brothers. Lieut. Turner looked at me with such a pleased smile I am sure he was thinking of his own sisters whom he has not seen for three years.

Saturday, 9th. Lieut. Turner, Cousin Johnnie [deButts] and Cousin French went on a raid today; after breakfast, Lieut. Turner said he was so sorry he had to go on a raid; he wanted to go to Glen Welby to give Miss Edith Carter a sleigh ride, Cousin John tried to persuade him not to go but only laughed and said "Duty first, pleasure afterwards, John." They expect to have a fight; I feel very uneasy about them.

Sunday, 10th. There was church at the Chapel today; when we returned we met Cousin Mit on the porch; she told us that Capt. Smith was killed, Lieut. Turner mortally and Mr. Boyd Smith slightly wounded, Lieut. Turner is in the hands of the Yankees.

I went into the parlour, Cousin John was standing by the fire looking perfectly miserable; he told me they were charging a Yankee camp near Harpers Ferry, when he suddenly missed Lieut. Turner, and one of the men telling him that he had ridden off wounded, he rode back to look for him. As he was inquiring for him, he heard him call him in such a low faint voice, he thought he must be dying, but when he found him he was still on his horse; he asked Cousin John as they were going to a house to take his watch and pistols. He had a ring Miss Edith [Carter] had given him, which was the only thing he wanted to keep. When he reached the house and was lying down, he told Cousin John to go. Cousin Johnnie begged him to let him stay, but he said calmly, "No, John, I am dying, go home and give my love to them."

John deButts told her of the January 10, 1864, battle of Loudoun Heights. Mosby lost two company commanders, Tom Turner and Capt. William R. Smith, Co. B, 43rd Battalion Virginia Cavalry, to mortal wounds.[4]

Letter of Richard H. Dulany to his daughter, Mary:

Saturday evening Jan. 10 [1864]
Camp Timberville

Seven miles west of New Market, in Rockingham County.

I wonder how my darling little May is enjoying herself this evening while I am trying with my stiff fingers to write her a few lines. As the evening is so beautiful I expect she and Fan have taken a long walk down the new road or with Cousin Mittie to make a visit to their Aunt at Mrs. Seaton's. I am anxious that both my daughters take regular exercise that their health and strength may be improved by it so that as they grow up they may be able to fill any station that may fall to their lot. The usefulness of a thorough education may be much lessened by the want of health.

You must not in attending to your studies think all your lessons are to be learned from your books. You must study yourself. Try and think at the close of each day how often you have given up your own will or wishes to those of your sister or brothers, or how often you have given way to your little tempers when you should have curbed it. We have all some besetting sin which we can only be conscious of by hard study, and not often then without asking of our Heavenly Father the assistance of his Holy Spirit to enable us to see ourselves in some degree as He sees us. The longer I live the more satisfied I am that real happiness is only attained in *striving* to do God's will and *trusting* to him to enable us to do it, for of ourselves we can do nothing.

I did not intend to read you a lecture when I commenced writing but the awful thought will flash across my mind sometimes, "Am I and my dear children to be separated from their dear Mother and their God in the next world after Heaven has purchased for us at such a price?"

I often wonder how our soldiers can be so brave when they have no hope of happiness if they fall. It must be because they do not think. And how brave a Christian should be when he knows that if he falls when doing his duty that his future home can never be invaded by an enemy and sorrow and death can never approach him.

I have just heard that Smith of Mosby's command and Turner were killed near Harper's Ferry. I cannot believe it. One of [Elijah] White's men says Turner was shot and not killed. This contradiction makes me hope the more that the report is false.

We have had a very hard march since I saw you. Some sixty of the men of the Brigade were badly frost bitten. We captured 45 wagons and about 250 mules and one hundred and ten prisoners and destroyed three forts or block houses forcing the Yankees to burn all their stores and arms. I lost one killed in my Regmt. Young Conrad was shot on the top of the head cutting the skin and leaving the bone bare for some two inches. The Drs. do not consider him in much danger.

Gen. Thomas L. Rosser and Gen. Fitzhugh Lee gathered sheep and cattle on a raid into Moorefield Valley, West Virginia, between December 31, 1863, and January 12, 1864.

Possibly Holmes Y. Conrad, who served in Co. D, 11th Virginia Cavalry, and on Rosser's staff.[5]

I enjoyed my trip very much although I suffered sometimes with cold. I think some of the nights were the coldest I ever felt. The constant exposure gave us good appetites. After feeding our horses and making a large fire we slept very soundly, wrapped up in our blankets on the snow. Genl. Rosser has been very successful since he took charge of our brigade. We cost the Govmt. nothing for mules or wagons and some of my companies are entirely armed and equipped with cap[ture]d property.

Did Hal get the paper I sent him with the account of Genl. Morgan's escape? I want you to read all the articles marked that I send in the papers to your Grand Father.

Gen. John Hunt Morgan of Kentucky escaped from the Ohio penitentiary.

Fan must consider this letter to her as well as to [you]; I will send the next to her. I hope you are both regular in the practice of your music. Does Hal show any wish to learn music? Is there any probability of your getting a music teacher this winter?

Ask Father please to try hard to get a thorough gardener this winter from Baltimore. I am very anxious that the garden and grounds should be kept in as good order as the state of country will admit. Remember me in kind terms to Mr. Weidmayer, to Cousin Armistead and all the servants. Give much love to my dear Father, Cousin Mittie, your Aunt Ida, to Fan the boys and Cousin Mary.

As ever your devoted Father
R.H. Dulany

I should prefer your not showing my letters except to your Grand Pa and Cousin Mittie.

From the diary of Mary Dulany:

Monday, Jan. 18th. I have had a sore throat all last week; we only heard once from Lieut. Turner, they say he is better, I wish I could believe it.

Thursday, Jan. 21st. Lieut. Turner died last Saturday, just a week from the last time I saw him.

Letter of Richard H. Dulany to his daughter, Fanny:

Moorefield, West Virginia.

Hd.Qrs. Cav. Brigade
Jan. 29th. 1864

My dear Fan

Tell your Grand Pa that I am much obliged to him for the inkstand but fear it will be a long time yet before I can use a pen. I have to hold my pencil between my second and third fingers to write at all. Thank him also for his long letter—he need not fear that I shall ever tire in reading letters written by his hand.

It gives me great pleasure to see how much you and Mary have improved in your writing. I hope I may find you both as much improved in all your studies. Every letter from Richland speaks of the great efforts your cousins are making to fit themselves for useful members of society. You must recollect that they have not half your opportunities for a thorough education.

You, Mary, and Hal, should each write at least once a week and lay your letters by until an opportunity offers to forward them to me.

Say to your Grandpa that I sent word to him to tell Mr. Weidmayer to tear his name J.P.D. off the check when he goes to Baltimore and put C.M.S. in place of it. The check was not to be paid by your Grand Pa.

C.M.S. is Charles Morton Stewart.

I hope May will continue to write her journal and send it to me. She should sometimes write her thoughts as well as mere matters of fact.

I see from the papers I send your Grand Father that while we are enjoying plenty for men and horse, Lee's army has been for a short time on short allowance of meat. Read Genl. Lee's address to the army. Our Brigade has gone to Western Va. for cattle for the army. On our last trip we brought in nearly five hundred and did not keep one of them for ourselves. I have been breaking a rule, "never to eat out of my command while on duty" which I have kept for more than two years. I have accepted three invitations to dine lately, and feel that each meal I make on turkey with a citizen saves as much beef to the army. I have never seen better beef than has been issued to our troops since our return to the Valley.

General Order #7, issued by Lee, says in part, "The commanding general considers it due to the army to state that the temporary reduction of rations has been caused by circumstances beyond the control of those charged with its support."[6]

Our men are in fine spirits and health although many of them have been entirely without tents so far. Our horses are suffering somewhat from scratches. My own are all in fine condition, Moses cleans them from morning until night. Col. Marshall and Clarence have gone with my regiment. I have been left in charge of the dismounted men and trains of the Brigade. I should have much preferred going with the Regiment but the Genl. required me to stay behind as Col. Marshall had been left on our last raid. I would not be much surprised if Clarence went West in the spring as my old friend Genl. Jones has applied for him as Adjutant for one of his regiments.

Ask your Uncle Armistead if he will not now agree with me that Genl. Jones has military talent? He has been the only successful Genl. of Cav. in South western Virginia—has captured in a few months nearly two thousand Yankees, several thousand mules and horses, besides many wagons and several pieces of Artillery and all this with but very small loss. I hear he has been made Major Genl. of Cav. and his praise is in everyone's mouth. Hurrah for my old much abused commander; may his success continue.

Has your Grand Father or Mr. W. made any efforts yet to get a professional gardener? You must all try and have as many vegetables [faded] as possible. Have the currant bushes all divided so as to set out a large number of new ones. I want you and Mary to make some wine next summer.

Remember me with much love to your Aunt Mary Eliason when you see her, also in kind terms to Mrs. Seaton.

We are all trying to prepare ourselves for a hard and bloody struggle in the spring and with God's help we hope to free our land of our enemies. Next summer and fall will either bring us victory and peace or we shall have many years of cruel war. May our Merciful Father give us peace and freedom in His own good time and restore me to my darling children prays your devoted father

R.H.Dulany

P.S. I received the cakes by Lt. McCarty. They were very acceptable but a little too hot. I also received the helmets. I will give Clarence his as soon as he returns. Welby deButts is with me; he had a chill yesterday and seems quite unwell this morning. You can scarcely tell how much I regret the death of Lt. Turner. I would have purchased his gray horse for Mary and you to ride if I had known it was to be sold. Welby tells me that John bought it. Tell Hal that I have his horse in camp; he is quite poor. If I part with him, I will give Hal a Black Hawk colt in his stead.

Lt. James W. McCarty was adjutant of the 7th Virginia Cavalry. On the original letter, Mary D. L. White later wrote, "These cakes were 'ginger' made of black pepper and very black molasses, no sugar, & tied up in an old drawer leg."

Has Mr. Haley brought the little colt from Freezland [sic] for the boys? If he has not I fear it will die, as it would require great care this winter.

Freezeland, near Linden.

I hope my friend Mr. Weidmayer may be successful in his courtship. He will have to win the father as well as the daughter and I expect that will be the hardest work. Give much love to all our household. Your devoted father

R.H.D.

From the diary of Mary Dulany:

Friday, Jan. 29th. I have written three letters to Papa this week and Grandpa has received one from him. Cousin Richard deButts, Cousin French, Cousin Johnnie and Mr. Slater were here today for dinner.

George M. Slater, also in Mosby's command.[7]

We went to see Cousin Maria [Conway] this evening and found her sick in bed.

Saturday, Jan. 30th. We expected to go to Oakley today, but as usual the rain prevented. Cousin Richard was here again today.

Sunday, Jan. 31st. Cousin Mit walked to church today through all the wet and mud, with Mr. Weidmayer. I did not envy her walk. Cousin French and Mr. Smith were here this morning. Cousin French showed me a nice letter from his sister Nannie which he received and answered today. Cousin Mit returned soon after dinner quite tired.

Monday, Feb. 1st. It is a beautiful day and as we heard that Cousin Robert Carter was at home, we learned some of our lessons at night that we might to see him tomorrow.

Tuesday, Feb. 2nd. We did not go today to see Cousin R as both Grandpapa and Uncle Armistead paid him a visit, and we hoped they would persuade him to come to see us. Uncle Hal and Capt. Wright spent the day here.

Wednesday, Feb. 3rd. Cousin Robert and Maj. White dined here today. After dinner we went to see Aunt Mary Eliason.

Dr. Lawrence S. Alexander, Co. B, a surgeon in Mosby's command.[8] Baron Robert von Massow, a Prussian, rode with Mosby.[9]

Sophia deButts Carter

Thursday, Feb. 4th. Dr. Alexander and Baron Massow (I believe that is his name) were here to dinner and remained all night. The Baron seems to be a very nice gentleman.

Friday, Feb. 5th. The gentlemen left this morning. I wrote a note to Cousin Sophy to ask her for some music which I think Mr. Mitler left at Glen Welby.

Partial letter of Fanny Dulany to her father:

Feb. 5, 1864

My Dear Papa

We have just had a visit from Baron Massow who is a Prussian and is with Major Mosby; it is very funny to hear Mr. Weidmayer speak German with him. He speaks French very well, and Mary and I spoke French with him almost always. We heard that General Rosser had whipped the Yankees some where in the valley, I hope you were not wounded.

Mary Dulany's letter to her father:

Feb. 7th.

Dear Papa,

You do not know how much pleasure your letter gave me, as it is the only one I have received since last March. We went to see Cousin Eliza on Saturday morning, and as it rained in the evening, we did not come back until this evening (Sunday).

Cousin Talcott saw Cousin William Eliason in Richmond. He was in wretched health and Cousin Talcott thought it impossible for him to live. I wish he would tell Aunt Mary, but he does not think she can stand it; I think it is a great pity.

Talcott Eliason

Aunt Mary L. (Carter) Eliason

Cousin Rutledge [Eliason] has come with some dispatches for Major Mosby, who has gone to Richmond.

I do not think Grand Pa, or Mr. Weidmayer either, have any idea of getting a gardener.

I am glad that you dine at the citizens' houses, as I suppose you must have a better, and much more comfortable dinner than you do in camp.

We will get Mr. Reardon to divide the currant bushes.

I am very glad that Gen. Jones has been so successful, and wish he was in Gen. Rosser's place again.

Mr. Weidmayer went to see Miss Jennie H. the day she came home, which was a week or two ago, but has not been there since; I am afraid that something is wrong.

I am sorry that the cakes were too hot. We will not put so much ginger in them another time. Mary and I are very glad that you got the helmets but were very much afraid that Cousin Welby would lose them. Uncle Armistead received a letter from Cousin Web Carter; he says when he arrived in Wheeling, the ladies were as kind as possible, and that Mr. John T. Carter had not been —[rest of letter missing]

From Mary Dulany's diary:

Sunday [February] 7th. We walked to Cousin Eliza's with Mr. Weidmayer yesterday morning, and as it rained, did not return until this evening. Cousin Robert has returned to camp. I wrote a letter to Papa this evening.

Monday, Feb. 8th. Coming out of school early today, I went in the parlour to practice, but to my surprise found it full of soldiers, none of whom except Baron Massow I had ever seen before. I felt a little awkward but thought I had better sit down and talk to them until some one else came in. I had not been in the parlour long before I was asked to "get up and play if I could" in such a very polite manner that I was not at all surprised when the Baron told me in French that the speaker was Major Mosby's brother, who like most copyists imitates the Major's manners but not his actions.

Tuesday, Feb. 9th. The Baron left this morning, the other soldiers yesterday evening. I am glad to say they were treated politely, particularly the Baron, as he is a gentleman. I am very glad of it. We went to see Aunt Mary this evening, Cousin Rutledge returned with us and played several games of chess.

Letter of Fanny Dulany to her father:

Feb. 13th [1864]

Dear Papa,

I am very glad to hear from you by Mr. Weidmayer.

William H. Mosby

Aunt Ida brought us some very pretty books from Baltimore; she got me four volumes of "Tales of a Grand-Father," and gave Mary and myself two books. Mine is called "Magnet Stories" and Mary's "The Earl's Daughter." Dick has a very pretty picture book.

You told me to tell you everything that I did from morning till night. In the morning as soon as I am dressed I draw my map if I have time, then directly after breakfast, we go in school and stay until dinner; then Mary practices two hours, and I go out of doors and stay until Mary has finished, then I practice till dark, then we all go upstairs whenever we remember and Cousin Mit reads the Bible to us, after which, I go down in the parlour and finish my practicing, then prayers are read, and as soon as they are over, we go to bed.

The Yankees were at Mr. Noland's mill on Wednesday, and two hundred went to Uncle Armistead's very early in the morning. I hope you, and your men, do not suffer from snow or cold. We expect Mr. Weidmayer back either Wednesday, or Tuesday. I have not any time to write more, but I will try and send you a longer letter the next time. All send love.

Your affectionate daughter
Fanny Dulany

Letter from Fanny Dulany to her father:

Feb. 28th [1864]

Dear Papa

Mr. Weidmayer came back from Baltimore yesterday morning. He brought us all some candy, which I think was very kind; he said that Mrs. Winn told [him] that she had received a letter from Aunt Mary, who said that Uncle Whiting had an attack of the same

Rebecca Winn, sister of John Peyton Dulany.

kind he had three years ago; please do not tell Cousin Clarence, as I do not think it is worth while to make him anxious about it.

Mary D.L. White noted, "Erskine was Pauline's husband, a worthless man, who coming home drunk, fell, and his face going into a mud puddle he drowned 'in the water you could have put in a bucket' Pauline told me. It happened near Lloyd's house, at the top of the hill!" Lloyd was the farm blacksmith.

Samuel C. Means, a Quaker from Waterford in Loudoun County, whose flour mill, crops and livestock were confiscated by Confederates, was offered a commission as captain of cavalry by Secretary of War Edwin Stanton. Means raised Co. A, Independent Loudoun Rangers, one of the few Virginia units to fight for the Union. Means was relieved of command April 13, 1864.[10]

Henry Erskine is going to take his departure next week; he has not done a single thing to the garden since he came back from Washington.

Mr. Weidmayer had an interview with Captain Means; he said he went in his tent to get his saddle, and found him very busily eating his dinner; his wife was in his tent with him, he asked Mr. Weidmayer if he would not sit down and take some-thing to eat, which Mr. Weidmayer declined, but Means insisted upon it and at last (Mr. W) took a piece of bread. Then as Mr. Weidmayer was going out, Means told him that some of his men were on the other side of the river who very "desperate" and that if they caught him they would hang him. Mr. Weidmayer then said, "Well, Captain, if that is the case I would rather get a pass from you as I suppose that your men would respect one of your passes more than one of the Provost Marshal's," and after getting one, he went off.

Mosby encountered Capt. J. Sewell Reed's detachment of the 2nd Massachusetts Cavalry near Dranesville, February 22, 1864.

Captain Mosby made a raid down in Fairfax County, and took "35" horses. Cousin Johnny has got one of them; he has gotten a substitute.

As Grand Pa is waiting for our letters, I must stop. Please answer mine as soon as you can. We are well, and all send their love.

Your affectionate daughter,
Fanny Dulany

Part of the Welbourne oral history concerns Cousin Johnny deButts, who was visiting there one night when the house was surrounded by Yankees searching for Mosby's men. Escape was

*impossible. Another cousin secreted himself in the
water tank atop the house, and Johnny was
hurried up to the childrens' room (above the dining
room). He hid beneath the covers of a large bed,
a heavy blanket was thrown over him, and several
children piled into the bed, pretending to be fast
asleep.*

*When the officers came to the bedroom, an old
mammy with candlestick in hand permitted them
to enter and search, but begged them to be very
quiet, as "her chillen was all asleep." When a
soldier approached the bed, the woman carefully
shielded the candle with her hand so as to create
even more shadows. Thus did Cousin Johnny
escape detection and remain free to participate in
many more raids.*

*Letter of Richard H. Dulany to Carlyle
Whiting:*

Hd Qrs 7th Va Cav
Mar. 28th 1864

My dear Carlyle

I owe this letter to Julia, but I am sure she
will not quarrel with me for making her wait a
little longer.

Since I have been in the army I have had
so little to read except Cav. Tactics that I have
almost forgotten how any other book looked.
You may imagine the pleasure of the arrival of
nearly a whole military library of choice books
gave us, as part of the fruits of Rosser's last raid
to western Virginia. After reading some
translations of French works on military
science, I picked up McCauley's essays and
after finishing the life and trials of Warren
Hastings had snugly fixed myself on my bed,
after the business hours of the morning, and
was becoming interested in the great efforts of

Frederick [the Great] to free himself from the combinations of his powerful foes, when in rushed one of Rosser's couriers with orders to saddle up and mount immediately & join the rest of the Brigade on the turnpike about two miles from camp. I assure you I laid down my book very reluctantly, thinking that nothing was the matter except probably Imboden's pickets being frightened by some of our scouts.

We had not gone far before I found I was wrong in my conjecture as the head of the column turned off the valley pike and took the direction of the Blue Ridge mountains. We soon learned that the enemy had marched through Stanardsville the day before with a large force of Cavy. and Artillery and were making for Charlottesville to destroy the bridge and public stores at and near the place.

As the Yanks had more than a day's start of us we had to march all night. The night was as dark as a wolf's mouth and the rain or mist fall continuously, freezing on the men's faces and beards. Two of my companies lost their way, and some of the men did not overtake us for two days. As for me I soon went fast asleep and slept a large portion of the way across the mountains where I waked up and found my horse had carried me away from my own regmt. and I found myself nearly at the head of the 12th [Va. Cav.] which was in advance.

We reached Charlottesville about sunrise cold, wet, and hungry, and were ordered into a piece of "black Jack" wood near the University "to make ourselves as comfortable as possible" while the Genl. and staff betook themselves to a University Hotel.

Neither myself nor men were in the most amiable humor for the next hour, but after finding some flat rails to make a floor and

Stanardsville is in Greene County, about twenty miles north of Charlottesville.

fixing a "shebang" of rails covered with our oilcloths to protect us from the rain, we were soon at the pleasant work of toasting our little pieces of bacon on the ends of forked sticks, and catching the melting fat on our hard crackers (to make them the more easy to swallow) as contented and happy as a set of fellows as you ever saw: how comparative are all our ideas of comfort and happiness, and how little we really require if we can only think so. Few Princes enjoyed their breakfasts as we did and my sleep before a bright fire but on hard rails, was as unbroken as an infants.

A soldier's term for a crude shelter.

We found that the Yanks under Genl. Custer had made a demonstration against Charlottesville the evening before we arrived and had been driven back by some of our artillery which was wintering near the town.

The day after our arrival at C. we received orders to move toward Hanover junction to intercept Kilpatrick who was said to be returning in that direction, then commenced a series of marching and countermarching, which for unprofitableness has only been equaled by a certain French king. Clarence has just informed me that he has written to his mother giving an account of our trip so I will change the subject.

In a clever ruse, Capt. Marcellus Moorman with 200 men of Stuart's Horse Artillery turned back 1,500 troops under Gen. George A. Custer at Rio Hill. As part of the deception, Moorman called out, "Tell Col. Dulany to bring up the 7th Regiment," even though the 7th was in the Shenandoah Valley at the time.[11]

The Dahlgren-Kilpatrick raid was an unsuccessful attempt to reach Richmond and release federal prisoners.[12]

After we returned to the west of the mountains Capt. Kennon, our inspector, told me that my furlough [for] which I had applied had returned approved, so I left the command at Waynesboro (where you ate so much apple pie and Dr. Rush and I saw such pretty girls) taking two men as a guard and started for home.

Richard Byrd Kennon, then the brigade inspector, served Jeb Stuart as asst. adjutant general from Apr. 26 to Nov. 19, 1863.[13]

The first night out a good citizen refused to let us have a room or to lend us an axe to cut some wood, so I had to encamp in or bivouack in his meadow and burn his rails to cook our supper and keep us warm. In the morning, *o tempora! o mores!!* I had a canteen of milk and an egg for breakfast which was only obtained by Alfred, being an earlier riser than the milkmaid and having better eyes than the Miss Rose of the establishment.

After breakfast, when I chided Alfred for milking the cow and not paying her for the milk, he very cooly told me that if the rafters of the barn had not been so high I would have had a fat hen for my supper, and that it was not stealing to take something to eat when the man refused to let us come into his house. That day we marched or rode as far as Luray and quartered in a church, determined not to receive another refusal—had a fine supper of eggs, bread and butter and boiled milk. Alfred filled the stove with bricking and then we went to sleep. About 10 o'clock I was awakened by some water splashing into my face and found Moses standing on the stove trying to put out the fire which had caught the ceiling from the stove pipe. After considerable trouble we subdued the fire and returned to our benches until morning.

We started early and reached our outside or advance pickets between Luray and Front Royal when we were overtaken by a courier from Genl. Rosser with my furlough disapproved because Col. Carter had been captured near my home. You may imagine my disappointment and the strong temptation to rebel but as I could not disobey an order from Gen. Lee, I sent Alfred on to Welbourne and I went to R.E. deButts.

On the following day I was surprised at the arrival of all four of the children in a driving snow storm. I feared that they had suffered with the cold but they seemed to have enjoyed their ride very much. Whenever they felt very cold Edward made a large fire on the roadside where they would remain until thoroughly warm when they would mount and ride on. I could not spend but two days with them and was sorry to part with the kind hospitality of Richard and Sarah. I left the house Friday morning and the children were to remain until Monday.

Richard and Sarah expressed great pleasure at the idea of entertaining you all at Grassland, and I hope nothing will prevent their having that pleasure. Father and the children could at any time make you a visit there and besides have the great happiness of feeling that I could add something to the comfort and, I hope, the health of you and my dear sister. More than this I think we owe it to our children to make them happy as possible and the bringing of ours so near to each other would give them social pleasures which none of them have at present.

If your goods and chattels could be brought to Fredericksburg & [illegible]—I should have no difficulty in getting them from that place to Grassland. Please let me hear from you immediately on this subject—one more summer may ruin the health of your children.

Clarence has not heard from Genl. Jones that he has made application for a Lieut. for him on his staff. While I shall miss Clarence very much it would be very wrong for him to refuse promotion. If Jones is made Major Genl. it will give C. the rank of Capt. I saw John deButts while at R.E. DeB, he is said to be one of the most gallant of Mosby's command and has been offered a lieutenancy two or three times. He refused promotion saying that he wants no responsibilities and is freer as a private. John is a fine boy, as liberal as a Prince, but I fear is rather inclined to be wild. I wish he was in the regular service.

Tell Julia that I sent her letters to Welbourne. If she would direct under cover to Lt. Col. Mosby through Genl. Stuart her letters would go quicker. I cannot yet write well with a pen, and but poorly at any rate, so you must excuse the inferior writing.

With much love to my dear sister, cousin Ellen, Julia, Nina and the other children. I am as ever your devoted friend and brother

R.H.Dulany

P.S. Dear C., I have written in great haste and with persons constantly coming into my tent so you must excuse mistakes &c.

Fanny Dulany wrote of the hazardous journey she and her brothers and sister made to visit their father. Portions of the account are missing, and it appears to have been written after the war, but it is still an exciting story.

One day a one armed soldier in our uniform rode up to the door & without dismounting, handed my Grandfather a rather dirty piece of paper upon which was written "Dear Father—I have obtained a week's furlough & will be with you in a day or two." Of course we were all in a wild state of delight at the prospect of seeing Papa who had been twice wounded & promoted since we had last seen him & was a hero in our eyes.

Our pleasure however was of short duration, for the next day an orderly arrived to say that the Gen. in command, having lost several of his officers in our immediate neighborhood by unexpected visits from the enemy, had forbidden Papa to venture through the lines, that he was then stopping at Cousin Sarah deButts on the other side of the mountain—about 20 miles from home—& it was his urgent wish that we children should go to see him.

My Grandfather said it was utterly impossible for us to do so. The country all around us was filled with soldiers & there was no one sufficiently familiar with the bypaths through the mountain to take charge of us, & no vehicle in which to send us. Bitterly disappointed—almost heartbroken—we dared not protest, as Grandpapa's word was law. Help came however from an unexpected quarter—my Grandfather's body servant, a colored man of more than ordinary sense, had come around the corner of the house when the Orderly appeared & had heard the message sent by Papa. After thinking a little while he approached & with his usual bow. "Master, if you'll [illegible] us dese children to me sir I'll [illegible] em safe an soun' & de shant no harm happen to 'em while I'm around."

The servant was Edward.

"How can you do that," asked my Grandfather, "you know every carriage & wagon has been burned & there is not a horse in the stable!"

" 'Cuse me, marster, that's 'cause they aren't no stable sir, but the two sorril mares are grasin' in the crick field & the horse what marse Richard lef' will mek de trip in no time & I'll come back 'fore sunup in de mornin' & tell you how Marse Richard look."

"Very well, very well," returned Grandpapa, "you can try it, but it is a most foolhardy expedition. I wonder Richard should have thought of it," & he turned to continue his walk up & down the long porch in front of the house with an impatient, irritated manner which made us all retreat with a general impression that Grandpapa was cross. Poor old gentleman, we did not then realize what a bitter disappointment the Orderly's message had brought to him.

We children were sent to bed early & at sunrise the next morning Mammy came in to call & dress us for our ride. After a hurried breakfast Edward appeared at the front door with Sally & Kate, the "sorril" mares—each with a dilapidated sidesaddle—& now arose a most serious difficulty. What were we to wear? The weather was bitterly cold—we wore calico dresses, no flannel, & our coats were very short & woefully thin. As for riding skirts—they had been cut up into jackets for our younger brothers long ago & we had no means of replacing them ... [Several pages missing.]

I was at last firmly tied up in my blanket & started ahead of the others down a narrow muddy lane—the little pools of water forming thin ice. Edward had talked so much of the danger which now beset us on every side—enjoining total silence on our part—that I felt quite nervous by this time & in a constant state of starting every time I heard a branch crack or a fall of ice from the limbs of the trees. I had only gone a few yards around a slight bend in the road when I felt something strike me right across my face & then pushed me back, back, until I slipped right down over Sally's haunches into a large mud hole, falling on my back, my feet hanging in the kind of swing made by the blanket fastened around the pommel.

I had sense or instinct enough to keep hold of the bridle so when I reached this point—I had pulled old Sally around—and there she stood quietly waiting and there I lay—dazed

Nancy Jackson was the mammy.

and scared—seeing nobody who could have pushed me off. Meantime I felt the ice breaking under my head & the cold dirty water oozing around my neck, which was anything but pleasant. Just then Edward—who of course had been delayed by mounting the others—came in sight & was even more scared than I at my sudden disappearance. The increasing mist & sleet made the whole atmosphere a thick impenetrable grey & he did not distinguish me, the horse being between us, until I called out to him not to ride over me.

After untying the blanket & helping me to my feet I was again mounted & then found my assailant to be the limb of a tree loaded with ice, which made it hang low over the road. [With] my head being bent down to keep the rain out of my face, I had ridden right into it without seeing it.

Picture to yourself what a sorry looking object I was, my back splashed red with red mud, my face cut & scratched by the branch of the tree, my clothes wet and rapidly stiffening in the bitterly cold wind, which whistled through the branches of the great old chestnuts, so that we could not hear each other speak without shouting, & this we dared not do, for fear we might be heard further than wished. I do not think the others found it so awfully loathsome, for there were two on each of the other horses & they could talk to each other, but the memory of that ride always fills me with the kind of fear that makes you look over your shoulder when you are in a room by yourself, or get through the door into a room *very quickly*, when you have come down a long, dark hall before reaching the door.

Once we saw a party of eight or ten men riding along the top of the mountain to our

right, and when they suddenly halted &
turned their horses in our direction we felt sure
we had been seen also. Edward immediately
ordered us to stand perfectly still. In a moment
there was a flash of light, a sharp whiz through
the air followed by a second one, and some
dead leaves and twigs fell around us. "Keep
quiet Miss Fanny—keep still children for de
Lord's sake, it's our onliest chance" whispered
Edward, & we were too used to that kind of
thing not to do just as we were told.

The men, thinking probably that they were
mistaken, for it was now dusk, rode on & we
could just distinguish their outlines against the
sky, as to our great relief they disappeared over
the hill.

Another hour brought us in sight of Cousin
Sarah's house and when we finally rode up to
the back door and Edward called for some one
to come out, we were almost worn out with
cold, excitement & fatigue. Some one lifted
me from my horse, and stood me on my feet,
but my limbs gave way under me, and I would
have fallen, had not papa caught me and called
someone to carry me in the house, his arm
being in a sling from a recent wound.

The others were in much the same
condition, and our friends feared our fingers &
ears were frost bitten. They made us each take
a swallow of some horrible stuff they called
"apple jack" which seemed to me more like
liquid fire than anything else. Cousin Sarah
was as kind as possible, keeping us well away
from the enormous wood fire which was
burning at the end of the long room, evidently
used as a sitting room, dining room and
parlour. After much rubbing, bathing our
hands & faces in cold water &c., we were able
to walk about a little and then we began to feel

ravenously hungry.

You will never, I fear, be able to appreciate the joy with which we sat down to that supper table—bountifully supplied with hot rolls, batter cakes, broiled ham & luxury of luxuries! a canteen full of "sawgum" given to Papa by an old dutch woman as he passed through the valley. Think of it, children—we had not seen or tasted any thing sweet for a whole year & here was sawgum for our bread & some to sweeten our tea with too. In this day, when sweet things are abundant, you can scarcely realize the pleasure which that delightful syrup gave us, or appreciate the jealousy with which we eyed the canteen as it was passed around the table.

Of course Papa was delighted to see us. We had taken him quite by surprise, as he had not expected us to come in such weather. Strange to say we suffered no ill effects from our ride & though every body remonstrated with Edward about returning that night, the faithful old man only tarried long enough to rest & feed his horse and was, as he had promised, in Grandpapa's room "by sunup next morning."

As spring approached, the 7th apparently moved to Rockbridge County, Virginia. Having ample pastures and being far behind the lines, the county was a frequent refuge for cavalry units.

Letter of Richard H. Dulany to his daughter Mary:

Staunton, April 22nd 1864

My dear Mary,

I wish I had time to write you a long letter but Mr. Phillips is waiting and a short letter must answer this time. I left Camp in

Rockbridge County day before yesterday. The first day I rode with two friends as far as North River to a Mr. Hamilton's where I received a most cordial welcome although a stranger to the family. We got a nice supper a comfortable bed and breakfast prepared for us before daylight the next morning so that we might ride to Lexington in time to take the stage to this place which we arrived last night. Mr. Hamilton gave us a pressing invitation to come to see him when we can and to bring our soldier friends with us. These invitations are very refreshing to a soldier, who has been living on 1/4 lb. of meat a day.

I am here as President of a Genl. Court Martial, a duty not at all pleasant. With love to "we all" as Hal says. I am in haste your devoted father

RHD

The court-martial was that of Major Harry Gilmor, who with his partisan command raided the B&O Railroad near Kearneysville, West Virginia, in February 1864. Some of his men robbed passengers and prisoners, which was against expressed orders. "The Northern papers made such an outcry against me for this raid, that General Robert E. Lee ordered me to be tried by court-martial," wrote Gilmor, who was acquitted. Colonel Dulany, whom Gilmor described as "a strictly conscientious man," presided.

Letter of Richard H. Dulany to Mary:

Staunton, 27th Apr 1864

My dear Mary,

I sent a letter to Mr. Weidmayer and being much hurried at the time, I sent him one hundred dollars too much. Please say to him that I have no recollection of seeing the papers

he wrote to me about. All my papers are in the
tin box in the safe and Father's bill of exchange
may be in the same box.

This morning the members of our Court
were invited to visit the deaf and dumb and
blind. The government requiring the large
buildings, which our state had prepared for
these poor unfortunates, for our sick and
wounded soldiers, a large number of them had
to be sent to their friends. About sixty of them
are left and they occupy a large house once
used for a female school.

The visit occurred at the
Staunton Female Academy. The
Virginia School for the Deaf and
Blind, established in 1839, was
being used as a hospital.

When we got into the house we found
three or four of the blind boys in the music
room. Two were playing on the violin and one
on the piano; afterward another boy joined
with the flute. They played very well together
and seemed to enjoy the music. After playing
several tunes a class of seven or eight girls
came in and joined their voices to the
instrumented music. They sang some
Southern songs with great spirit, and sent a
little comic over which they laughed heartily.
One or two of the girls were very pretty, but
most of them it was painful to look upon.

We were taken into another room where
some twenty deaf mutes were reciting. The
instructor was also a mute. He had a very
intelligent face and was teaching two classes
at a time. The classes were arranged on
opposite sides of the room before black boards.
The teacher would look toward the older class
and by signs read to them a few lines from
American history when they would turn to the
black boards and write it down with the
greatest rapidity. To the younger class he
would make signs telling them to write "a frog
jumps into the water," "a green frog jumps into
the river," &c, &c, which they would write

Col. Michael G. Harman of the
52nd Virginia Infantry,
quartermaster at Staunton until the
end of the war.[14]

Waynesboro is in Augusta
County, between Staunton and
Charlottesville.

Possible referrence to the end of
the Red River campaign.

down very quickly and seemed to be much
amused at their lesson.

The teacher married a mute some years ago
and has now two boys. Col. Harman who was with
me told me that when the parents found their first
child could speak or rather cry, showing it had a
voice, they were wild with delight.

Both the boys can speak but understand
the language of signs before they could talk.
Some of the children draw very well. I think
the most interesting sight was to see the blind
boy read by feeling the raised letters. Two of
them read very correctly, one of them reading
French and translating it into English.

In the evening, we (the members of the
Court) called on Col. Harman and took tea
with him, after tea we had ice cream & part of
the company played cards. It was very amusing
to see the blind music teacher playing, he
would play as quickly as any of the party and
would clap his hands and laugh whenever he
won a trick. I did not get to bed until after
twelve o'clock, so you may judge that I spent
a pleasant evening.

I expect to be here about six days longer,
when I shall return to my regiment which is
now in camp near Waynesboro. I suppose we
shall be ordered east of the mountains as soon
as Genl. Grant makes his attack on Genl. Lee
or as the soldiers call him "Marse Robert."

Our men are in fine spirits and will give the
Yankees a bloody reception whenever they
come. Our successes so far this year are very
encouraging. We have whipped them every
time we have met, since Jan. have taken some
six thousand or more prisoners.

If the late news from Mississippi is true we
have gained a very decided victory, but I never
rely upon news from that quarter until it is official.

You must try and find out how a blind man can play cards. Please ask cousin Mittie to have me a pair of pants made as soon as she can as I shall send Alfred for them before long. If Baldwin goes to Alexandria write to him to purchase for me two yards of the *best* grey cloth, as I shall want a coat before many months. I will pay him in wheat or greenbacks.

This makes the third letter I have written since I came here. I sent the Baron's money by Mrs. Grigsby, who promised to deliver it on Monday. Ask Mr. Weidmayer to add 2 doz. proof cotton socks to his list for me. You must all have long letters ready by the time Alfred comes home. Let me know how every thing looks on the farm and in the garden. If we drive the Yankees back so as to get to our homes, we shall expect to have plenty of vegetables after living on salt meat for so long.

I want you and Fan and Hal to read the papers I sent to your Grand Pa, especially the extracts from the Richmond papers. [Illegible, paper creased.] I have been very fortunate in having so many opportunities to write home of late.

I hope you and Fan go frequently to see your aunt. When did you see your Aunt Ida? I hope she is well. You must give her much love when you see her. Has Hal commenced with music yet? Does he like it? You all require a little more application if you desire success. I wish Mr. Weidmayer would send me monthly reports of your studies.

Say to Mr. W. that if Mr. Harrison will send Hatcher's receipt I will collect the money for him.

With much love to Fan, Hal, and Dick, Cousins Mittie and Mary, I am as ever your devoted father

R.H.Dulany

Baron von Massow had been wounded in a skirmish in late February and had to retire from service. He apparently remained in the area to recuperate.

*During the battle of the Wilderness—May 5,
1864—Rosser's brigade, including the 7th
Virginia Cavalry, fought General James Harrison
Wilson's cavalry division at Todd's Tavern. Col.
Dulany was in Staunton and missed the battle
itself, but in the following letter he describes the
aftermath.*

*Letter of Richard H. Dulany to his daughter
Fanny:*

Bivouac 17 May 1864

Dear Fan

I believe I owe you all at Welbourne letters,
except your Grand Pa to whom I wrote after
our great fight on Thursday last. I enclose a
draft of our fortifications and those of the
Yanks. The inner lines are ours and the outer
the enemy's.

The draft of the fortifications has
not been found.

Our first engagement was between General
Ewell and Grant shortly after the latter crossed
the Rapid Ann. It continued for two days,
Ewell repulsing him with great slaughter. On
this occasion we captured three Genls. Our
loss was very small.

Gen. Richard Ewell, commander
of 2nd Corps of the Army of
Northern Virginia.

Rapid Ann was a common pun for
the Rapidan River.

The enemy having been driven back for
several miles, tried on the 6th. to turn our right
flank when he was met by Genls. Longstreet
and [Micah] Jenkins and whipped a second
time.

On Sunday 9th. Genl. Early attacked the
enemy's right and drove them from their rifle
pits killing a great number. The enemy,
holding a very strong position near the ground
over which they were driven by Early's troops,
then shelled the woods in which a great
number of their dead and wounded lay so that
we could neither bury the dead nor bring off
their wounded. The woods were at last set on

fire by the bursting shells and the dead and wounded burnt together.

The day on which I last wrote, the enemy having moved from the opposite hills, I rode over the battle ground. It was the most awful sight I ever witnessed, many of the dead had been entirely consumed and wounded who had been burned lay with arms and legs in every possible position showing the great agony in which they died.

After making some of my own men bury some of the dead, a number of prisoners were sent in by a scouting party—when I put them to work and buried many more, but these men broke down before half the work had been completed, so many a poor fellow who enlisted to subdue us and make a farm is not even honored with a grave.

Our loss on Thursday, the day of the great battle, was two Genls. captured, some fourteen hundred men captured, and twenty two hundred killed and wounded. The enemy's loss is put by Genl. Lee at between forty and forty-five thousand up to this time, although the New York *World* estimates their loss at fifty thousand. Our whole loss of killed, wounded, and captured is (11) eleven thousand.

Losses at Spotsylvania, May 12, 1864: Union 6,020 casualties and 800 missing; Confederate 9-10,000 wounded and 4,000 captured. The captured generals were George Steuart of Maryland and Edward Johnson.[15] Two other generals, John M. Jones and Leroy A. Stafford, were mortally wounded.

We have been expecting another attack ever since Thursday but Grant's army seems to have been too severely handled to recover yet. He is a brave, rash and desperate man and I do not think will leave before he makes another fight. Prisoners say that he has burnt some of his pontoons and then told his army that if he did not take it on into Richmond, that all [that] would be left could cross the Rappahannock on a log. The larger portion of their army is now massed on our right.

I enclose an order received from Genl. Lee

The order has not been found.

last night which will [give] all the good news, and save me some writing.

I have not had time to ride down our lines to see many friends I have in the army although I am not two miles from the center of our army. Genl. Lee requires every man to be at his post and I cannot tell at what time we may be called to the front.

There are two things which would give me great confidence in our success if I had not many other reasons. One is that there is a deep religious feeling among a large portion of our army and I have been in no part of our army without seeing men reading their Bibles with great attention. Another is that the Yankees seem to have perfected a system of lying. Their prisoners tell us on all occasions of orders read to their army without the foundation of truth.

Benjamin F. Butler launched an expedition from Fort Monroe to the Bermuda Hundred in an attempt to capture Petersburg. William F. "Baldy" Smith, commanded the XVIII Corps of Butler's Army of the James.

They have told this army that Richmond and Petersburg have both fallen, and are in possession of Butler & Genl. Baldy Smith and that Lee is the only obstacle to our entire subjection, and that then will come the confiscation of our lands and property to be subdivided among their victorious troops. Our Heavenly Father will never bless a lying nation or a lying person.

On May 6th, Longstreet was mistakenly shot by his own men near Chancellorsville. Micah Jenkins of South Carolina was killed by the same volley.

I suppose you have heard that Genl. Longstreet was wounded & Genl. Jenkins killed by our own men mistaking them for Yankees within a short distance of the place where Genl. Jackson was killed.

None of these rumors were true. Gen. David McMurtrie Gregg commanded the 2nd Division of the Federal Cavalry Corps.

It is reported in camp that Genl. Meade was killed in one of the last fights and that Genls. Custer & Gregg were killed in the fight with our Brigade.

Susan Grayson Hall.

Give much love to your cousin Eliza Carter, Aunt Ida and cousin Sue, also to each member of our family. Write frequently and so have letters ready to send me when ever an opportunity occurs.

I have not seen a Richmond paper for several days so have none to send.

Ever your devoted father

R.H.Dulany

[P.S.] Ask Cousin Mittie if I have any socks or shirts, please to send me two shirts and a pr. of socks by the first safe opportunity.

Wednesday, 18 May: I went to see Genl. Ewell last evening and found he had taken Genl. Rodes' division to drive in the enemy's right to get some of our wounded that we found in the morning inside the enemy's lines. The fighting commenced about sun down and continued during a portion of the night. At sunrise this morning the firing was very brisk but has now (7 o'clock) nearly ceased, except the artillery—I think we are driving the enemy as the firing is more distant. We are saddled and ready.

Robert E. Rodes

On May 19th, General Wade Hampton, taking with him Rosser's brigade, cooperated with Ewell in this attack. On the 21st, Hampton proceeded to Milford, about twenty miles SSE of Fredericksburg, and met the Federals at Wright's Tavern. Hampton fell back toward Hanover Junction, until relieved by the arrival of Lee's infantry. The cavalry division was posted on Lee's left.[16]

Letter of Fanny Dulany to her father (Margin note: "Please excuse my stupid letter. F.D."):

Caleb C. Rector joined the
Dulany Troop in July 1861.

Charles E. Grogan, second
lieutenant of Co. D, 43rd
Battalion Virginia Cavalry.

May 20th 1864.

Dear Papa,

Grand Pa has just received a letter which you wrote before Alfred came, and sent by Mr. Rector; it is dated April 29th.

I agree with you perfectly about going back in the Union, I would rather die first.

We all went to Oakley last Friday as Jenny Powell & Kate Noland called for us.

We went to church on Sunday, and heard a very good sermon. The text was "but they that wait on the Lord shall renew *their* strength, they shall mount up with wings as eagles; they shall run and not be weary, *and* they shall walk and not faint." We spent quite a nice time, but there are always so many soldiers there. I hardly like to go, particularly while Mr. Grogan, who is one of Mosby's men, stays there; the best description of him is that of a *very* frisky woman.

I learnt a piece of poetry in Longfellow's, which I think will suit us so well, that is all but two or three lines; you know you told me that you preferred my learning poetry in some other book, but I do not think you will have any objection to this piece, I will copy it. It is called "Hymn of the Moravian nuns of Bethlehem at the consecration of Pulaski's banner."

When the dying flames of day,
Through the chancel shots its ray,
Far the glimmering tapers shed,
Faint light on the cowled head,
And the censor burning swung,
Where, before the altar, hung
The blood-red banner, that with prayer
Had been consecrated there.
And the nun's sweet hymn was heard there while
Sung low in the dim, mysterious.

Take thy banner; may it wave
Proudly o'er the good and brave,
When the battle's distant wail
Breaks the Sabbath of our vale,
When the clarion's music thrills
To the hearts of these lone hills,
When the sword in conflict shakes,
And the strong lance quivering breaks.

Take thy banner and, beneath
The battle's cloud encircling wreath,
Guard it, till our homes are free!
Guard it, God will prosper thee!
In the dark and trying hour,
In the rush of steeds and men,
In the breaking forth of power,
His right hand will shield thee then.

Take thy banner! and if e'er.
Thou shouldst press the soldiers bier,
And the muffled drum should beat
To the tread of mournful feet,
Then this crimson flag shall be
Martial cloak and shroud for thee.
The warrior took the banner proud,
And it was his martial cloak and shroud.

Do you not think it very pretty, and suits
our cause very well, all but the first verse, and
the one which I left out which is this:

Take thy banner! and when night
Closes round the ghastly fright,
If the vanquished warrior bow,
Spare him!—by our holy vow,
By our prayers and many tears,
By the mercy that endears,
Spare him!—he our love hath shared!
Spare him!—as thou wouldst be spared!

We heard that one of the Armisteads had been killed and that it was Cousin Walker. I hope it isn't so. We heard also from a soldier that Cousin Johnnie was very ill, but the Yankees who were in Upperville yesterday said he was walking about. We do not know which to believe, but I hope what the Yankees say is true. We all want to see you so very much. Please write soon and tell us every thing about yourself.

Your affectionate daughter,
F. Dulany.

Letter of John Peyton Dulany to his son:

Welbourne Hall, 29th May '64.

My dear Son,

I have just heard that Rector starts for the army in the morning and I do not like to let any opportunity pass without letting you know that all are well at Home, and to say how very anxious I am to hear frequently from you. I only received yours dated of the 13 and 14 Inst. on yesterday. We are kept in such a state of anxious suspense about the safety of those we so fondly love that it may seem unreasonable of us to expect to hear from you more frequently.

Mr. Weidmayer left home last Wednesday fortnight for Baltimore and has not yet returned. I much fear that he is in trouble as Miss Charlotte Hall told me yesterday that she heard Judge Bond say that Mr. W. should have been arrested when he was here purchasing money. I hope that Charles Stewart may not be compromised as I think it more than probable that Mr. W. will be searched, and he had a good many business papers for Stewart. This has annoyed me very much but I will try and hope for the best.

On April 28, 1864, John Peyton deButts, surprised by a squadron of the 2nd Massachusetts Cavalry under Col. Charles R. Lowell, was wounded in the shoulder and arm and captured in Leesburg. He was sent to Old Capitol prison and later to Fort Delaware.[17]

Charlotte Hall, age sixty, of Linden, lived with Thomas S. Hall, age 49. Her occupation is noted as "knitting &tc." (1860 U.S. Census)

John deButts is getting well very fast. Dan'l Dulany went to see him several times and he prevailed upon the Col. to let John stay in Alexandria until his wound was healed. However much Dan'l may want principles he certainly has kind heart.

Your stock at Welbourne are looking *too well*; it would be a great temptation both to the Yankees and our agents who are in want of good beef. I heard only a day or two since that the sheep on the mountains were very poor and suffering for the want of salt. I purchased a sack for which I had to give twenty-six dollars in greenbacks, which has reduced my purse very low in that currency. Haley and Triplett are plowing corn; they will get over the first plowing some time this week. The weather has been adverse to farming operations, I have never known such a spring, continual rain and cold weather. I fear very much that your bays & horses have been very uncomfortable.

The garden is looking very well altho vegetation is more backward than I ever remember to have seen it. I have had your grapery attended to by Mr. Carter's gardener, who appears to be very clever and understands his business perfectly. I wish you could have met with him sooner. He says in two years we may *expect* to have a plentiful supply of grapes "man never *is* but all/was to be blest." I do not know if this is a literal quotation but it expresses my meaning.

With respect to your colts, I am really at a loss to know what is the best thing to do with them. I think they are safe where they are as they would be on the mountain, and I think there is a very little encouragement to send stock to the mountains, as they always return look[ing] much [more] worn than when sent.

Daniel F. Dulany, of Rose Hill near Alexandria, served as a military aide to Francis Pierpoint, governor of West Virginia. He was captured on September 28, 1863, by Mosby's Rangers, among whom was his own son, French Dulany.[18]

George Carter of Oatlands.

I delivered your message to Armistead. He is very much depressed, looks badly. Mrs. Conway gives him a great deal of trouble. She is sometimes quite outraged, so much so that the House servants threaten to leave if she is permitted to remain much longer. So you see we are none of us exempt from annoyance, and perhaps it is best for us that we are not, it ought to teach us that this is not our resting place, yet with all our disappointment, bereavement, &c, &c, how hard it is to wean our affections from the too great love of this world and nothing but chastisement will drive us to that better Country where alone we can find true happiness that we so vainly search for here.

I requested Mittie to write to you, but she says you have not even acknowledged the reception of her last; do write to her. Eliza Carter requests [that I send] her love. You see, my beloved Son, your Father has become quite a garrulous old man. Farewell, may our good God guide and guard you from every evil is the prayer of your fond Father

J.P.D.

From Mary Dulany's diary:

Friday 3rd June. Baron Massow & Mr. Knapp returned from Oatlands today, both sick, the Baron had chills & fever & Mr. Knapp a sore throat, the Baron must be very sick; he fainted several times on the road, and has a very high fever. Mr. Knapp went to Oakley this evening.

Probably Ludwell Knapp, Co. A, 43rd Battalion Virginia Cavalry, who had enlisted November 21, 1863.[19]

Saturday 4th June. Aunt Ida & Mr. Knapp rode here on horseback this morning. Aunt Ida looked prettier than usual. Baron Massow is much better today. Mr. Weidmayer returned from Baltimore this evening; he brought a great many things for us which we were very much in want of.

Sunday, 5th June. We went to church in Mrs. Seaton's ox-cart today. We saw Cousin Eliza & Aunt Ida, they both sent their love to Papa. The poor Baron had a very violent chill today.

Monday 6th June. Dr. Gunnel [sic] was here yesterday and left some medicine for the Baron who is much better today though in dread of a "chilly" as he will call it, tomorrow.

William Presley Gunnell, who is known to have lived with William H. Dulany of Fairfax County in 1850.

Tuesday, 7th June. There was a report of the Yankees this morning but it was false as usual. The weather was very warm today and has been so for several days.

Wednesday, 8th June. Today was my fifteenth birthday, I did not have a picnic. I did not want one, but I received presents from everyone.

Letter of Richard H. Dulany to his daughter, Mary:

Near Atlee Station, 8 June.

Atlee Station is about six miles NE of Richmond.

My dear May

I should like very much to be with you on your birthday and enjoy with you your fried chicken after being so long confined to bread and bacon. We are doing a little better now than for a long time before, as we get sometimes an onion or beans for dinner, and today is the second time we drank coffee and sugar [line illegible].

Everything is very quiet in our front, Grant's having become tired of [having] his men slaughtered by sending them against our breastworks. A Yankee prisoner told us yesterday that Grant had lost more men than

A reference to the assault ordered by Grant at Cold Harbor, June 3, 1864.

William E. "Grumble" Jones was
killed at the Battle of Piedmont
on June 5, 1864.

Clarence Whiting was serving on
Jones's staff.

all their Genls. together who have
commanded their Potomac armies.

The Yankees getting to Staunton is very
provoking, but they will be attended to in due
time. Were you not sorry to hear of the death
of my old friend Genl. Jones. He was killed
near Staunton. I have applied to have
Clarence assigned to my regiment. I have
several companies badly in want of officers.

Say to your Grandpa that Genl. Lee, having
now successfully repulsed every effort of what
the Yanks call the greatest living General and
by far the mightiest army every raised, he must
now consider our cause stronger and our
prospects brighter than ever. Our
Government [here lines are effaced].

With much love to all our household I am
very truly your devoted father

RHD

[P.S.] If you can have me two shirts made
send them to me together [illegible] or
Sergeant [illegible] who will deliver them.

From Mary Dulany's diary:

Thursday 9th June. Aunt Mary & Mrs.
Seaton spent the day here, and Aunt Mary
stayed all night.

Friday June 10th. Aunt Mary went away this
evening. I walked to Mrs. Seaton's with
Cousin Maria today; she behaved very well,
and made herself quite agreeable.

Saturday June 11th. Aunt Ida & Uncle Hal
ate breakfast here this morning, on the way to
Oatlands, and Mr. Weidmayer went with
them. I was afraid that Mr. W. had offended
Mr. Knapp by ordering him away the other
day, but he returned this morning in a very

good humour and spent the day.

Sunday June 12th. Baron Massow went away this morning but said he would return before going to Richmond. Mr. Knapp brought us a letter from Papa today, he writes in very good spirits and his account of the army, its provisions particularly, raised Grandpapa's spirits to twice their usual height.

Monday June 13th. As Mr. Weidmayer has not yet returned from Oatlands I taught the other children, besides learning my own lessons which kept me [in] school much longer than usual. Mr. Weidmayer returned just before dinner, & brought a beautiful magnolia he gave me and a bouquet destined, [I] suppose, for Miss Jennie.

Letter of Mary Dulany to her father:

Monday, June 13th.

My Dear Papa,

We received your very welcome letter yesterday morning, it confirmed my hopes, & relieved Grandpapa's fears; why don't you say something about Moses in your letters sometimes? You don't know how sorry I was to see in the paper the other day that Gen. Jones, (our Gen. Jones) had been killed. I hope that Cousin Clarence was not hurt. Have you heard from him lately?

There is a Mr. Henry Smith from Maryland with Mosby now who hearing some one mention me at Oakley & thinking I suppose that I was grown, persuaded Miss Grayson to send me a bouquet, that he might have some excuse for coming here; Saturday morning while I was practicing, a soldier came into the parlour, with some flowers which he said Miss Nannie Grayson had sent Miss Dulany &

Possibly Henry Smith, Co. D, 43rd Battalion Virginia Cavalry.

which I received with much pleasure as they were very sweet. He stayed a few minutes and then went away & told every body "that after all the trouble he took he did not see Miss Dulany but only her *little* sister." Don't you think I got the best of the bargain?

My fifteenth birthday came last week; I received my presents from nearly everyone in the house. Grandpa gave me a box of figs, Mr. Weidmayer some oranges & candy, Fanny a book, the boys a set of chessmen, & Julia a bouquet. I did not have a party; I did not think it was right to have one at such a time.

The garden is looking very well, I think we will have a plenty of vegetables this year, they look very well now. I have just finished a very pretty drawing for you and am learning a beautiful piece, which I hope to play perfectly by the time you come home.

From Mary Dulany's diary:

Tuesday, June 14th. There has been no one here today so we have heard no news, though we feel quite anxious to hear from the army.

At this time thirteen-year-old Fanny Dulany began to keep a journal. On its cover she wrote: "Open this not for you will find/Something that will not suit your mind."

From Fanny Dulany's journal:

Tuesday, June 14th 1864. Grandpa insists on my writing a journal, but I am afraid this one will be very stupid.

We rose rather late this morning and I found it very difficult to rise at all, for I was very sleepy. When dressed I went down and

The log cabin at Old Welbourne ca. 1940.

The remnants of the cabin at Old Welbourne in 1991.

Plate 1

A painting of Welbourne as it appeared ca. 1836.

Welbourne as it appears today.

Plate 2

Col. Richard Dulany (dark hat) and others in front of Welbourne in the early 1900s.

Major John Pelham scratched the words "G C Walker Oct 28 1862 J" on a parlor window at Welbourne. Walker was his aide-de-camp. Before he could complete his own name, thirteen-year-old Mary Dulany came to fetch him for breakfast. Years later Mary named her own home Pelham after the gallant young officer.

Plate 3

Richard Henry Dulany is shown as a fair-haired youth in this painting that hangs at Welbourne.

This miniature of Richard Henry Dulany was done in Rome in 1851.

Plate 4

This painting of Richard Henry Dulany in his uniform as colonel of the 7th Virginia Cavalry, C.S.A., hangs in the parlor at Welbourne.

Colonel Dulany ca. 1864. In this pose he has hidden his wounded left arm from the camera.

Plate 5

Col. Dulany's hat, gloves and sash remain in the family. His saber was stolen in recent years.

Colonel Dulany, shown here in the early 1900s, remained active until his death in 1906 at age 86.

Plate 6

Colonel Dulany rode regularly,
even into old age.

This painting of
Colonel Dulany was
done about 1905, not
long before his death.

Plate 7

Rebecca Ann Dulany, wife of Colonel Richard Dulany, died in her 30th year in 1858, before the war arrived on the doorstep of Welbourne. She left him five children to rear, but he never remarried.

Rebecca Ann Dulany with one of her daughters.

Plate 8

Mary Carter Dulany, born in 1849, was the eldest of the colonel's children. She was twelve years old when the war began.

Although called upon to care for her father while he recovered from his wounds, her diary and letters give a teenager's view of the war.

Seen here in middle age, Mary Carter Dulany Neville lived in a home she called Pelham not far from Welbourne. Her father built it for her as a wedding present.

Plate 9

Frances Addison Carter Dulany, called Fanny, and her elder sister, Mary, in a daguerreotype made prior to the war.

Fanny Dulany as a young woman.

Plate 10

A drawing of Fanny Dulany by
an unknown artist, based on a
photograph taken in 1866.
Fanny and her descendants
eventually inherited Welbourne.

J. Southgate Lemmon and
Fanny Dulany were
married in 1873. The
Lemmons lived in
Maryland when the war
began, but South served in
the Confederate army. A
letter he wrote to his
mother describing a
harrowing trip from
Maryland into Virginia is
included in this collection.

Plate 11

Henry Grafton Dulany, called Hal, born in 1854, was seven years old when the war began. He died in 1890 at age 37, having never married.

Richard Hunter Dulany, called Dick (1856-1917), the colonel's youngest son, was only five years old when the war began. He eventually inherited Old Welbourne.

Plate 12

John Peyton Dulany, the colonel's father, took care of his young grandchildren and other family members and saw to the management of the Dulanys' various farms and other business while his son was away.

John Peyton Dulany died in 1878. The photos on this page were taken at Matthew Brady's studio in Washington, D.C., before the war.

Plate 13

Mary Ann Dulany Whiting (1818-1895), the colonel's sister, spent much of the war traveling between Richland, her home in Stafford County, and Welbourne. Her husband was ill during much of this period. Several of their eleven children were still at home and others, particularly Julia and Nina, spent extended periods of time at Welbourne.

George William Carlyle Whiting, known as Carlyle, was Mary Dulany's husband and a close friend of his brother-in-law the colonel. Whiting died at Welbourne in 1864.

Plate 14

Henry Grafton Dulany, called Hal, was the brother of Rebecca, the colonel's wife. He served as a lieutenant in the Dulany Troop, but left the army with an eye injury in 1862.

Mary Eliza (Powell) Dulany, better known as Ida, was Hal Dulany's wife. She spent the war at their home, Oakley (below), near Welbourne. Her diaries offer a vivid eyewitness account of daily life in Mosby's Confederacy.

Plate 15

Richard Earle deButts
was one of Mosby's
Rangers. Colonel
Dulany was a frequent
visitor to his home in
Warren County.

Sarah Hall deButts,
wife of Richard Earle
deButts.

Plate 16

John Armistead Carter, "Uncle Armistead" in the letters, lived at Crednal (below), across the road from Welbourne. His son, Richard Welby Carter, called "Cousin Welby" (right), was colonel of the 1st Virginia Cavalry.

Plate 17

John Peyton deButts, "Cousin Johnny," was Colonel Dulany's nephew. He was one of Mosby's most daring rangers until his unfortunate capture at Leesburg.

C. E. Weidmayer, who lived at Welbourne during the war as the children's tutor, was a Swiss national. Because of his alien status, he was permitted to pass through the lines and was able to conduct business and obtained much-needed supplies for the family in Washington and Baltimore.

Plate 18

John Singleton Mosby, the famous Gray Ghost of the Confederacy, formed a bold band of partisans that operated in Loudoun and Fauquier counties. Many of his rangers visited and, for small periods of time, stayed at Welbourne. This photograph, signed by Mosby, is a prized possession of the family.

Heros von Borcke, a Prussian who served on the staff of Maj. Gen. J.E.B. Stuart, was wounded in June 1863 near Middleburg, thus ending his Confederate career. Long after the war he returned to America to visit his Confederate comrades. Colonel Dulany was his host at Welbourne.

Plate 19

Gravestone of Richard Henry Dulany, colonel of the 7th Virginia Cavalry, in the family cemetery at Old Welbourne.

Gravestone of Rebecca Ann Dulany, who rests beside her husband in the family cemetery at Old Welbourne.

Plate 20

Mr. Weidmayer had prayers; we then had breakfast, after which we went to school at half past nine and got out at half past one. I went upstairs, washed my face and hands, fixed my hair, went to the wardrobe, took out the first vol. of dear Mama's journal, went down in the arbor, which is very sweet now as the honey suckle & roses are all in bloom; and read until Mary had finished her music lesson, then went to take mine.

In the meantime Mary went fishing with Mr. Weidmayer, and as soon as I had taken my lesson I went to see Cousin Maria Conway with Hal. I found her reading to Armistead the *Life of General Jackson*. Armistead is in bed suffering from the effects of poison oak. I sat with him for some time and then came home.

The *Life of Stonewall Jackson* by John Esten Cooke, published in Richmond in 1863. Cooke served on General J.E.B. Stuart's staff.

From Mary Dulany's diary:

Wednesday, June 15th. Mr. Weidmayer went fishing with Uncle Hal today, so I had to teach again, as Cousin Mit is busy making our dresses. Mr. Knapp spent the day here, he told me that Lieut. Grogan had been arrested for going to see Cousin Sophie instead of being ready to go on a raid; I wish I could let Cousin Welby know.

Sophia deButts Carter of Glen Welby married her cousin, Col. Richard Welby Carter, after turning down both a Methodist minister—who shot himself as a result—and James K. Boswell of Gen. Jackson's staff.

From Fanny Dulany's journal:

Wednesday, June 15, 1864. We rose at half past six this morning, had prayers & breakfast & then went to school at a quarter of nine. Mr. Weidmayer went to Oakley this morning to go fishing with Uncle Hal for Fall fish. He came back tonight after supper & seemed to be very tired. Mr. Knapp came here today. He seems to be very fond of Mary, for he comes here very often. Indeed, I believe he comes almost every other day. Mr. Grogan has been arrested for going to see Cousin Sophie Carter, who is now on a visit to Warrenton, instead of being with Mosby on the road. Grand Pa went to Upperville & heard that Col. Mosby & eight of his men had been captured down near Leesburg. I do trust it is not true. I wonder what the Yankees would do to him if they were to catch him.

Oh me I will be so glad when our vacation comes. Mr. Weidmayer is getting crosser & crosser every day in school—never mind though, vacation will be here in fourteen more days & then we will *all* have a good, long rest, both teacher & scholars.

How I do wish dear Papa could be with us during our whole two months although I would not like him to leave the army now. Of course we feel anxious about him, but I will trust to "Him who doeth all things right."

Thursday 16 [June]. I rose very late this morning & in consequence was not down to prayers for which I was sorry.

We went to school at the usual hour, half past nine; I got out at a quarter of one. Grand Pa went to Upperville today & heard that the Yankees were on the mountain, where I do hope they will stay.

I would despise that horrid old wretch Hunter to come here. Geary was bad enough, but in one of Papa's letters he says that Hunter is almost as bad as Beast. The Bible says "love your enemies, bless them that curse you, do good to them that hate you and pray for them that despitefully use and persecute you." But indeed, I *cannot* love such a horrid, savage, mean, dirty, unprincipled, cruel—I do not

Geary had raided Welbourne in April 1862.
Gen. David "Black Dave" Hunter was executing a raid in the Valley that targeted civilians—the first such tactic of the war.
"Beast" was Benjamin Butler's nickname.

know what to call them, the word wretch is too good for them—Devil is the only name by which they can possible be called with justice.

I won't believe the Bible ever meant the Yankees.

Partial letter of Richard H. Dulany to his daughter Mary:

Bottoms Bridge 22 June 1864

Bottoms Bridge is on the Chickahominy River, NW of Charles City Court House.

Dear Mary

I received your journal by Brown, but not the long letter referred to in it. Add to your journal each day how you have been occupied—what you have read—what, and how many, lessons recited that I may know each day's progress, and as your journal is only to be seen by me, and as you can have no friends to whom you are so dear, I should be glad to have you express your thoughts on many subjects, especially upon yr. daily progress in yr. religious life that we may try and aid each other in the only road worth travelling. But this may only be done with yr. own *free will* and *consent.* You will find through life that there is no love so unselfish as that of a parent for a child. As anxious as I am for yr. physical and mental improvement, I would rather see you deaf and blind to every enjoyment on earth than see you fail in the only object worth living for. Do you ever converse with my darling Fanny upon religious subjects?

I have been very fortunate in having such a companion as Col. Marshall, but his life is a constant rebuke to me; he seems constantly to enjoy what to me are but too often cold formal duties. I would write you news from the army but that I send you papers with fuller accounts

The battle of Trevilian's Station, June 11-12. Rosser was wounded, and Col. Dulany assumed temporary command of the Laurel Brigade.

The White House plantation on the Pamunkey River was owned by Gen. W.H.F. Lee. It is about twelve miles NE of Bottoms Bridge.

Confirmed by James Wood, Co. F, 7th Virginia Cavalry. In his diary entry of June 16, 1864, he writes, "Move on after Sheridan. Came to Gen. DeJarnett's house find 7 Y. plundering kill 6 take one prisoner whom saved himself by taking a little girl in his arms when he came up to surrender."[20]

than I could give.

We (cavalry) are still between Sheridan with the larger portion of the Yankee cavalry and Grant's army to prevent their uniting. We have had several skirmishes with him since our fight on Sunday week, but he does not seem willing to come far beyond the protection of his gun boats on the Pamunkey.

We attacked him yesterday near the White House and drove him back some distance, killing one captain and several privates and capturing one captain, one Lt. and fifteen privates. We lost one man killed and several wounded, one of our wounded has since died.

Seven (7) of our scouts (one a preacher) were following the enemy day before yesterday when they came upon seven Yankees robbing a house and killed three of the thieves, wounded two and brought the remaining two off as prisoners. The parson would have shot one of them but the man caught up a child and held it before him as a shield.

You can form no idea of the desolation produced by this raid of Sheridan. Having been driven back by Hampton in his attempt on Charlottesville, he has allowed his soldiers to rob and plunder every poor family within his reach. There is scarcely a family along his line of march left one pound of meal or meat—a chicken, cow or hog. In many instances after taking all they could carry away, they destroyed every particle of clothing in the house. I think orders will be given to take no prisoners, hereafter, when found plundering defenseless women and children. You will see in the papers that the Government has at last found a way to prevent the cowardly shelling of Charleston. As I have filled my paper I must [rest of letter missing].

For about ten days near the end of June the Laurel Brigade was active in defending the important railroad lines northeast of Richmond. When the Federals left the area, the command settled down for some much needed rest at Stony Creek Station on the Petersburg & Weldon Railroad, about sixteen miles south of Petersburg.

Letter of Richard H. Dulany to his daughter Mary:

Stony Creek Station July 5th 1864

My dear Child,

I received your unfinished letter and journal two days since. I am much pleased to see how much you are improving in your hand writing but both you and Fan are getting a little careless in spelling. In your last letter or journal you forgot the r in church. I expect you must have been talking to your Cousin Charles [Whiting] or Chew. I fear you find much difficulty in reading my letters as I cannot yet use a pen. But they will answer as a [word illegible] as well as to inform you that I am well and in good spirits as I can be so far away from all I love—no, not all—my duty and my country's cause are ever present, and which at times makes me forget all else.

How is your Uncle Armistead, and in what spirits? He was your mother's best friend and should be very dear to my children. Cultivate his friendship by little delicate attentions to his comfort, which he may seem not to notice, but he will appreciate them.

Mr. Henry Smith's mistake was quite amusing. You must not forget that you are Miss Dulany's "little sister" for the next five years, and then Miss Dulany herself. Your ideas in regards to parties are very proper—it is now no time for gaiety and pleasure when our country is daily pouring out the blood of her best and noblest sons as an offering for peace—deep humility, and earnest prayer, is far more rational in a Christian people. If our people could be induced to humble themselves before God, I believe He would give us our liberty and peace in less than time it will take this letter to reach you.

It is not sad to confess, that while I can thus write, that I am so very, very far from what I think it the duty of others to be and do—alas, poor human nature. If we only taught others to reach our own attainments, how low the standard would be. Your own dear mother and my own were the only persons I have ever known who seemed properly to appreciate the gift of time. It will be a great source of happiness to see you and my dear Fan follow their example.

Ask your grand-father to allow you, Fan, Hal, and Dick a certain allowance of meat a week-day—3 or 3-1/2 pounds each—and deny yourselves a portion of it each day for the poor of Richmond. There are hundreds if not thousands in that city who live on bread and water alone; and while many of our soldiers have given all their meat for two days out of five to the poor women and children of the city, our country people are sending theirs to market at from five to ten dollars a pound and if anything has been sent from the country as a gift I have not heard of it. It will not do to think "that the pound or two that I can spare will amount to nothing;" that pound or two would be of great value to the poor child who had none. Recollect, the ocean is made of little drops of water.

Don't think that I intend to scold my own darling, but look in your Bible under what our

Heavenly Father promises to those who remember the poor. I think that unless we deny ourselves the gift is worthless.

Alfred starts for home in the morning to take papers and letters to see his wife and to try and get me a horse. I am glad that you have ... [letter creased, illegible] I am very fond of the music and many of my happier associations are connected with it. Do you think Hal will ever play well? I expected he would be fond of music. I suppose Dick's thoughts are not raised far above a terrier puppy yet. I expect him to make a man yet if he lives, there is something in him if he can be properly trained. His self-will will make him selfish unless [he takes] great care to direct it.

And what is my dear Hal thinking of? Is he filled with the wish to be a man that he may ride a fine horse and own a dog and gun? These things are well enough in their place, but I want my boy to have a higher mark than to be a drone in this busy Confederate hive of ours. We have lost too many of our working minds and hands for him to be content to idly live on the meat and bread others have earned without adding something to the common store.

Hal is only ten years old, and Dick is seven.

Tell him with my love that he is to fill Johnny's place as well as his own, and to do this he has no time to be idle. He must now study hard to fit himself for whatever place he may be destined to fill, that he may live not for himself alone but for his country, for our glorious Old Dominion as our part of it. His best foundation for this is, to have a constant desire to be *just* and *truthfull* [sic]—to "love God with all his heart and his neighbor as himself."

Johnny had died ten months earlier.

Since our rout of Genl. Wilson we have had two or three days of comparative rest having nothing but picket duty to do. The enemy have fallen back from the Petersburg and Weldon R.R. and it is being rapidly repaired. I have heard from Clarence—he is now, I suppose, with the army of the Valley and is well. I look to have him with me before long.

Say to cousin Mittie that I received her note and thank her for sending me the socks, shirts & collar; I have not yet received the other package.

Moses has been with the wagon train for some weeks; he came up with the train three days ago. He is much more afraid of flying musket balls than Alfred. Alfred usually goes with me to every fight and remains usually with the ambulances. He ran off during a fight and when I scolded him about it he said, "He staid long enough to put one wounded and one dead man in the ambulance and on looking up saw some Yankees coming over the hill and that he thought it was time to leave and save his mare." Moses says "that he has nothing to do with the fight anyhow," and he ain't going near the bullets. With much love to Fan, who shall have the next letter, to Hal and Dick. I am very sincerely your devoted father,

R.H.Dulany

P.S. Moses desires me to thank you for mention of him—sends his kinds respects and [letter creased, illegible] Old Master and he will bring her the watch he promised her. Give much love to Ida and your cousin Eliza Carter & Sue Hall and always to your Uncle Armistead.

Letter of Richard H. Dulany to his daughter Fanny:

Stony Creek Station July 6th

My Dear Fan

Alfred started this morning before I was well awake, so I forgot to correct a mistake you seem to have made in regard to my promotion. I have had a Brigade to command since Genl. Rosser was wounded, but this does not increase my rank. I am still a Col. and shall return to my regiment as soon as the Genl. recovers. I have but little desire to change my old position. I am much attached to the men and Officers of the old 7th.

I have lately lost several of my best Lts. Granville Smith of Capt. Hatchers comy. wounded in the stomach but is now recovering and Lt. Vandiver, who lost his right arm and part of his shoulder within twenty yards of the place I am now writing.

1st Lt. Granville T. Smith, Co. A, 7th Virginia Cavalry, survived wounding at the Wilderness, May 5, 1864.

Vandiver is a noble fellow and a splendid soldier. When wounded the Dr. told him he would lose his arm. "Well, Dr.," he replied, "I have no right to be exempt from what other men have suffered." I called to see him yesterday with Mr. Carson. He asked Mr. C. to write to his mother and "tell her that it was not as bad as it might have been," and then said to me, "Col., I am greatly blessed in having this cool room and a kind nurse to attend to me." I need not add that the Lt. is a Christian.

2nd Lt. Charles H. Vandiver of Co. F, 7th Virginia Cavalry, enlisted at age 21 and was wounded numerous times; he lost an arm at Sappony Church, June 28, 1864.[21]

Theodore M. Carson was appointed chaplain on January 6, 1863, succeeding James B. Avirett.[22]

If he lives it will be owing to his perfect resignation and courage. Ninety men out of a hundred would die. Ask yr. Grandfather to send me a bottle of sherry wine for him as it is impossible to get any pure wine in this country. Write longer letters and with less hurry.

Vandiver survived.

Your devoted father

R.H.Dulany

Sappony Church, built in 1728, is ten miles west of Stony Creek Station, at the end of White Oak Road, about five miles east of the Boydton Plank Road.

Letter of Richard H. Dulany to his niece, Julia Whiting:

Sappony Church, July 10, 1864

My dear Julia,

Do I now owe you one or two letters? If two I must plead the difficulty I still have in using my hand, although I am glad to say I hope before very long to have the full use of my arm again—although I fear I shall never have the free use of my first finger and thumb. I still have to hold my pencil between my second and third finger.

We have had the most active campaign of the war during the last eight weeks. On the 12th of June we met Sheridan, who had some ten thousand cav. at Trevilians on his way to join Genl. Hunter after he should have burned our stores and R.R. stock at Charlottesville,

The battle at Trevilian Station

and gave him a severe thrashing, killing, wounding and capt. nearly two thousand of his men. Our Division sent five hundred to Richmond. Sixty died and one hundred and twenty five wounded men fell into our hands, I do not know the exact number capt. &c by Fitz Lee. Sheridan in his official report says he lost one hundred and twenty five men and although stating that it was or had been his intention to join Hunter in the Valley after destroying the R.R. stores etc. at Charlottesville, he turned back because forage was scarce and his ammunition gave out.

Matthew C. Butler had lost a foot at Brandy Station, but returned to lead his troops into battle armed only with a silver-mounted riding whip.

Pierce Manning Butler Young of South Carolina.

The South Carolinians under Butler lost pretty severely in this fight and if it had not been for Rosser's timely blow on the enemy's flank recapturing a large number of the S.C.s and a part of Hampton's train the Yanks would have capt. nearly the whole of Young's Brigade. This was on Saturday and on Sunday they threw their whole force against Butler

and were handsomely repulsed. Rosser was
wounded in this fight and I have had
command of the Brigade since.

After the fight at Trev. we followed
Sheridan nearly to Charles City C.H. when
Sheridan, thinking we had sent off the greater
part of our number, suddenly made a counter
march and attempted to cut us off from
Richmond by getting between us and
Richmond and fortifying all the roads.
Hampton dismounted and attacking drove the
Yanks from their breastworks, again killing
and capturing a large number in the fight they
lost a large number of officers among them
three Cols. killed and capt.

Charles City Court House is about
twenty-five miles SE of Richmond.

We then followed Sheridan until he found
shelter of his gunboat at the White House
where we only capt. fifty two of his men. I
cannot say how much were killed as we were
driven back by the gun boats.

Sheridan moved northward
toward the Pamunkey River.

Having driven Sheridan to the water we
quickly crossed the James and turned our
attention to Genls. Wilson, Spear, Kautz, who
had been making sad havoc of our railroads
and robbing defenseless women and children
of every particle of food, and in many instances
of all their clothing. These last raiding parties
have been more destructive of property than
any that have heretofore desolated our land.
There was nothing of too little value to be
stolen or destroyed. When Hampton reached
Stony Creek Station on the Petersburg and
Weldon R.R. he had barely time to post his
command before the head of the returning
column (Wilson's) struck us.

Samuel P. Spear and August V.
Kautz

It at first recoiled, but after bringing up
their artillery they made an obstinate attack
upon our line, especially on a road on which
they were going to Grant's army. At this place

The battle of Sappony Church

our troops commenced to waver as the enemy were using grape and canister which we could not return as they had posted their artillery in a lady's yard, the lady and her children all being at the house at the time.

My regiment being in reserve was ordered forward on foot to the weak point. The old 7th came up with a rush, and with a yell that seemed to put new courage into the troops that a moment before gave strong symptoms of giving way. Our whole line taking up the "infernal yell" as the Yanks call it, pressed forward with the 7th and drove the enemy from their advanced position.

Lt. Charles H. Vandiver

In this charge I lost one lt. (arm taken off at the shoulder) and seven men. During the night the yanks made three other attempts to break through our lines but were repulsed every time. At daybreak our brigade attacked their left flank and Hampton pressing them at the same time in front he broke them and drove them in great disorder for several miles.

Our men were so close during the flank movement to the enemy that there were several hand to hand fights. Mott Ball tried hard to kill a Yank who was rather too strong for one of his men but the fellow beating Mott's men severely, held him between Mott and himself until he surrendered. Another of our best men I fear may die from a blow over his head with a musket.

Mottrom Dulany Ball of Fairfax was the son of Mary Dulany and Col. Spencer Mottrom Ball, a nephew of William H. Dulany.

Reams Station was ten miles south of Petersburg, on the Petersburg & Weldon R.R.

Gen. William Mahone

The enemy, said by their papers to be six thousand strong, fled toward Reams Station ten (10) miles distant, but were there met by Mahone and Fitz Lee, whom Hampton had had placed there knowing that if we whipped them they would retreat in that direction.

They charged Mahone's infantry and captured sixty of them when Lee struck them in flank, recaptured the poor footmen and routed the whole party, capturing seven hundred negroes (not in arms), three hundred fifty Yanks (350), all their wagons, ambulances, a large number of horses and thirteen pieces of artillery.

Our Division composed of Butler's, Rosser's, and Young's Brigades captured three pieces of artillery, one caisson, a large quantity of ammunition for artillery and small arms, one hundred and sixty-three negroes, about one hundred and fifty horses, most of them broken down, and eight hundred and three (803) live Yanks. I do not count the dead or wounded.

Matthew C. Butler, Thomas Rosser and Pierce Young.

This has been the most successful cav. engagement of the war. Since Sheridan's advance in June (11th) to Wilson's rout on the 29th of the same month, the Yankees have lost not less than ten (10) thousand horses, most of them shot by themselves to keep them from falling into our hands, and six thousand men. Genl. Hampton thinks *at least* (7000) seven thousand men. This self-same Genl. Wilson, when his rear was attacked some weeks since by Dearing's men and being informed they were Confed. Cav., pretended to hold them in so much supreme contempt that he would not leave the room he was eating in. Has he not verified the proverb [part of letter washed out].

General James Dearing

Our boys say he had not met the Laurel Brigade before, but this is not the case, for Rosser had whipped Wilson twice before with our Brigade when Wilson had a Division, and on each occasion Rosser received the thanks of Genl. Robert Lee in General Orders.

After the death of Genl. Jones, Clarence's commission became void. I have made application for him to command one of my companies, but Genl. Lee requires him to go through a certain form before he can be again commissioned.

Copy of application not found.

I enclose a copy of my application as Rosser's endorsement will, I know, give Carlyle pleasure. I have heard once or twice from C. since Genl. Jones's death; he was well and anxious to be with my regiment.

I suppose Clarence is now in Md. as I have not heard of him since Gen. Ransom, who has Jones's troops, went down the Valley with Genl. Early.

Gen. Robert Ransom, Jr.
Early's men were in Maryland, moving toward Washington.

July 16th. I suppose you have heard of our troops being with in a few miles of Washington and of Baltimore after Early had badly whipped Genl. Wallace, commander 6th Corps and captured Genl. Tyler. Yankee papers say that our shells are falling within two miles of the center of Washington, and our army is in line of battle on the prolongation of 7th St. and a portion of it [section washed out].

On July 9, 1864, Early engaged Maj. Gen. Lew Wallace at Monocacy, who was reinforced by elements of the Federal Sixth Corps. Early reached the outskirts of Washington but did little damage. Gen. Erastus B. Tyler, who commanded the defenses of Baltimore, was not captured.

I enclose a letter from the children. I fear Fan's heart is not as tender as her father's. The verse she objects to expressed my sentiments exactly. I was obliged to leave three wounded Yankees (shot through the body and the Dr. said must die) laying in the road with the woods on fire on each side of them after our last fight, and I felt it more than I have done the death of some of my own men because I could not help their being killed, but it did seem cruel to leave the poor fellows to be roasted. Our ambulances had our own wounded in them.

See the verse on page 155.

I cannot ask yr. mother to write to me as she must have more than her hands full, but really I think Nina, Alice, or Mary might let me hear from them sometimes. As the country is now all open to Welbourne I do wish you could move Carlyle there and after a good long rest to Grassland, if yr. mother [section washed out].

How is Ellen? Give her my love. Tell her I heard from Burwell yesterday, the Yanks had treated him badly, taking almost every thing from his farm [in Clarke County].

Much love to my dear Sister and the children and Carlyle. Yr. letters have not been sent to me as there is no mail.

R.H.Dulany

Letter of John Peyton Dulany to his son:

12th July 1864
Welbourne

My Dear Richard,

I begin to feel anxious about you, it has been five or six weeks since I have had any tidings of you, do let me hear from you as soon as possible. Clarence, who will be the bearer of this, will be able to give a more satisfactory account of every thing transpiring here than I can by letter. With respect to Welby deButts' horse, he was stolen out of the field about the time Brown left. I have no doubt but Brown was the rogue, but stealing horses has become so much the fashion that few think there is any impropriety in it except those that lose.

Vegetation is suffering most intensely— there will be no oats made, and I fear if we have no rain in a few days there will be no corn made. I have never witnessed anything like it—there will be very little wheat, hardly enough to supply the wants of the farmers. Persons from the lower counties have hauled nearly all the bread stuffs from Loudoun. I cannot help looking forward to the winter with dread for the suffering poor of the South.

I have tried every way that I could to get you a horse, but in vain; the Southern money will hardly pay for anything here. They ask for a common horse from two thousand to three thousand dollars, in Northern money from three hundred to four hundred. If I can meet with such a horse as I think will suit you, I will not stand on price.

I wish I could give you some information respecting the movements of our army but everything concerning them is wrapt in mystery. In a few days I presume their intentions will be known. I very much fear that if our army should have to return to Virginia, the Yankees will make a clean sweep of every thing in their route and leave us destitute of everything they can find. As Clarence will not leave for some days I will lay aside my pen, in hope that I may have something to communicate.

Alfred has this moment arrived with your most welcome letter, and I try, my beloved son, to feel grateful to that Being who continues to watch over you and preserve you in the hour of danger.

I have anticipated your request having desired your overseer in the mountains to have your black colt. I am told that he is a splendid horse but it will require some time to make him fit for service—if you allude to the bay mare you purchased to match Lady May, I do not think she will answer your purpose. She is now at Welbourne and is only fit for harness.

I regret that so many of Mr. Weidmayer's and my letters have miscarried. I am sure that at least six of mine you have never received.

With respect to the wool, I have made no disposition of it. You had better write to

Early's army was, at this time, on its way back to Virginia.

[illegible] on the subject. I have purchased cloth for you and the servants and regret that I could not procure buttons or I would have had them made up for you. I will send you by the first safe opportunity a very handsome coat and waistcoat that were made for Turner, which I hope will fit you.

I hear Major Foster is not at Grassland. As soon as I can find out his whereabouts, I will send him your letter. In the mean time, if I can possibly find a horse to suit you I will buy him if I can send him to you immediately, for it is very dangerous to keep anything of any value on the farm. They are constantly stealing my sheep in spite of all I can do. We are without law, and people here are without honesty.

Possibly Maj. Thomas R. Foster of The Plains, who served as commissary, purchasing supplies for the South.

I commenced this letter with the intention of informing you of the arrival of Carlyle and Mary, and on the same day Clarence made his appearance, very much to the delight of his parents, but I presume Mary intends to give you an account of herself and I need not say anything more of her. I heard from your sister Julia by Welby, who did not give me an opportunity of writing to you. She and her family were well.

With respect to your request of selling your old cows and oxen to the Government, I do not think you will be able to get as many as you wish. The only cow at Welbourne that will do for beef is Dairymaid; the oxen will make beef in the course of a month or two. Haley says Dairymaid will have no more calves. I do not know what they have on the mountain farms.

I saw [illegible] a few days since. He informed me he had the cattle you purchased on the farm. We have finished harvest with a very poor turn out. We shall not make more than enough bread for the family and for seed.

If we have not rain soon it will be impossible to fallow this fall, the ground is almost as hard as marble.

The girls and Mr. Weidmayer have just started in the wagon to pay a visit to Oatlands. I am always glad when I can offer them any amusement; if they do not enjoy themselves now they never will. Carlyle is the most emaciated person I ever saw. Dr. Leith saw him yesterday. He thinks there is very little chance of his ever recovering. Poor fellow, how much he has suffered from his [illegible]. If you could hear what your sister has gone through, you would indeed deeply sympathize with her.

From present appearances there will not be enough corn to feed the hogs. I have never in my long life known so long a drought—if we have a much longer continuance of it it will be impossible for any corn to be made, at least in this part of the country. Under the circumstances, do you not think it will be better not to send off the cattle that perhaps the family may stand in need of? Many families are suffering for the necessities of life. I am told between this and Richmond the suffering is intense. Loudoun has been supplying the lower counties with bread stuffs and meat for several months. The drain has been so great that it will hardly leave enough for the inhabitants.

As Clarence and Welby are very unexpectedly to take French leave I have to bring my scroll to a finish, so good by my dear son

As ever your truly
J.P.D.

Letter of Fanny Dulany to her father:

July 1864

My dear Papa,

Mr. Weidmayer took Mary and I down to Oatlands last Thursday in the wagon. We started at 6 in the morning with as Hal calls her "the white-stocking mare" and the one which you bought to match Lady May; when we had gotten near Mr. Reardon's house, you know there is a little hill formed by two large stones. The white stocking mare commenced balking, and then the other; at last after rearing and a great deal of backing, Mr. Weidmayer succeeded in getting them to the bottom of that steep hill on the side of Mr. R.'s house where they would not take one step, in spite of patting, whipping, and jerking. Nina, Mary & I had to get quietly out of the wagon, and walk back. We started off again with the white mule and Lady May's match, and arrived at Oatlands at about six. We had a very pleasant visit in some respects, but poor Uncle Hal was down there, and Oh! Papa, he was *drunk*, the whole time.

If you had heard him speaking of his soul, he said that he believed that if he was to go to Heaven he would go, but if he was born to go to hell, he would go there. I did feel so sorry for him, the tears were in his eyes the whole time he was speaking. Please write to him about drinking so, for I believe you are the only one who has any control over him. He came away from Oatlands this morning with a bottle of whiskey, & in passing by here he stopped and drank until he was as drunk as he could be.

We started from Oatlands also this morning after hunting for the mule and horse in vain which have been stolen by our *own men* with two of Mr. Ben Carter's horses, and met two brigades of Early's men getting right in the center and covered & almost suffocated with the dust.

I am ashamed to send such a badly written, and badly misspelt letter, but we came late this evening and did not know until a few minutes ago.

Please write to Hal next time, for I think he is getting a little jealous. We expect Hunter through here tomorrow morning early. Good-night.

> Your affectionate daughter,
> Fanny C. Dulany

Letter of Richard H. Dulany to his daughter Fanny:

Rowanty Creek is SW of Reams Station.

HdQrs Rosser's Brigade
Rowanty Creek, July 18, 1864.

My dear Fan,

I received yesterday letters from Mary and you dated May 10th. They have been a long time on the way but were very welcome.

The poetry you quoted from Longfellow is certainly good, but the sentiment you seem to object to, as contained in the last verse is the best of the piece, as it is the most Christian. We are trying every means in our power to rid our country of our civil invaders, but I do not think it right to encourage a spirit of revenge against them. I have never yet seen a captured Yankee maltreated by one of my men, although we have frequently caught them with the plunder they had taken from the houses of defenseless, helpless persons. Our scouts have killed them when caught in the act of robbery, and in that I think they are justifiable. You know who says "Vengeance is mine and I will repay."

I have several letters here from Richland for Clarence, and as I suppose he has gone to Maryland, and that you may probably see him on his return, you must let him know where his letters are.

We have had little to do except light picket duty since we so completely routed Genls. Wilson, Spear, and Kautz near Stony Creek.

We have been in this camp, on the banks, or rather dry swamp, of Rowanty for a week to-day. The weather has been so dry and the nights so cool that so far as we have escaped both chills and mosquitoes. Since our feint upon Baltimore and Washington seems to have the desired effect of taking troops from Grant's army, I suppose there is some chance of our leaving this country before the latter part of August, which is the commencement of the sickly season.

We have had plenty of fine fish, and riding on our outposts a day or two since, I found a deserted house, and in the garden a plentiful supply of cymblins from which I brought three days supply. The people are very kind, but their hospitality is sorely tested where there are so many soldiers. I rarely eat out of camp—have taken but four meals under a roof since I left home. Tomorrow I am invited to shoot Woodcock, and in the evening to a fish fry. I do not know if I can yet use my gun, but I can at least eat the fish.

Cymblins are vegetables of the squash family.

How much I should like your Grandfather and Mr. Weidmayer with me a few days during my partial holiday. Alfred, I hope, brought my letters safely to Welbourne, and is by this time nearly ready to start back with a return mail.

Have you heard lately from your Aunt Julia and has she heard from John deButts?

John Peyton deButts was a prisoner at Fort Delaware.

Rebecca, the younger daughter of
Ida and Hal Dulany of Oakley,
would have been six years old.

I hope you will visit your Aunt Ida
whenever you can. Give much [love] to her,
your Uncle Hal, and the children when you
see them. Does Rebecca grow much? Tell her
that she must not forget me. We are all too
quiet to furnish any news, so I must look to you
as I suppose Mosby and his men have returned
from Md. and Genl. Early is again south of the
Potomac. If Alfred has not left, send by him a
small package of black pepper. I suppose the
great drought has injured the garden very much.

With much love to my dear father, to May,
Hal, Dick, and your Cousin Mittie, I am very
sincerely your devoted father

R.H. Dulany

[P.S.] Remember me kindly to the
Servants.

July 25th. I have had no opportunity to
send this letter until today. We have had
several fine rains lately which I hope have
reached Loudoun. Alfred and Clarence have
taken me quite by surprise. I had not expected
Alfred to return for some days. I was much
disappointed by his not bringing me one of my
young horses. If we do not move further North
soon I shall send after my black colt.

It gave me great pleasure to learn that your
Uncle, Aunt and Nina were at last at
Welbourne. Give much love to them, and say
to your Aunt Mary that Grassland is at her
service whenever she can take possession. She
would have to give one room to the overseer
until I can get a short furlough, which I shall
apply for as soon as Genl. Rosser takes
command of his Brigade. I will answer Mr.
Weidmayer's and your Aunt's letters the next
opportunity.

R.H.Dulany

Letter of Julia Whiting to her uncle, Richard H. Dulany:

Richland, July 27th '64

Dear Uncle,

I can hardly find words in which to express my pleasure at receiving the package of letters for me today by some person unknown.

Neville and I were busily engaged in our morning reading of Rollin, deep in the campaigns of the great Cyrus, but since the arrival of your letter, we are neither of us in the mood for enjoying the achievements of any soldiers but our own gallant Southerners. We see very few Richmond papers; our accounts of the various engagements and raids which have taken place this spring and summer are therefore nearly always given by the Yankee papers, so that independently of the pleasure of hearing from you, it has been a great gratification to receive the description of all our successes from an eye witness.

How shall I thank you for having written such a good long letter, and that too when writing must be so disagreeable to you. I cannot consider you in my debt any longer although I have written repeatedly since last March, knowing that you would like to hear from Father and mama. Yours, as Grandpapa tells me of his, would cancel a great many of mine. I wish I had May and Fan at my side to enjoy with me the success of the Laurel Brigade and above all that our own regiment. I should like so much to see you at the head of the Brigade if it could be gained in some way but by the death of Gen. Rosser, who is too valuable an officer for us to lose. I am always anxious that those soldiers who have fought bravely for our freedom should live to see it won.

Neville is her brother.

Cyrus, king of Persia, conquered Babylon and liberated the Jews.

Julia had wished that the colonel would be promoted to general.

An amanuensis is one who writes what another dictates.

Possibly Maj. Thomas Conway Waller, 9th Virginia Cavalry.

I think, though, that my ambitious wishes that you laughed at in Amherst [County], are in a fair way of being realized. I shall not have the pleasure, though, of writing your letter of acceptance this time. I quite envy your amanuensis his office.

I see that Major Waller has never delivered [to] you my letter sent by him in the beginning of this month. I am particularly sorry that he did not as it contained news from Welbourne much later than you had received when you wrote and I had enclosed it in a letter from Fan written the third of this month. As the mail is so uncertain at present that you may not yet have heard from Welbourne I will run the risk of repeating what you may chance to have heard before receiving this.

Father, after resisting all our persuasions and reasonings until we fairly gave up in despair, suddenly concluded to follow the Dr.'s advice and in your wagon, comfortably reclining upon a stretcher, started for Loudoun accompanied by Mama and Nina. They reached Welbourne about two o'clock on the third day after starting. Father bore the journey remarkably well, and Mama wrote me word that he was so much excited by the arrival that Grandpapa could not believe her account of his previous weakness.

The 30th of June must have been a day of surprises at Welbourne for a few hours after Mama and Father arrived Clarence made his appearance most unexpectedly to all parties. It must have been an intense relief to Father, for since the news of poor Gen. Jones's death he had been suffering great anxiety about C.

May and Fan wrote that all at Welbourne are well. I sent Fan's letter to you and cannot imagine what Major Waller could have done with it. Should you meet with him, please inquire about it; several letters for Clarence were sent by him at the same time.

Father expected to stay at Welbourne for some time and then visit Clarke [County]. Mama intended returning to look after us in October; what their subsequent plans may be neither I nor they could tell while the country remains so unsettled. In the meantime, I am left here enthroned as vice queen, but feeling very much as if I were in an honorable exile and very willing to be relieved of my office.

I miss Mama so much and as the unhealthy season draws nearer—if any season in Stafford could be called healthy—I do not like to think that the responsibility of taking care of seven children lies upon my shoulders. You could [not] tell how much good you were going to do me by writing, but your letter has been the first thing I have had to cheer me since Mama left, and I have been in the depths of the blues.

I grow weary of the river, beautiful as it is, and long for our own mountains and a breath of pure delicious air from them. The atmosphere here is enervating.

We had a visitor a week since whom I was quite pleased to meet, having heard so much of him from Coz Henry Arthur and Coz Eliza—Mr. Dunlop, formerly on Gen. Armistead's staff. You may remember him, as he was for some time at Coz H.A.'s while wounded. He brought his wife to the neighborhood, and I invited them to stay until they could cross the river, as they were on their way North.

Mr. D., having left the army on account of his health, was returning to England. His wife was a sister of Col. Maury of the Cav. and cousin of the Maury's in Richmond. As they

Henry Arthur Hall

William Dunlop was a *chargé d' affaires*.

Col. Dabney H. Maury

were just from Richmond and acquainted with all of our friends and relations there and in Baltimore, their visit was an agreeable interlude in our quiet life.

Mr. D. spoke with a great deal of affection for Coz Wm. Herbert and said that Coz W. had been for some time giving evidence of religious feeling and had been since he entered the army perfectly steady. I have been so fond of Coz William ever since my childhood and have regretted his unfortunate life so much, that such news of him was very pleasant. What happiness it would give Coz Mitt to see Coz W. a consistent Christian.

It seems doubly hard to live as a Christian in times when all one's feelings of indignation, hatred and revenge are daily roused by tidings of some fresh atrocity perpetrated by the Yankees in the once happy homes of the South. Deprived too as we are of all the ordinances of religion at the very season when we need them most. None of the family here have been within the walls of a church for three years; and during all that time there has only been divine service once in all this portion of Stafford.

Monimia "Nimmie" Fairfax (1820-1875), daughter of Thomas 9th Lord and Margaret (Herbert) Fairfax, and wife of Archibald Cary.

I wish the children could have had some religious influence brought to bear upon them during all the time of Father's illness when mama was unavoidably forced to neglect them, such influence as Nimmie Fairfax exercised in her family or Miss Law in Cousin Sarah's.

I long for the time when we shall be again settled near our own relations and friends, for one might almost as well be north of the line as here. When do you expect Grant to be driven from Virginia? He certainly has more tenacity of purpose than any Northern general has yet exhibited. I hope nevertheless he may meet with the fate of his predecessors.

I'm afraid my feelings would accord better with Fanny's than yours with regard to the Yankees. I certainly never could say "Spare him, he our love hath shared." If I would have our own men spare them, it is rather that I wish our soldiers to treat them according to their own dignity than to their foe's deserts.

The ruffians who have ravaged our land can only be punished fitly by those who could equal them in baseness. I would not have our Christian soldiers sully their laurels by a single action resembling those of our enemy.

I hate to think of our men destroying private property across the line, though I know that necessity compels us to retaliate. Of course everything depends upon the spirit in which it is done, yet I cannot help fearing that in thus retaliating our men may lessen the high honorable feelings which they have displayed during the war. I love the honor and glory of our own army more than I hate the Yankees, much as I detest them.

I will not ask you to write to me again as the way is now open to Welbourne and you will have enough to do to write to Grandpapa and the children, only let me know when you are made Brigadier. Aunt E. sends her love in which the children join

Your attached niece
J.B.W.

In early August 1864, Dulany continued in command of the Laurel Brigade, which had a rare period of rest with plenty to eat in the area of Stony Creek. Captain Frank M. Myers of the 35th Battalion Virginia Cavalry reported that "for a

rarity, when Col. Dulany commanded the brigade, no drilling to do."23

Partial letter of Richard H. Dulany to his sister, Julia Roszell:

Hd Qrs Rosser's Brigade
Sussex Co. Aug 3rd 1864

My Dear Sister,

Gen. John Bell Hood replaced Johnston as commander of the Army of Tennessee and began a series of costly offenses against the troops of Gen. W. T. Sherman.

The Crater, July 30, 1864. Dulany is in error about the black troops. They were the last to charge.

I feel anxious about Atlanta. I cannot help having doubts as to the wisdom of removing Johnston. Hood has made a hard fight and captured many guns ... but still Sherman threatens the city.

The Yanks made a desperate assault upon Petersburg on Saturday morning, after mining and blowing up an advance earthwork. After the explosion the negroes led the attack crying "No quarter, no quarter." Our troops were driven back from the first line the enemy holding it for some [time] when we attacked, Mahone leading, and drove them out of the works, punishing them so severely that they have been perfectly quiet ever since, at least we hear no guns here. A gentleman told me that when a courier told General Lee, that the enemy had blown up a battery and had capd. our outer works, he did not even get out of his chair, but simply said to one of Beauregard's staff, "Go and tell Genl. Beauregard to drive those people out of our works." It is not hard to imagine such coolness, and such perfect confidence in our troops.

Letter of John Peyton Dulany to Richard H. Dulany:

Welbourne, August 6th 1864.

My dear Richard,

As I do not know at what minute I may
have an opportunity of sending a letter to you,
I think I had better try and have one ready in
case I should meet a soldier going to the army,
although I have found them to very unreliable
mail carriers. You say you have written
frequently to me; I have not had one item from
you since Alfred was here. A few days since
Fan received a letter from you dated 6th July,
but neither papers nor stamps accompanied it.
I suspect the letters written to you have been
equally unfortunate.

The information you received from
Clarence about your bonds was incorrect. Mr.
Weidmayer had nothing to do with them. I
regret that you have not received his letter
enclosing a statement of your business
entrusted to his care. You are, I have no doubt,
informed of Charles Stewart's having left
Baltimore for Europe; it is expected that he
will return about September.

The Bank in New York has refused to cash
the check you drew in favour of Mr. W. for I
believe $200. I let him have that amount in
greenbacks. I have told him what you said in
your letter about his mare. He has not yet, I
suppose, made up his mind on the subject as
he has said nothing to me about it.

I heard the other [day] by R[ichard]
DeB[utts] that your black colt was in good
order, but do not know of any opportunity of
sending him to you. The man that brought
your letters appears to be very uncertain when
he will return. I can supply your wants as far as
a hat and very indifferent pair gloves will go.

Bar was here some days since; he paid me
eight hundred and eight dollars in Bank of
Virginia notes and I think $150 in

Having left her home at Oatlands on October 20, 1861, Mrs. Carter was living at "Bellfield," near the town of Bloomfield, when this raid occurred.

Confederate notes for his crop of wool. He says he had no choice, he had either to sell or let the Yankees have it. He complains very much of the Maryland soldiers, he says they treated him worse than the Yankees. Such conduct is certainly a disgrace to our soldiers.

You are misinformed with respect to the Yankee raid, they came no nearer to Welbourne than Mrs. George Carter's. They searched her house, took her watch from her side, nearly all of her trinkets, which she had hidden in some secret place in the House, but they knew exactly where it was, no doubt some of her servants informed them. They carried off all the meat and horses they could find.

In two of my letters I requested to know if I should let Dairymaid go with the cattle that could be spared from the different farms to the army (Haley thinks she will have no more calves), and to whom are the cattle to be delivered? I think if possible we ought to keep some of the cattle for beef, as we shall have very little corn to fatten the hogs. We are suffering very much from a long protracted drought. When the Yankees were here last, I sent all the cattle we could spare to the mountains, but as the cattle always return from the mountains much poorer than when sent, I shall have to send for them again, and take the chances of losing them.

We are surrounded by rogues. Bar informs me that it is impossible to prevent their taking the stock and particularly sheep. He says that he shall have to sell the hogs, as he will not have corn to fatten them. The times are gloomy indeed. I often wish that I were in the army, or anywhere else than in the power of the Yankees. What do you wish done with the wool on the mountain? Do you not think I had better exchange it for linsey for the servants? It is certainly very unsafe where it is.

William Whiting was here the day before yesterday. He says that [Harry] Gilmor's men were guilty of almost every outrage. I really think his conduct ought to be represented to Gen. Lee. If we are to be treated so by men who ought to be our protectors, what can we expect from our enemies.

Gilmor's men had harassed the citizens of New Town (now Stephens City), Va., eight miles south of Winchester.

I have returned from riding through the corn fields on the Welbourne farm and at Millsville. That at Welbourne, if it should rain in the course of seven or eight days, may make one 1/2 crop, and about 1/4 of one at Millsville. I do not think I have ever known so severe a drought in my life.

I very much fear there will be great suffering in the country this winter, already the people are daily sending from the more Southern counties for bread stuffs and meat until we are nearly exhausted—our wheat crop is very small, the corn ground almost everywhere has been a failure. There have been no oats made; the lot near the house did not produce one bushel. We can only trust to Him who sends the early and later rain, and who has promised that our bread and water shall be sure. I am plowing for wheat at Millsville, running both plows there. I am at a loss to know whether to send the corn to be ground or not; it has not paid for sending for the last two years.

It is unaccountable to me that our land will not produce now without manure. It was predicted some years ago that it would be the case, that guano would in the course of time leave our land in a much worse state than it found it.

Sunday morning. I have just been informed

that Lieut. Smith will leave tomorrow for the army. I will try if I can prevail on him to take your hat and gloves to you. The girls would have written if they had been at home; they went yesterday to Mr. Bolling's to spend two days with the Miss Harrisons (daughters of Henry H. of Leesburg), two very entertaining girls. Whiting, Mary thinks, is improving. If he recovers it will be indeed a miracle.

Charlotte Hall is Henry Arthur Hall's aunt.

Miss Charlotte Hall is perfectly deranged. She is with Henry Arthur, has to be kept in confinement. All well at Welbourne and send their love, the servants send their respects. Had a little rain last night which will keep the corn from being entirely burnt up.

I have managed to fill up my paper and have hardly room to tell you my beloved son how fondly I love you.

J.P.D.

Letter of Richard H. Dulany to his father, John Peyton Dulany:

Hd. Qrs. Rossers Brigade
Sussex Co. Aug. 9th 1864

My dear Father

I sent Moses home last week for a short holiday, and to take letters and papers to Welbourne. As Mr. Hatcher will leave in the morning for Loudoun I want Moses to return with him, although this will give him a longer time at home than I intended but it will also give him an opportunity of preparing my horses for their trip to camp. He should feed on *old* grain and *hay* and give them a thorough cleaning every day. Every thing is very quiet here, we have nothing to excite us except now and then a little picket fighting. I hope Moses succeeded in getting you all the late papers as he passed through Richmond.

The Northern papers are very doleful since their attempt to blow up Lee's army and then capture Petersburg. The largest estimate of our loss is I believe is twelve hundred, while they confess a loss of nearly six thousand and you know that they always under-rate their losses. You will recollect that Sheridan states his loss at Trevilian at 160, when we had sent to Charlottesville 500 men besides 100 wounded and upward of 60 of their dead fell into our hands.

The New York *World* says that this defeat ends the summer campaign. This may be so, as it regards heavy fighting above P. & Richmond, but if Early can hold his own, I hope to see the war carried into Africa before the summer ends. The march upon Washington and into Pennsylvania with the battle at Petersburg has made many peace papers in the North. If we can only get Washington and make its destruction as complete as Sodom, we will have struck our best blow for peace.

I know how hard it will be for you to see the Capital destroyed, but what is stone and mortar compared to the lives of hundreds of brave men. Ask Cousin Armistead if he would not hold the handles of a plow which should turn broad furrows from the Navy yard to Georgetown. If corruption makes g— land, what a crop we should have.

I feel some anxiety about Early, as Lincoln must have sent a very large force against him, and I hear that a large portion of the Yankee army is at Charlestown, which would threaten Early's rear.

It is very hot here and our men would be glad to receive orders to march north.

Maj. Roger Preston Chew's Horse Artillery.

Admiral Franklin Buchanan was wounded at the Battle of Mobile Bay, August 5, 1864.

Roasting-ears and water-melons are just in season, but I am so much annoyed by farmers complaining of the depredations committed by the soldiers that I almost wish that the corn and melons would become bitter to the taste.

Two of my men were slightly wounded by the guard in a cornfield and one man from Chew's battery killed. It seems cruel to kill a man for taking a few ears of corn, but we are all fighting to assert and protect individual rights, and it would not be consistent to allow our soldiers to become the oppressors of our citizens.

I am sorry to see that our gallant little navy has met with a reverse at Mobile and that Capt. Buchanan was badly wounded and captured with his ship. This is one of the few reverses we have met with in the last twelve months.

I send some papers for Ida; please send them to her when you have read them. The dear little woman, how much I do want to see her and her little ones.

We have a long drought, but the corn is looking remarkably well. The land is sandy, but yields well in oats and makes with very little labor from two to four bushels of corn. Some fields near us will make six blls. The corn does not seem to be at all injured by the drought. A great many melons are usually grown, but they are very late this year and when there are so many soldiers they are becoming quite scarce.

I am quite pleasantly situated with Genl. Rosser's Staff, but I shall be very glad to see the Genl. back again, that I might return to my regiment. My ambition ranges no higher than to make the old 7th the best regiment in the command. I enclose a letter from [part

missing] I fear with her views she would make
a [illegible] soldier a politician. I wish very
much that Julia and the other children would
be brought from Richland before September.

With much love to Carlyle, Sister Mary,
Nina, and my dear children, I am as ever your
devoted son

R.H.Dulany

Mr. Hatcher will return about the 25th
instant. I wish Moses to return with him unless
he finds some other person [portion of letter
faded and illegible].

*Rosser reclaimed command of the Laurel
Brigade on August 23, 1864, and Dulany
returned to the 7th Virginia Cavalry.*

*Among Dulany's papers is the following
account of the battle of Reams Station, August
24-25, 1864, in which Grant attempted to cut the
Petersburg & Weldon Railroad, Lee's supply line
to the south. Dulany mentions obtaining the
sixteen-shooters during the Cattle Raid, which did
not occur until September 1864. McDonald's
Laurel Brigade correctly identifies this as the
Wilson Raid and quotes all but the last line of this
account.*

I was ordered by Genl. Rosser to report with
my regiment (7th Va) to Genl. A.P. Hill near
Reams Station on the 24th of August 1864.
When I found Genl. Hill, he told me that he
was very anxious that the federal forces, who
were entrenched at Reams Station, should not
know of his presence until he attacked their
earthworks, and to that end he wished me to
drive in all the cavalry in his front. Not
knowing what was before me, I ordered Col.
Marshall to advance with a squadron and

attack any forces he came up with. I followed with the rest of the regiment.

We had not advanced more than a mile when I heard firing, and Col. Marshall was brought back badly wounded. I immediately rode to the front and, taking command of the advanced squadrons, charged the enemy and drove them behind their earthworks. We were so close on their heels that two of my men, unable to control their horses, followed the federal cavalry into the fortifications. One of the men was Pendleton of Baltimore, the other I do not remember fell dead in the trenches. I do not recollect what other loss we suffered.

David E. Pendleton of Baltimore, Co. A, 7th Virginia Cavalry, charged his horse over the breastworks, was captured, sent to City Point and later to Point Lookout, Md. He was exchanged at Cox's Landing, James River, Feb. 14-15, 1865.[24]

Genl. Hill was repulsed in his first attack with a heavy loss. On the morning of the 25th Hill ordered me to protect his flank with the assistance of (I think) a portion of Wright's command while he made his second attack. When he carried the earthworks sixteen (or twenty six) hundred men, and six or eight new three inch rifle guns. During the fight the federal cavalry made three efforts to get at his flank, but we drove them back every time.

In *Laurel Brigade* this reads "twenty-six or eight hundred men."

As Hill sent his prisoners to the rear the federal cavalry again attempted a flank movement and with more stubborness than their first attempts. We had a number of sixteen-shooters captured during the Cattle Raid with Hampton, and our fire was so rapid that Hill became uneasy, and sent an Aide to know if we needed any assistance. I asked for two Howitzers, which he sent me, and immediately after a portion of Genl. McGowan's command.

In *Laurel Brigade*, this has been corrected to read "Henry sixteen-shooters recently captured from Wilson's cavalry."

They came at a "double quick," and the Genl., being a large man, was pretty well blown. He asked [me] to put his men in position as he did not know the ground. As the

Gen. Samuel McGowan's South Carolina brigade.

Howitzers were all the help I wanted, and I desired my own men to have all the credit of the frequent repulses of the enemy, I told Genl. McGowan that there was a stream in the wood in our rear where, if he would take his men, they would be near enough if we required their assistance.

After this Genl. Hill ordered me to move forward and take possession of the battle field to secure the guns and ammunition left by the enemy and to bury the dead. While carrying out these orders, a squad of Cavalry under a flag of truce came asking for permission to bury their dead. I had orders to refuse any such application, and they retired. Genl. Hill wished to get back to the army before the enemy should know that he had left Reams Station.

R.H. Dulany

In the following letter, Richard Dulany reviews events that occurred while he commanded the Laurel Brigade.

Letter of Richard H. Dulany to his son Hal:

Hd. Qrs. 7th. Va. Cav. 29 Aug. 1864.

My dear Hal,

It has been some time since I have written to you, but if I can give you but a short account of the time since Moses left with letters to the family, my letter will be longer than a half dozen of yours. As I suppose you prefer to hear from this Brigade and the 7th Regiment, I will try to give you an account of our engagements since I have had command of the Brigade.

On the 11th of June we fought Genl.

Sheridan's force at Trevilian when he attempted to march on Charlottesville. On this day Genl. Rosser was badly wounded and I then took command of his Brigade.

On the next day 12th, Sheridan attacked us behind our rail breastworks and after a half day's desperate fighting we repulsed him, capturing five hundred prisoners, two hospitals containing more than a hundred wounded, and sixty of his dead were left on the field.

We (Genl. Hampton's command) followed Genl. Sheridan until he took refuge under the protection of gun boat at the White House. One of the South Carolina regmts. here drove in the Yankee infantry pickets and captured forty of them. This was on the 20th June. Genl. Hampton then withdrew his troops in the direction of the James River, when Genl. Sheridan, thinking we had sent a portion of our men across the river, thus weakening ourselves, threw his whole force between us and Richmond so as to prevent our returning to the city unless we first drove him out of the way. This we did most effectually, whipping him badly and capturing three hundred of his men. I commanded a flank movement with about a hundred and fifty of my men.

We charged the extreme left of their works and drove them from them. I lost but eight men in the attack, one of them a cousin of Mott D. Ball's. As we turned their flank Genl. Butler dislodged them in front and then we ran them for four miles capturing about three hundred prisoners beside many wounded & dead. If we could have run our horses we would have captured many more, but we had nearly all broken down and had to stop to rest.

After this fight we crossed the James River in time to meet a large force of Cav. and

Artillery under Genl. Wilson who, with the assistance of Genls. Kautz and Spear, had done great injury to our railroads and had treated our defenseless women and children with great cruelty, taking all along their route not only the horses but in many instances every particle of clothing and food, leaving whole families to beg or starve.

With Genl. Fitz Lee's assistance we whipped and completely routed the whole party, capturing eight hundred negroes, a thousand prisoners, many horses, small arms, thirteen pieces of Artillery and all their ambulances, many of them being loaded with clothing and plate taken from citizens and churches.

After this fight, in which I lost one of my best officers and several men, we had quite a long rest doing light picket duty and drilling and sometimes fishing. Genl. Hampton went a few miles from camp with a small party deer hunting and killed three in four days. I cannot shoot with my right hand yet but as my arm is gaining strength I hope my fingers may yet be strong enough to pull a trigger and when the war is over you and I may be able shoot many partridges together during your fall vacations. But I must continue my history.

About the 1st of August we were ordered to Gordonsville, and we all supposed that from that place we should go to the Valley, which caused great rejoicing among my men as the most of them lived in that part of the county & had not seen their families for many long months. Then, within one day's march of Gordonsville, a courier overtook us with orders from Genl. Robert Lee to march back to Richmond as the Yanks had sent a large force to the north side of the James River and were threatening the city.

Gordonsville is in Orange County, about twenty miles NE of Charlottesville.

Gen. John R. Chambliss, Jr.

Union cavalry under Gen. David
M. Gregg attacked up the Charles
City Road on August 16.
Chambliss rode toward the front
and was killed near White's
Tavern.

Maj. Edward McDonald

We returned immediately and after three
days march came up with Genl. Chambliss'
Brigade, which had engaged the enemy nine
miles southeast of Richmond. Genl.
Chambliss' brigade is only a portion of Genl.
W.H.F. Lee's Division. The whole Division
was engaged & driving the enemy when we
came up with them. Genl. Chambliss rode into
the enemy's lines during the fight and was
killed; his horse escaped to us.

That evening we rested and the next night
my command was ordered to get on the
extreme flank of the enemy and make a night
attack, but not to attempt to carry their
breastworks if they were strong. I sent Col.
Marshall and Major McDonald with the
advanced line of skirmishers to make the
attack, but the enemy withdrew before them
until they could get behind their fortifications,
when I recalled my men as ordered and we all
went back two miles & encamped.

The next day there was to be an attack
along the whole length of the enemy's line and
we were all ordered to take our positions as
quietly as possible and then wait for a signal,
which was to be six shots from a cannon on
our right answered by one shot on the left—
the signal was to be given about eleven o'clock.

As I was moving the Brigade to its position,
one of my scouts reported a number of Yankee
Cavalry on my left flank. I immediately rode
to an open space in the woods through which
we were marching and saw within 250 yards of
our column about 30 cavalry gathering
watermelons. I ordered everyone to keep
perfectly quiet until I could send a Squadron
to get between the rogues and the Yankee
army & thus capture them. Unfortunately,
one of our horses neighed just as the squadron

started, this alarmed the Yankees and they mounted & started back with their plunder with our boys after them at full speed. If the Yanks had not barricaded a gate, which prevented our men from getting through for about a minute, we would have caught them—as it was, we got all the melons which they lost in the chase. They must have been pretty well loaded as one of my men got three.

As I have but little space left I will finish in a letter to Mary. Take more pains in your writing, there is no reason why you should write in a hurry.

That God may bless my dear boy with perfect truthfulness and pure religion which embraces all good is the sincere prayer of

your father
R.H.D.

The next scrap of incomplete letter from the colonel to his daughter Fanny may have been written about this time:

[Missing]... Clarence bought me a poor chicken ... for which he paid six dollars. I made Alfred tie it by the tent peg and had expected to make it very fat before eating it. A few moments ago it got into a yellow jacket nest and was so badly stung I had to have it killed to keep it from [word illegible].

If everything remains quiet here, in a few days it is possible we will be sent nearer to Loudoun. I hope we may not be disappointed again, for I then may have an opportunity of seing you and all the dear ones of Welbourne. We have a large number sick who might be benefited by leaving this climate.

I sent you a recipe by Mr. Read by which I wish you to make me a half doz. bottles of Catsup.

With much love to your Aunt and Uncle and Nina, to your Grandfather, Mittie, cousin Mary, Mary, Dick, Hal and Mr. Weidmayer. I am as ever, my dear Fan, your devoted father

Undated letter of John Peyton Dulany to Richard H. Dulany:

Welbourne

My dear Richard,

I have written so recently to you that I have very little to communicate. Mr. Weidmayer has returned from Baltimore, and was fortunate enough to lay in some groceries which we were very much in want of.

The children have all been very sick with sore throat, but are recovering. I am still very weak from my recent illness, but hope to soon to be well again.

I regret very much your not being here as we have had no Yankees for the last two weeks; I should, however, have been painfully anxious about you, so perhaps it is best that you were away. Major Mosby has been severely wounded in a raid on Sunday—if he should not recover it will be a serious loss as his place could not be filled. From what I gather from reports I think the Yankees do not intend to fight until the fate of Charleston is decided—if they are successful they will bring their whole force against Richmond. I sincerely wish this business could be decided in some way or other.

By the way, Charles Stewart informed Mr. Weidmayer that he had received two letters from England for you, but did not think it safe to send them. Clarence is here, intends joining

Mosby had been wounded in the groin in early September 1864 in Fairfax County. The wound did not prove fatal. He returned to his command on September 29th.[25]

the army next week—his arm is still stiff. I wish you would get someone to write for you, as I long to hear from you. Do tell me how your arm is getting, I fear it is not doing as well as I could wish. We are doing very little in the farming way. The Yankees burnt all our fences again, the farms are of course very much in common and the crops exposed.

Farewell my beloved Son, as ever your fond Father

                                                                    J.P.D.

[P.S.] I have not heard from Mary Whiting since I sent Julia home. They are all well at Julia Roszell's.

Letter of Richard H. Dulany to his daughter Mary, written at Gravelly Run, due west of Reams Station:

Head Quarters 7th Va. Cav. on
Gravelly Run. Sept. 3rd. 1864

My dear Mary,

I have received your letter of the 15th of August. I have to find the same fault with you that I did with Hal—you write too hurriedly and thus injure your handwriting. Some of the letters show that you have much improved, but you must not grow careless. For my writing there is some excuse as I have still to hold my pencil between my third and fourth fingers and having no desk or table have to hold my paper on a book on my knees. I fear I also misspell some words, as I scarcely finish a line without being interrupted by someone on business.

A farmer wants a guard to protect his

fences—another wants a guard to protect his fruit and vegetables—another says that the guard reads the newspaper while some of the men steal his sweet-potatoes. I send a new guard and the old one returns with a man who happened to be present, to prove that the citizen has made a misstatement, that he has done his duty, and that the citizen is as mean as a Yankee, that after guarding his fruit for days he had sold him a little green watermelon for a dollar and a half and the only peaches he could get he paid ten dollars a basket for.

I paid the man the other day nearly a thousand dollars for three acres of corn. In this lot we had dug some rifle pits from which we had repulsed the Yankees—they attempted to flank Genl. Hill during the battle of Reams Station and the man wanted me to pay for the damage done to his land, when one day's work with four men would have replaced all the earth, and besides I lost forty men killed and wounded in driving the Yanks from this farm and repulsed them when attempting to return. You see I have many things to interrupt me, although I have stated how to attend to all regimental business.

It provokes me very much to see some rich farmers make more fuss about a few hundred rails destroyed than many of my poor fellows do at the loss of a leg or arm. A soldier has just called at my tent to hand me a letter from Father. It is dated 16th Augt. I am sorry to see he is not in good spirits, I will answer his letter this evening or tomorrow.

I will resume the history which I was writing our late cav. engagements for Hal:

Aug 16th ... At the very time father was writing his letter I had all my men except two Squadrons dismounted and standing in a drenching rain waiting for Genl. Lee's signal gun to make our combined attack on the Yankee lines north of the James River.

My brigade was on our extreme left, and the balance of our Division had, under Genl. Butler and Col. Wright, marched beyond me so as to threaten the enemy's rear while Genl. W.F. Lee and my brigade attacked the front and flank. The signal was to have been fired at eleven o'clock, but it was delayed hour after hour until five in the evening. While the long suspense was far from being agreeable to me, I could not help being struck with the cool indifference of many of the men. Some sat and chattered over their captured watermelons as if they were at peaceful homes and without a care. Some laid down and slept wrapped in their blankets, on the wet ground, while others seemed restless and would come for permission to creep through the woods to find how the Yankees were posted and to find if we had to attack Cav. or Inf.

When nearly five o'clock, I began to think it probable that Genl. Lee had changed his plans, and we should return to camp without a fight. I must confess a sense of relief at the thought that there would be no more dead or wounded among my men for one more day—and then it is impossible to know where we have to fight in thick woods or [if] the enemy is hid behind breastworks, whether we shall be successful or whether we shall be broken and driven back by overwhelming numbers, having to leave our dead and wounded in the hands of cruel enemies and beyond our care and sympathy.

These thoughts were soon interrupted by two shots from cannon far away to our right, and many thought they were fired near

Petersburg and could not be signals, but soon we heard two more and then two again, the six we expected, and the loud, clear, and unmistakable answer of one shot from our battery plainer in fortifications a mile in our rear for our protection in case of being [line faded]. Later I heard small arms on our right [that] showed that Gen. W.F. Lee had made the attack. I was [word illegible] ordered the skirmish line forward under Lt. Col. Marshall, one of the bravest Christian soldiers of our army, and I followed straight eighty yards distance with a line of two dismounted Regmts., a third bringing up the rear as support.

Genl. Butler was to have made an attack, so as to occupy the enemy's attention while we charged their flank, but my skirmishers drove those of the enemy in so soon that we could not wait for Genl. B. With yell after yell the men rushed forward, firing as they ran, drove the Yanks from their slight breastworks, capturing two captains and thirty men, and by the time Genl. B. came up we had driven the enemy fully two miles upon their infantry and artillery support. We were still driving them when we received orders to fall back lest we in turn should be flanked by Yankee infantry.

This fight brought a congratulatory order from Genl. Robert Lee for the success of his Division (Genl. Butler's) and as our Brigade did all the fighting I called upon Genl. Hampton for Genl. Butler's report of the fight and received the enclosed letter which you will give to your Grandfather. I think it will gratify him since he has much more ambition than I have. I have never seen a number of boys after a rabbit more enthusiastic than the men were in this charge, and the result was but small loss on our side as we only gave the Yankees a chance

The dispatch from Hampton is on page 216.

for one volley before we had routed them.

Two days after this the Yankees crossed to
the south of the James, and on the 20th we also
crossed. On the 22nd we camped on the
Rowanty, four miles from Reams Station on the
Petersburg and Weldon railroad. The enemy
had taken possession of this road from Reams
Station to the Yellow Tavern, three miles from
Petersburg, and Genl. Lee had made two
attempts to drive them from it. At the first
attempt we were quite successful, capturing
some three thousand prisoners and the Yankee
papers [admit] that this Corps' loss [was] killed,
wounded, and missing: five thousand. The
second attack was not so successful. We were
repulsed with a loss of nearly five hundred, most
of them killed and wounded.

On the 23rd I was ordered by Genl. Butler
to relieve Lt. Col. Kacker from picket duty and
as the pickets had been driven in, I supposed
merely by cav., I took two Regmts., the 7th and
11th to drive the enemy back that I might
reestablish the line. After crossing the
Rowanty bridge and getting within a mile and
a quarter of Reams, I came suddenly upon the
Yankees, who had just taken position behind
some rail breastworks on the crest of a hill,
giving them a very strong position; they also
occupied some houses on the hill.

The first intimation I had of their presence
was from Kaskin scouts rushing back on my
column and a brisk fire poured upon us from
eighty or one hundred yards distant. Several of
my horses and two or three of the men were
wounded, and Col. Kaskin, who was riding by
my side, was shot through the leg.

I withdrew about three hundred yards, as
the enemy were too strongly posted to charge
mounted, and dismounted the two Regmts.

and after forming a line of battle marched on either side of the road to within two hundred yards of the enemy's line, the 7th having the right and the 11th the left of our line and here halted, having a good position in the edge of a wood, and sent back for reinforcements as I was satisfied that the enemy was far stronger in numbers and position than we were.

I had scarcely taken position when the Yanks moved out of their breastworks and came directly upon us. The 7th met them with such a steady fire that the part of the line opposed to them first halted and then fell flat upon the ground to avoid the fire. I was not so fortunate upon my left, for Major McDonald sent to me that the Yankees were flanking [the] line and he could not hold his position. I rode to him as quickly as possible and found that the enemy's line overlapped our left by a hundred yards and that they were coming up on our left flank and driving our men before them. As soon as the left was broken, the right had to be slowly withdrawn.

I met Genl. Butler as my left was giving way, who informed [me] that he was bringing reinforcements. I ask him to halt his men and form a line about a hundred yards in my rear, so as to check the enemy until I could reform my men when they should be driven past him. To this he objected and said we must fight it out where we were and rushed his men forward among mine, who were being driven back now rapidly—the result was his men were whipt in two minutes, leaving ten of his dead and some wounded in the hands of the enemy.

Just at this time the enemy charged with their cav., but fortunately the 12th Regmt. of our Brigade had come up and dismounted and reformed then in an open field and ordered

Major Knott to check the enemy until I could rally and reform the two broken Regmts. This order was most promptly obeyed, the Major not only checking the advance but gallantly driving them back into the woods.

This gave time to reform our line when we again advanced, capturing some prisoners from the 4th NY heavy artillery (acting as infantry) from an infantry regmt. and also several cav. who were shot or taken prisoners when they charged us. The enemy retired beyond their first position, which I then occupied. Genl. Butler, being largely reinforced, marched on another road [and] had tried to flank them, but they gradually fell back to their earthworks on the railroad and were here too strong for him.

The Genl. kept up his fire until near ten o'clock at night, taking one line of slight works which withheld during the night. In the morning we retired, leaving our pickets on the line the enemy had occupied in the morning before. During this engagement I lost about forty wounded and not more than five killed. I cannot tell what the enemy lost. I buried three of their dead, and a Mrs. Hargrave told me that they brought twenty-three wounded and one dead into her yard and that they took her wagon, buggy and cart to assist in taking off their disabled. As their fortifications were within a mile, their ambulances could have taken off a great many without the taking of which from citizens.

Finding the enemy had so large a force here, Genl. Lee sent Genl. Hill with a large number of infantry and artillery to drive them away as they were destroying the railroad. All the cavalry except my regmt. was sent with Genl. Hampton to Malone's Crossing. Genl.

Maj. John Locher Knott, 12th Virginia Cavalry, would be killed at High Bridge, April 16, 1865, on the retreat to Appomattox.

Rosser resumed command of his Brigade and I returned to my regiment.

This map is sketched in the top margin of one page of the letter.

At Reams Station the Yankees had thrown up earthworks covering or surrounding some twenty acres around the station. From the fortifications they would send out strong parties to destroy the railroad, and if attacked fall back, as on the 23rd, on their stronghold. Genl. Hampton came up with their cav. and a portion of their infantry at Malones three miles below Reams and attacking drove them to Reams, capturing between five and six hundred.

About five o'clock Genl. Hill ordered me to drive in the Yankee pickets on the road on which he was advancing to Reams. We attacked and drove in the Cav. picket and captured a captain and infantry picket. We drove the cav. behind their earthworks. In this charge Lt. Col. Marshall was shot through the shoulder, Violett [sic] of Hatcher's company was killed and several of the men and horses wounded. After this I was sent to Genl. Hill's left flank to protect that from cav. and saw no more of Hill's fight. The Cav. made two slight efforts to drive me away, but they were easily repulsed.

Genl. Hill carried their works just before dark, capturing sixteen hundred prisoners and nine pieces of beautiful artillery. The next morning I rode over the battlefield. There

Marshall would be killed on November 26, 1864. He is buried in Winchester.

James Elijah Violet enlisted in Co. A, 7th Virginia Cavalry, at Middleburg on March 4, 1862.[26]

were still lying unburied about 100 Yankees
and eight or ten of our men. In one small piece
of ground were thirty six dead artillery horses,
killed by our guns.

I will send you papers in which you will find
a chance account of the battle. I write what I
suppose will interest you most.

Hancock says he *supposes* that his loss will
reach 1500, but that his men have not yet been
organized and then claims a victory, which the
Yankee papers say was one of the bloodiest of
the war, and this afternoon had received a flag
of truce from Genl. Gregg asking permission to
bury his dead and who had counted 2300
prisoners beside the killed and wounded. I was
left in charge of the battlefield and had my
pickets a mile *beyond* the position that Genl.
Hancock claimed to hold after the battle.

I cannot imagine a Christian people
(professing), even daring, to hope for success
if their cause was religious, when they
persistently and outrageously violate every
principle of truth. Many of their own soldiers
say they had to wait for Genl. Lee's reports
before they can be satisfied as to the true
results of their battles.

I will send this letter and the papers by the
first safe opportunity. I fear many of our letters
are lost, but I have written to every member of
our family including a long letter to sister Mary
in the last six weeks.

Your Grandfather wrote to me that Fan
and you are invited to parties to which your
Aunt Ida wishes you to go. I have not written
to you on this subject because from your letters
to me in regard to your birthday you express
[word illegible] agreeing such [here two lines
are blank] that I [blank] exposing our lives and
foregoing every enjoyment of home or

comfort, to be feasting, fiddling, and dancing. How would the thought of the torn and bleeding body of one of our brave fellows affect one of these gay, and certainly the thoughtless, parties? And yet they are to be sure in [word illegible] and household every day. In one hospital alone in Richmond the [words illegible] nearly three thousand of these noble fellows who gave up wife, children and home rather than submit to Yankee rule. There cannot be less than thirty thousand wounded men now in Virginia.

[Here a section is faded out.]

Give much love to both and tell them how much pleasure it would give me to be able to add to their comfort.

As soon as we can have a little quiet I shall apply for a furlough.

Remember me kindly to your uncle Armistead and Aunt Mary Eliason. Take the newspapers to your Aunt after your Grand-father has read them.

Let me know if you take regular exercise. Do not forget that I wish Fan and you & Hal to take great care of your teeth, and if you must have someone in the day or [illegible] upon which [illegible] clothing and mend them when they require it.

Phrenology, the study of the bumps on the skull, was popular in this era.

Has Fan's "bump of order" grown any? It requires a little enlargement unless she has changed much since I was at home.

I suppose your vacation is over by this time. If any of Mosby's men come to Welbourne, treat them politely and give them bread and meat as soldiers, but they are not to be associates of my children. Poor Turner was one of the very few gentlemen I have met with in that command.

Neither the manners nor the ideas of

propriety of the young ladies of Upperville are such as to benefit either you or Fan. You see I am growing sensitive and particular, but I never fear that I shall become more so, than your own pure instinct teaches. You must overlook your dear sister and brothers and try to become their confidant and friend in all their little troubles. Nothing would distress me more than either of the boys should learn bad habits. Try to teach them to be open and candid in all things. They will commit faults, but may be willing to confess them freely and never to hide or cover them over.

Remember me in kind terms to Mr. Weidmayer. Does he visit much in the neighborhood? When did you see your cousin HAH and wife? Give much love to them and to Eliza Carter and your Aunt Ida.

Henry Arthur Hall.

Clarence is well. We mess and "tent" together, except on picket, when each of us rolls up in our own blanket and oil cloth. A few nights ago I got soaking wet on the side on which I lay, but the oil cloth kept the upper side quite dry. A hot fire and a cup of coffee soon made me forget the demi-bath although it had deprived me of several hours of sleep.

Alfred is well and sends his respectful regards. You must be tired by this time of the long letter, at any rate I am so good by my [here one line is blank] direct every thought word and act of your life prays your devoted father

R.H.Dulany

HdQrs 7th cav 4 miles from Reams

Sep 4th 1864.

The next letter is the enclosure mentioned above. Letter of Major Theodore G. Barker to Col. Dulany:

Riddell's Shop skirmish, June 13, 1864.

Head Quarters Cavalry Corps,
Army of No. Virginia, August 31, 1864.

Colonel.

Genl. Hampton directs me to say that no formal report of the engagement on the 18th. inst. on the Charles City Road, in which Rosser's Brigade took the leading part, has been made to him by Genl. Butler. A note hastily written to him during the night after the fight was over, informed him that the Brigade had gallantly attacked the Enemy and, under your command, had vigorously pushed them a mile and a half beyond Riddell's Shop.

Great credit was given to the conduct of the Brigade and especial praise to yourself on that occasion, both in the note and in subsequent oral communication from Genl. Butler. His note was forwarded to Genl. R.E. Lee.

Genl. Hampton also desires me to say that in the recent fight at Reams Station where you guarded the left of the infantry of Lt-Genl. Hill, it gave him great pleasure to hear the terms of high commendation in which Genl. Hill spoke of your services in driving in the Enemy's Pickets, and afterward in repelling the attack of the Enemy's Cavalry on the Stage Road when the flank and rear of our Infantry was seriously threatened.

As you were detached from the Cavalry on that day and were under immediate orders of Lt-Genl. A.P. Hill, he has requested Genl. Hill to include you and your command in his report to Genl. Lee.

I am, Colonel, Very Respfy., Yr. obednt. servt.

Theodore G. Barker
Maj. & A.A. Genl.

Letter of Richard H. Dulany to his father:

Gravelly Run, Sept. 5th. 1864.

My dear Father,

Yours of the 16th Aug. was handed to me yesterday. I hope your fears in regard to Genl. Early have been relieved. I can well understand how much more anxiety persons beyond our lines or out of the army suffer than we do by my short experience at home last year. Banded together as we are gives us a sense of security unknown to persons isolated as you are.

Early had been detached from Lee's army to command troops in the Shenandoah Valley.

I can give you no idea of Genl. Lee's plans. He seems to be perfect master of his position. With all Grant's boasted skill at flanking, he is met at every turn and most severely punished. The occupation of the Weldon railroad is claimed to have been his best effort, as I believe it is, still Lee has taken from him on this road an immense number of prisoners. In two days they must have numbered more than ten thousand. During the fight of the 25th under Hill and Hampton we captured 2300 and these were picked up on the next day. This does not include either their killed or wounded who fell into our hands.

I saw a church and out buildings at Reams filled with dead and wounded, beside 150 dead that lay in the trenches unburied. One of their Drs. came the morning after the fight to get our men to take provisions to their wounded left on the roadside as their troops fled from the battlefield. With the usual proportion of wounded to the killed, Grant's loss here must have been over five thousand, and we see Hancock claiming a victory and supposing his loss to be 1500. Now take this as a basis and what must have been their loss on Thursday,

Oak Grove Methodist Church at Reams Station.

George Pendleton (Ohio) was nominated to run as vice-president at the Democratic convention in Chicago.

when they confess that they lost (5000) five thousand? You must see that my calculation of 10,000 in two days' fighting is very moderate. How long he can stand such drafts from army he alone knows.

What do you think about Chicago [line illegible]. I heard Pendleton make the strongest argument I have ever heard in this last U.S. Congress in favour of Southern Rights.

I have written to Mary on the subject you mentioned in regard to her visiting, etc. Rest assured, my dear father, that there is no one in whose opinion and judgment I so perfectly rely as upon yours, and if you cannot confide your trouble to me without annoying me I must be very unworthy of your confidence.

I expect the pork from the mountain will more than counterbalance the flour drawn from Welbourne. My impression is that both Nolls and McEwin had already drawn their portion of flour. Let them have no more.

I hope to get home some time in October to make arrangements for sister Mary to commence housekeeping either at Grassland or at Millsville in the house occupied by Triplett as she may prefer. I am very anxious to make her as comfortable as possible before winter.

I have just heard that Atlanta has fallen. If this is true it is a great blow to us. Our continued successes for the last twelve months was rapidly increasing the peace party in the North and our Gov. stock was selling for much more in London than that of the U.S. Gov. This may continue or prolong the war, but I am fully persuaded that a Merciful God will give us peace and independence in his own good time.

Mr. Carson has preached some most

interesting sermons of late. I think him much improved. We have prayer meetings every night when in camp and they are very well attended. I hope much good may come of them.

We all expected to start to the Valley today but have been disappointed. Genl. Hampton cannot be spared and I suppose he is unwilling to part with our Brigade. The officers are getting up a petition to Genl. Lee, but I have refused to sign it as much as I should like to see you again. Genl. Lee knows best where we should be.

Rosser is again in Command of his Brigade. His being wounded deprived him of promotion. After Bradley Johnson's surprise and loss of men and horses, the War Department wanted a man at once to fill my poor friend Jones's place as Johnson could not do it.

Lomax was sent as Rosser could not then move from his room. I think Rosser one of the first Cav. officers of the Confederacy. I fear, though, he will not succeed here as well as if he had a separate command. We have to fight here on foot on account of the wood, and this Rosser detests. The last order he gave me after he turned over his command to me at Trevilian was "Col. fight with the men mounted. Let the other Cav. fight as infantry."

Hampton I think is superior to Stuart in prudence, good judgment and in military [line illegible] not the extreme dash (sometimes costly as at Dranesville) and perseverance for which Genl. Stuart was remarkable.

I send you papers in which you will find an account of Hood's failure to hold Atlanta. Genl. Joe Johnston seems to have been right after all.

Johnson and Gen. John McCausland burned Chambersburg, Pa. Pursued by Union cavalry, they reached Moorefield, but prematurely relaxed their guard, losing four guns, 420 prisoners and more than 400 horses. Both generals escaped, but Johnson was eventually relieved of command.

Lunsford Lindsay Lomax was colonel of the 11th Virginia Cavalry; he later commanded a brigade under Fitzhugh Lee. He was appointed major general August 10, 1864, and commanded Early's cavalry in the Valley.

The battle of Dranesville, about twenty miles west of Washington, December 20, 1861. Stuart did no reconnaissance, and the affair was mismanaged.[27]

With much love to the dear children, sister Mary, Carlyle, Nina, Mittie, Mr. Weidmayer, and kind regards to Julia, Nancy, Emily and the other servants. I am your devotedly attached son

R.H. Dulany

Please give Major Barker's letter to May after you have read it.

Partial letter of Richard H. Dulany to his daughter Fanny:

HdQrs 7th Virginia Cavalry,
9th September 1864

My dear Fan,

Mr. Read may have been a younger relative of "old Uncle Read" mentioned earlier.

I sent letters to all of the children but you by Mr. Read. At the receipt of this letter you will all be in my debt.

You must think me very amiable to be contented to receive little lambs for my sheep. I shall have to require two for one in future unless you hasten to give better measure.

Both Mary and you should keep a journal of each day's occupation—you need not fear to weary me with repetition or sameness—so that I may know how you are employed. I may also become your father confessor by your journal's telling me your thoughts, how often you have failed to put your room or clothes "to rights" after driving, if you forgot this morning to clean your nails or teeth before leaving your room, or if you have indulged yourself with a morning nap so that you had to hurry down-stairs without having time for your morning devotions—or if, on looking for your brush or comb [and] finding it has been removed by Hal or Dick against your orders, you may not have given way to some little temper or pettishness for which you were afterwards sorry—if on finding yourself wrong or in error you have not been *tempted* to frame excuses or to state only a portion of the fault or mistake thus changing the true color of the act. If you have not been thus tempted, my darling child, you have been very much blessed, and have been much more fortunate than your father.

It may be *one* reason why I place so high a value upon *perfect* truthfulness is because I know by experience how hard, how very hard it is to attain.

Your journal must also state at what hour you breakfast, when you got up—what lessons recited—how well—indifferently—with or without pleasure!

This portion of my letter is for Mary as well as for you. Do you not both think that with a determination to agree to my suggestions, for I do not intend them in any other light, that you will be more careful, attentive and industrious? I have not the slightest doubt of it, for I know that you both love me and would be very sorry to give me pain or uneasiness.

With these thoughts look a little further. Is there not One who whether you wish it or not sees every even the slightest deviation from truth or right—knows all our *intentions* and who will hold us to an account for all the blessings he grants us and even as to the benefit we have received from his chastisements. He gives no talent that He does not require an account of. To be often reminded of these things is necessary to us all, and the longer I live the more conscious do I become of it.

As for my own time, the days are pretty much alike unless the Yanks stir us up by driving in our pickets, and we have to saddle up sometimes at midnight and be ready to meet them if they become too demonstrative or Genl. Lee wishes to know the position of their infantry, if it has changed to the left or from the right to center, etc., when we have to drive in the enemy's Cav. and run in upon their infantry. Having gained the information, we return to camp, bringing with us usually some half dozen or dozen blue devils and one or two of our advance guard for whom we have to dig a grave, the service is read, the grave filled, and with the next excitement they are forgotten except in some distant home where a mother, sister, or wife mourn their dead.

Sometimes we have to fight both infantry and cavalry on foot, and our men are becoming almost as much accustomed to fight as infantry as cavalry. When everything is quiet, the bugle sounds for roll-call at daylight. I have then to get up and dress so that I may be ready to receive the officers as they come to report the condition of their companies. I then wash and read a few psalms, say my prayers and get ready for breakfast, which Alfred usually has ready about sun-up. If Alfred is not ready I frequently after dressing roll up in my blanket and take a short nap to make up for an hour or two lost before day when I was waked by the cold and lost about that length of time. Yesterday I got an extra blanket and last night I slept more comfortably.

Our breakfast usually consists of a cup of coffee without cream or milk, a couple of quite nice biscuits and a little piece of fat middling instead of butter ... [An entire section here is not legible because of fading] This is a digression.

After business hours I read the newspaper or my Bible, almost the only reading matter we have in camp, write, or lounge in my tent. We dine on soup made of a piece of middling with tomatoes (when we can get them) or beans and a biscuit. Sometimes we have a roasted apple for dessert. We keep in fair condition on this diet. If the day is very long and gloomy we have a cup of tea at night—but this is rare, two meals usually sufficing. I think Clarence ate six biscuits this morning; how many more he would have eaten I do not know. As Alfred seems to know exactly how much we *require*, he has no trouble in taking care of what is left. After dinner we take a ride or walk, at sunset have music from our band—at dark have roll call ...

[The rest is missing]

Letter of John Peyton Dulany to Richard H. Dulany (a note at the top says, "I have at this moment received your letter of 12 July"):

Sunday 18th. Sept. 1864
Welbourne

My dear Richard,

As Mr. Read will leave in the morning for the army I will write to inform you of what is passing in the neighborhood. In the first place, the Yankees paid the mountaineers a visit on Friday morning before our boys were up. They took a good many horses, some estimate the number to be between sixty and seventy. They behaved, however, better than they usually do, as they passed around the houses without disturbing the sleepers.

William H. Chapman led the pursuit into Snicker's Gap on Sept. 16, 1864, took eighteen Union prisoners and forty horses.

Mosby had been wounded in a brief skirmish with five Federals near Centreville the day before. He recuperated at his father's home in Amherst County.

Capt. Chapman followed on and captured (report says) between thirty and forty men with their horses etc. Several of the Yankees were killed and one of our men. I regret to inform you that Col. Mosby was wounded in a fight and has gone South.

I presume before this you have received the sorrel mare. I hope she will suit you—she walks and trots remarkably well. I had to give a large price for her, your brown mare and one hundred dollars in cash after the war. The colt will be worth more than the sorrel a year hence. I was glad to part with the colt as the Yankees would certainly have gotten her in the course of time. They let nothing escape them.

I am very sorry to hear that there is a great deal of excitement in the North between the war and peace parties; I had some faint hopes that Abe Lincoln might have been beaten in the coming election, but now I have none. I fear that a great majority in the North are in favour of a continuation of the war. Lincoln has put a stop to the draft, but this is only a political measure to secure his election. The present party in power has the cunning of the old Boy, they make any sacrifices to secure their ends.

The report here is that the peace party intends to call another meeting to nominate a peace candidate, but it is too late; they were hardly strong enough when united, and they certainly will be too weak when divided. It will be playing into Lincoln's hands just as he would wish it—it really appears to me that everything conspires to help the Yankees.

I see by the papers that England has withdrawn her troops from Canada for fear she will give offense to the United States. I sometimes think that all the world is against us. I see that France declines to acknowledge our independence without we abolish slavery.

The hands commenced seeding on yesterday. They have finished the lot by Mr. Rutter's and the orchard near the house. On Monday they will go to Millsville.

Haley has not yet returned, it is feared that they have sent him to Fort Delaware. It is strange they should have sent him as he had taken the oath. They do not make any distinction, one of their officers told a neighbour that they were commanded to take all that could crawl.

Robert Carter sent for Eliza. He is quite sick at Richard deButts's. Mott Ball and William [H. Dulany] have called; they are both well. Moses still very low, it will be some time before he will be able to join you. Ball thinks it probable that you will be sent down the Valley as Cavalry is much wanted by Early. 'Tis said the Yankees outnumber us three to one.

Carlyle is no better and I fear never will be.

I have nearly worn out my pen and your patience, so I will bid you good by—

J.P.D.

Colonel Dulany received a note from General Hampton, commending him on his gallantry at the battle of Reams Station:

Head. Qrs. Cavly.
Sept 19th 1864

Colonel

Lieut. General A.P. Hill has requested me to express to you and through you to your gallant Regiment his obligation for the efficient services you rendered on the 25th Aug. at Reams Station and his great admiration of the gallantry displayed by yourself & your command on that occasion.

Whilst I am much gratified by the commendation bestowed upon your Regiment, I am not at all surprised by it, for its conduct on previous occasions under my own eye, made me confident that it would sustain its high reputation and that of the "Laurel Brigade."

I take great pleasure in extending the thanks of General Hill to you and I confidently hope that your Regiment will always maintain its high character.

I am Colonel

Very Respy. Yrs.
Wade Hampton
Maj Genl

Most of the members of the Laurel Brigade were from the Valley, so it was with great joy that they received orders on September 26th to join Early. On September 27th, Colonel Dulany moved the brigade out of their camps south of Petersburg and began the long and fatiguing march. By the time they reached camp at Bridgewater, about six miles southwest of Harrisonburg, on October 5th, the command was worn out and reduced in number.

Dispatch of General Jubal A. Early to General Thomas L. Rosser, in the possession of Colonel Richard H. Dulany:

October 4th, 1864.

General—

The commencement of the turning by the enemy & his having his troops in dress parade this evening, which is seen from the heights near here, probably indicates a movement & it may be an advance—Be on the look out & prepare for any thing which may happen—If

the enemy move back I wish you to follow him
at once & do what you can to annoy him.

J.A. Early

Lt. General

*On October 9, during the battle of Tom's
Brook, Richard Dulany was wounded again, this
time in the arm. The wound was severe enough
that surgeons wished to amputate the arm;
however, a resection said to have been performed
by Dr. Hunter McGuire proved successful.*[28]

*Not yet informed of his son's wounding, John
Peyton Dulany writes the following undated letter
from Welbourne:*

My Dear Son,

As Alfred will leave for the army in the
morning I feel like writing a few lines if it is
only to say that we are well—as every day
passes much alike I have very little of interest
to communicate. The Yankees have only paid
us one visit since you left, as they found very
little worth taking. I hope they will not think
it worth their while to come this way again.

We are all very anxious to hear from your
army as it has been reported that Genl. Meade
was on the advance. I think everything will
depend on the next battle in the West. I regret
to hear that there is so much dissatisfaction
among our officers.

I send by Alfred the coffee & sugar you
desired. He will inform you of every thing that
has transpired since you left. We not only lose
our property by the Yankees, but by our own
men. I am sorry to tell you that your bay colt
that you left with Haley has been stolen by
some (I presume) of the stragglers that are now
infesting the County.

Tell Clarence that I have tried in vain to

In Mosby's "Greenback Raid," October 14, 1864, several of the Rangers robbed civilians on the B&O Railroad. Each received $2,100.

procure him a pair of boots. The first opportunity I have I will try and get him a pair from Berlin, as there has been no capture made in the way of Wagons for some time.

[After] the last raid made by Mosby, the men divided $1200 each; I fear it has had a very unhappy effect on the young men. They generally take everything the prisoners have without the least ceremony.

I had written this far when I was interrupted by the cry, "the Yankees are in Middleburg." It has driven out of my mind everything I wished to say to you. I am almost weary of life by the constant excitement I have.

Farewell my beloved Son, may our God protect you from all danger

J.P.D.

Letter of Fanny Dulany to her father, Richard H. Dulany:

October 20th was a Thursday.

Friday, Oct. 20th.

Dear Papa,

Barbee's Crossroads is today known as Hume, Va. It is about twenty miles SSW of Welbourne.

We heard the other day, that you were at Barbee's cross-roads. Please try and come to see us. Grandpa received a letter from Cousin Julia yesterday, saying that Uncle [Carlyle] Whiting was no better. Aunt Mary is going to run the Blockade to Washington.

Major Mosby made a very successful raid two or three days ago, of which Mary will give you the particulars. Mary and I have had no opportunity of going up to Cousin Richard deButts.

We have been fortunate enough not to have any more visits from the Yankees, since you went away.

Cousin Mit has improved the garden very

much, and has had one of the honey-suckles planted on one side of the arbour, which makes it very pretty.

Yesterday Aunt Ida's carriage passed by, full of the young ladies, (who were staying at Oakley), on their way to Oatlands, to stay until Monday, and then Aunt Ida is going to leave Cousin Sophie here until Cousin Mary Welby comes after her. Cousin Mit received a letter from Margaret Sweeny, saying that she reached Berlin in safety, and that as the person who was with her took all the responsibility upon himself, she was not even asked to take the oath.

Sophia Carter and her mother, Mary Welby (deButts) Carter, wife of Richard Henry Carter of Glen Welby.

I hope your arm is getting better, and that you will soon be able to answer our letters.

Julia, Aunt Emily, Mammy, and Ellen, all send their love to you.

Your affectionate daughter
F. Dulany.

Letter of John Peyton Dulany to Richard H. Dulany:

Welbourne Nov. 2, 1864.

My Dear Son

Events crowd so rapidly on each other I hardly know how to begin to chronicle them.

In the first place, [Willis] Hanson, his wife and one other family belonging to Hal were making their way to the Yankees. They were intercepted by some of Mosby's men and I presume carried South. General Augur sent three hundred men to make enquiries after Hanson, who it appears was a very important person in the Genl.'s estimation.

Gen. Christopher Augur

Not finding him, and Hal being from home,

he carried off Ida, altho' it was raining. She was taken to The Plains, where she remained all night; next morning she was set at liberty and the same day arrived safely at home.

After this, hearing from Ida that the Yankees were falling, it was supposed, back to the Orange [& Alexandria] railroad, we were congratulating ourselves on the probability of having at least a resting time for some months, when who should pounce down on us but a brigade belonging to Sheridan's army—it seems they came from Front Royal—they have stript us of everything they could find. We have lost fifty-one of our best cattle and my horse. I think they must have taken more than two hundred head, and I know not how many sheep. I presume they never made so successful a raid before; it is surprising that so large a number should have surprised us so completely. Armistead Carter had every head of cattle that he owned taken, and one of his horses. Lauck faired in the same way.

Mitty, Mary, and Fan went to the turnpike and got three of the cows—altho' Mary accomplished little, she says, she could not condescend to ask a favour of a Yankee even for the sake of milk and butter.

Mary Whiting and Mr. Weidmayer left Welbourne a fortnight since for Washington. Mr. Weidmayer intended to go as far as Baltimore to attend to some business affairs of mine (I fear I shall lose considerably as I have been informed that the Government has confiscated all deposits made by Southerners). As they have already over-stayed their time, I begin to feel some uneasiness about them.

Carlyle Whiting is declining, he is as weak as an infant. I do not think it possible that he can last much longer.

I regret that I cannot send Mary to you immediately. She is in want of clothes and there is no knowing where the Yankees are, for really they appear to be ubiquitous. When you remove to Noland's, I will send her by the first opportunity.

Alfred has this moment come in from Middleburg; he declines setting out for the army fearing that the Yankees might catch him. I will, therefor, lay aside my pen for a day or two as something may transpire that might be interesting to you.

A servant of William Whiting, who has been staying with his brother in the absence of Mary, has this moment arrived with the sad news that his son was killed yesterday. It seems that Carlyle with two others had taken nine prisoners but failing to take their arms with them, was shot, Carlyle and one other killed, the third was wounded but made his escape. The Yankees ran off leaving their horses. This is the second or third time I have heard of a similar case; when will our young men learn prudence.

Nov. 4th. William Whiting, who left on Thursday to attend the funeral of his son, has just made his appearance. He was driven from Clay Hill by the Yankees, who are in that neighborhood in considerable numbers. It is strange that when the Yankee army comes in, ours are always on a raid somewhere else.

Col. [Elijah] White was here, it is said in search of cattle left; went to Little Washington without driving any off. The Yankees came next day or two afterwards, drove nearly three hundred away. The very next day, I believe, Col. White returns to pick up what the Yankees left. So it goes.

Mary Whiting has not yet returned, I fear

Dulany has apparently asked that Mary be sent to help nurse him in Harrisonburg.

Maj. R. Noland in Charlottesville was a friend.

Carlyle Fairfax Whiting, nephew of G. W. Carlyle Whiting and son of William W. Whiting of Roseville in Clarke County, serving in Co. A, 6th Virginia Cavalry, was killed near Sperryville.

Clay Hill was the home of Francis B. Whiting in Clarke County.

"Little" Washington is in Rappahannock County.

Rev. John Landstreet.

John deButts was still in Fort
Delaware Prison.

she will find some difficulty in getting away.
Moses is getting much better. Henry Dulany
has to leave home, how much better it would
be if he had remained in the army.

Lincoln's reelection will give us another
four years of War. I am afraid my friend
Landstreet has gone crazy. He writes me that
there will be peace between this and
December next. I hear occasionally from your
sister Julia—they are all well—also John P.
deButts, he does not complain of his treatment.

I send you by Alfred two bottles of brandy
and one of old whiskey. I fear I shall not be
able to send you another supply as it is now
impossible to procure anything from
Yankeeland. Our only hope is in Mr.
Weidmayer's success. As I expect every
moment that Alfred will be here on his way to
the army, I must hasten to close this letter. I
was in great hopes I should have been able to
announce the arrival of your sister. I begin to
feel very restless about her long stay—on
Wednesday next it will be three weeks since
she left Welbourne.

Remember us all very affectionately to
Clarence; if he can get leave of absence he had
better come and see his father, as I am sure it
would be a great gratification to see him. I have
tried hard to find matter enough to fill up my
paper but have not been able to succeed, so I
must say God bless and protect my Son,

As ever your devoted father,
J.P.D.

Letter of Mary Dulany to her father:

Welbourne Hall, Nov. 11th. [1864]

My Dear Papa

I expected to be with you by this time, but

as Mr. Weidmayer has not yet returned, I will be obliged to content myself with writing to you all that has occurred since my last letter. Last Tuesday Boyd Smith came here in the morning, intending to stay all day, but as there was a report of the Yankees, he left about eleven.

Grandpapa had all the cattle driven off, & he & Cousin William went on the Hill. About a half an hour afterwards, hearing a great noise I went to the window, & had the pleasure of seeing about two hundred Yankees riding rapidly through the yard. I was very glad to hear Grandpapa's voice just then, as I did not like the idea of their being no gentlemen in the house if the Yankees searched it. They rode by, however, without stopping; I was congratulating myself, as I saw the last one disappear leading Cousin William's old horse, on our safe escape, when the servants who had driven off the cattle returned with the dismal news that the Yankees had captured all the cattle, including every cow & calf on the farm; and not long after the rogues returned driving our beautiful heifers & cows before them; Cousin Mit, Fan & Nina went out in the yard & begged them to leave the cows, but the Col. told him that he had no authority to do so, & they had better go to the toll gate & see the General.

Grandpapa then told me to have his horse ordered, & brought to him at the stable. I very reluctantly delivered his message to Sandy, for I was sure the Yankees would take the horse, & Sandy with many tears saddled him & led him out of the cellar. No sooner, however, than he reached the barn yard, the Yankees dismounted him & took away the horse; Sandy, instead of going to Grandpapa, ran screaming & crying as loudly as possible in the direction of the cornfield.

The toll gate was at the Little River Turnpike (U.S. 50) and the stone bridge over Goose Creek, near Rector's Crossroads.

Cousin Mit then proposed to go herself to the Yankee General, if Grandpapa was willing, and as he did not object she started for the toll gate in company with Fan, Hal, Dick, Mr. Ward & myself. Just as we reached the turnpike gate, about seven officers passed by (the Yankees were on their way to Upperville). Cousin Mit asked one of them for the General. They told us that he had just passed & was a little way up the road. On hearing this, Cousin Mit said that she would walk on until she found him.

As we walked along, Cousin Mit told the officers what we came for, & after a little conversation among themselves, a young man rode up to us & said politely, "Ladies, if you will follow me, I will get you some of your cows." "Only two or three," called out one of the other officers as we all turned back & followed the young man through the regiment that were coming slowly up the road. I was afraid that with all his politeness, this Yankee Captain, who was quite good looking, was going to play us some trick, & kept as close as possible to his horse's heels. All the way the soldiers kept up a running fire of remarks about "dismounted Cavalry," "High tempers," & "contemptuous looks," to which I paid no attention, having eyes for nothing but the Capt.'s blue coat as we followed him in & out among the horses & men.

We passed on very well until we reached the bridge, which was so full of soldiers that after the first two or three yards I was obliged to walk on the stone wall on the left of the bridge all the way. I did not think of it then, but when I was on the other side I wondered that my head did not swim as I walked along the narrow wall with the swollen creek running rapidly beneath. When I reached the other side I found the Capt. waiting for us at the toll gate, & as Cousin Mit & the other children were some distance behind, we waited there until they came up.

We then went to the hill beyond the toll gate & Mr. Ward went to look for the cows, which were not very easy to find among the angry animals, who were running in every direction, goring each other & bellowing as loudly as possible; while he was gone the Captain stood looking as with the most smiling face; when the cows were found he rode away, leaving a man with us to see that we were allowed to carry them off.

We got three cows safely home, & two or three returned that the Yankees had not seen; we lost about sixty head of cattle in all. Uncle Armistead lost all his cows but one, & nearly every one in the neighbourhood lost several of their cows.

I am going to Oakley this evening with Cousin Rutledge!

All send their love,

Your devoted daughter
Mary Carter Dulany

Rutty Eliason was wounded in the leg at Spotsylvania on May 5, 1864,[29] and was recuperating at home.

According to a note by Mary D.L. White on the following letter, Colonel Dulany was nursed after his wounding at Tom's Brook by a Mrs. Zirkle, who may have been the mother of two of his men, David P. and Harvey (Henry), who enlisted in Harrisonburg and served in Co. B of the 7th Virginia Cavalry.[30] Mrs. Zirkle sent the colonel's sword to his daughter Fanny at Welbourne.

Letter of Richard H. Dulany to his daughter, Fanny Dulany:

Mrs. Zircles [sic], Nov. 27th. 1864.

My darling Fan

I owe you several letters but as I have so many to answer you must not hold me to too strict an account. I expect to leave for Charlottesville on Tuesday if the weather is as bright as it is this morning. Gen. Rosser has gone on a raid and has left this line so exposed that I shall feel a little uneasy until I get off.

Capt. Richard Blazer of the 91st Ohio Infantry, with a special force of a hundred men, was detailed to seek out and destroy Mosby's command but was bested in Jefferson County (now W.Va.). Blazer was captured.[31]

When you see Col. Mosby congratulate him for me on his complete success in destroying the band the federal government had been to so much trouble to form for his capture. The Northern press seem much mortified at Blazer's failure.

I hope Mary may be able to meet me at Charlottesville soon after I get there. If she goes in the spring wagon she should take plenty of food for the horses, for herself for the trip, and two nice hams for me. If Pris has my chickens and they are fat she can send me two pair of them, as they will keep [in] this cold weather.

I have just heard that some of my friends in Hardy [County] have sent a box to Harrisonburg. Is it not complimentary that I should receive so many evidences of good feeling from people I have seen but twice and never but one (Mrs. Hatcher) from the country in which I was raised. I have received an invitation from Mrs. Vandiver to come to her house and she would take good care of me until I am well.

Mrs. Hatcher was the mother of Daniel and Harry.

The conscript officers must be more active in Loudoun, as many young men are joining the army who until now have refused to do their duty. I hope every one of them may be driven to the ranks or to the Yankees.

When you write again let me know what

you are studying and what you are reading. Make it a *rule never* to commence reading a second book until you finish the book you have already commenced.

Never leave your room until your teeth and nails are as well as your hair and clothes and in perfect condition, and never, my dear Child, lay in bed so long as to be obliged to hurry through your morning devotions. This is a direct insult to your Maker. Let me see if you can govern yourself so far when I return as to have made up your mind to get up every morning at an appointed hour. After you try this a week you will not find it such hard work.

I cannot send you a receipt [word illegible] growing so fast, but you will have to study hard to keep your body from getting in advance of your mind.

I hope your Aunt has returned by this time; give much love to her, your Uncle, Nina and all other members of the family. Do you ever see your Cousin Sue Hall? Remember me most affectionately to her and Eliza Carter as well as your Uncle Armistead. I wish you always to treat your Uncle with marked attention and affection. He was a true friend to your mother and she loved him in place of a father.

My arm is getting slowly better—it gives me some pain at night but not much in the day. I fear it will never be of much use to me.

How does your Grandfather like the horse I sent him? I hope he may suit him. Give much love to Hal, Dick and Cousin Mittie and Cousin Mary, write soon.

                                Your devoted father

                                    R.H.Dulany

Mary Seldon Kennedy

Carlyle Whiting, son of William
Whiting.

Gen. William H. Powell

*Letter of Nina Whiting, who was at
Welbourne, to her sister, Alice Whiting, who was
at home at Richland in Stafford County:*

Welbourne Hall

Nov. [no date] 1864

Dear Alice

I received your letter day before yesterday,
which was dated September. I was exceedingly
sorry to hear that you all had been so sick, but
hope that you are now quite well again. Mama
and Mr. Weidmayer left here for Richmond
two weeks ago, and we expect them this
evening. I suppose mama told you that Uncle
Wm. stayed to nurse Father during her
absence. Yesterday his servant Charles [Ford]
came bringing a note from Mrs. Kennedy,
informing him of the death of our poor Carly.
I never felt so sorry for any one in my life. How
terrible it is that he should lose his only, his
idolized son. He bears it much better than I
thought he would, but he cannot now realize
it.

Saturday Nov. 19th. I put off finishing my
letter that I might tell you of Mama's return
but have been disappointed as Mr. Weidmayer
returned Thursday night alone. As I suppose
Mama is now with you at home, tell her that
Grandpa is unable to send for her as the Yankees
have taken his horse during her absence.

A few days after Mr. Weidmayer and
Mama left for Washington, Gen. Powell's
command of Averell's Command came to this
neighbourhood and carried off the stock
which they could find. From here they took 52
head of splendid cattle, also Grandpa's riding
horse and the white mule, also Uncle Wm.'s
horse; Father says Mama will have to come in

Uncle Richard's drag, and with her horses. I suppose she can get Charly to drive her up. If Mama does not come up directly, I shall be in a state of Nudity and will have to stay in bed; I have to stay upstairs every time anybody comes.

Boyd Smith, Rutledge Eliason, Mr. Charles Rozier and Mr. Horner, are down stairs tonight and have been here all the evening, but as usual I have not been down.

We heard to-day that Capt. Richards of Mosby's Battalion had captured Cap. Blazer and 30 of his men and killed and wounded 25; the fight took place near Rippon. Uncle Wm. returned on Thursday. He succeeded in getting poor Carly's body and having it buried in the Chapel grave yard near Millwood.

What do you all think of our having Negroes to fight for our independence; what a back down it is on the part of our Government. I really think the South must be pretty far gone if she has to have Negroes for soldiers.

You must excuse this horribly written letter but I am in a great hurry to finish it that Boyd Smith may take it to Col. Mosby's headquarters. Tell Mama that Cousin Eliza's house is being rented and occupied.

Every body here thinks you all will get along a great deal better where you are than you would up here. Father has been very unwell for last few days, but today I think he has been better. How much surprised you must have been to see Mama land from a gun boat. I hope she found you all well and with plenty to eat and wear.

We heard from Uncle Richard the other day; he is getting along very well and expects to go in a few days to Charlottesville where Mary will join him. I expect she will stay there all the winter, at Major R. Noland's, who is a

The Confederate Congress began to debate the use of black slaves in the Confederate armies in December 1864. The act passed on March 13, 1865.[32]

friend of Uncle Richard's.

With love to all,

I remain Yours affectionately,

Nina C. Whiting.

Mary, who was all of fifteen years old at this time, arrived at Charlottesville on Sunday, December 4th, to stay with her father during his convalescence.

Letter of Mary Dulany to her sister Fanny:

Dec. 5th. 1864.

My dear Fanny

We arrived here safely Sunday evening; I have been trying to write to you ever since I arrived but have not had an opportunity.

Papa is looking thin but better than expected; I take my meals with him but sleep in the room with Mary Davis who is just your age. Miss Betsy Hill lives here to take care of her, as her mother has been dead six years. I like them both very well, though I think I shall like Dr. Davis more than Miss Hill when I become better acquainted with him.

I shall write both you and Nina long letters by the first opportunity.

Give my best love to all.

Your affectionate sister
Mary Dulany

Partial letter of Fanny Dulany to her sister Mary:

December [17,] 1864

I have not been to Oak[ley] since you left, although I hope to go next Christmas—still I don't expect to go! Julia told me yesterday that George had told her, cousin Richard deButts

Dr. John Staige Davis was the surgeon at Charlottesville General Hospital in the absence of the surgeon-in-charge, Dr. James L. Cabell.

had told him that Cousin Sophy had broken her engagement with Cousin Welby, not because he had been accused of being a coward, *that* she did not believe, [but] because he had been drunk.

Lucy is dancing, and laughing, and jumping and bowing and "jumming jim crow" and going at such a rate, that I can scarcely write.

Grandpa has just come in the dining room and told us that Uncle Whiting is *dead,* so good night my dear Sister until tomorrow. Uncle Whiting's funeral will take place Monday morning.

Tuesday. Uncle W.'s funeral was delayed until this morning, in case one of his brothers should come.

Boyd has just arrived, with letters from you to Nina & Jennie, but none for me. If you knew how much disappointed I was at not even receiving a message from you, I'm sure you would have written; it is very hard for me to be separated from you anyhow, as it is only the second time in my life that we have been parted; therefore, I think you might comfort me with a letter from you !!!!!

December 30, 1864. It has been some time since I added anything to my scribble, but we have all been so busy in getting things ready for Christmas & also for Aunt Mary and Nina to wear, that I have not been able to do so.

What a lovely day Christmas was, so bright and beautiful; the only thing besides gifts which we wanted were our two dearest ones to be here, you & Papa.

We have at last been able to find [clothes] for Aunt Mary and Nina to wear. Cousin Mit cut our brilliant skirts up & made a very nice dress for Aunt M., and Nina has also made herself a black cloth bodice out of an old coat

Despite the *contretemps*, Sophia and Welby would be married in 1866.

G.W. Carlyle Whiting died at Welbourne on December 17, 1864, and is buried at Old Welbourne Cemetery.

of her Father's, which she wears with cousin Julia's black and white plaid, which Aunt Mary brought up with her.

December 31, 1864. The Yankees went to Oakley last Wednesday, and behaved outrageously.

Aunt Ida had locked and bolted all the doors, and barred all the windows, and when the Yankees came, instead of going down to meet them, everybody stayed upstairs, and let them bang and beat at the doors. At last, finding that they were determined to come in, Aunt Ida went down and unlocked the doors. No sooner was this done than they rushed into the house, kicking everything that came in their way (they succeeded in breaking the panels of two doors). They rushed into the parlor, and deliberately kicked the doors off the étagère which is in the west corner of the room. They then went upstairs, took two very handsome blankets, Uncle Hal's white buffalo robe, and several counterpanes. In trying to pull a counterpane from a Yankee he struck Aunt Ida on the back, but she paid him back for it by giving him a good thump.

While this was going on upstairs, others were no less busy downstairs. They had broken open the storeroom door, but first they went down in Uncle Robert's room & ripping open his pillows, emptied the feathers on the floor; then they went up into the storeroom & filled the pillow ticks with flour. Would you not want to eat the bread? They took all Uncle Hal's clothes, boots, shoes, & everything that they could lay their hands on. They also took Aunt Ida's pretty blue poplin & a silk dress, and after spreading them on the floor, with other things, they threw a quantity of grease on them, & then trampled on them. They also poured a good deal of her molasses on the floor!

They treated the Quakers no better. In one house down in the Quaker settlement there was a sick girl in bed! The Yankees rushed in her room and dragged her out of the bed, telling her that she had something hid under her. They then took her sister and shook her as hard as they could. I suppose they wanted to see if any[thing] would jingle or drop. They also tried to pull the rings off of one of the Miss Hatchers' fingers.

January 1, 1865. Cousin Mit received your letter today; of course, there was only five lines for me. I *really* think you might write to me, by *a good opportunity* It seems as if I was doomed not to get any letters from you at all. This is the last which you will receive from me.

Give my best love to Papa; and tell him that though he must let you read this miserably written letter to him, more than half of it is for him. Aunt Mary started for Richlands last Thursday.

> Your ill-humored sister,
> Fanny Dulany

With the county under Union control and with no means of delivery at hand, the following letter of John Peyton Dulany to his son was written over a period of about two weeks:

December 1864

My Dear Son

Smith handed me your very welcome letter on yesterday informing me of your improvement. I hope ere long you will be yourself again, but you must not think of

On December 21, 1864, Mosby
was dining at Lakeland, the home
of Ludwell Lake, south of Rector's
Crossroads, when the raid
occurred.[33]

Lt. Charles Grogan was wounded
at Kinloch, home of Edward
Turner near The Plains, on
December 20, 1864. He was taken
to Glen Welby to recover.[34]

The "Burning Raid"

returning home. Last night, as bad as the weather was, the Yankees were out hunting.

They found Col. Mosby sitting by the fire, shot him through the window; the Colonel told them he was a scout. I presume they thought him mortally wounded, and strange to say they left him.

I received a letter this morning from Doct. Eliason—he thinks Mosby will recover. They also shot Lieut. Grogan, breaking his leg. I have not heard the particulars.

The Yankees passed by Rectors X roads last night, none of us knowing anything about it until about an hour ago. The day Mary Dulany [Whiting] left home the Yankees returned and made a clean sweep, burning the barn they had previously left—there was about one hundred bushels of wheat and fifty bushels of potatoes in the barn; they also burned about one thousand bushels of wheat at Millsville, drove off the cattle with the exception of a few young cattle; they broke into the meat houses and took some of our meat.

We were in great hopes that Sheridan's army would have taken up their winter quarters in Maryland, but I fear that they will remain in or near Winchester; the sufferings of the people this winter I fear will be very great.

Poor Whiting died the day before yesterday after suffering agony for more than two years. His death is not to be regretted on his own account or his family's. Mary had fortunately returned from Richland a short time before his death—poor girl, her future is very dark. If the Yankee army should ever leave Fairfax and I can get possession of it, I will give it to Mary for a resting place.

Friday 22 Dec. Haley has this moment informed me that a large force of cavalry has gone up the Valley, and their destination is supposed to be Charlottesville. I shall feel very anxious to hear the result of their raid. I sincerely hope that they will not put you to any inconvenience—you will, I hope, have due notice of their approach.

Robert Carter was here a few days since. He does not appear as hopeful as he did some months ago. He is very much afraid [of] the Yankees capturing him.

I hear occasionally from John deButts; he is well, but very tired of his captivity. Richard deButts told me that Welby deButts was riding out near his house, and was halted by a Yankee picket—altho. Welby was unarmed, he charged the Yankee, who dropt his gun and ran. Welby got the gun and carried it to Richard deButts' house as the fruit of his valor.

24 Dec. Mr. Norris called on his return from Philadelphia—he informed me that the Yankees were sending a great many troops from Harper's Ferry in the direction of Washington. Lincoln has made a call for 30,000 men. He saw the Miss LaRoches. Anna is to be married in a short time. They send a great many kind messages.

28th. The Yankees have returned (this is their fourth visit) in large force, their object is to find Mosby and drive off what cattle they can find—every time they come they commit greater outrages. They went to Hal's, broke the furniture and even went so far as to strike Ida, broke the windows—in fact, they have done everything but burn the House. Hal had to escape without hat or boots. The last two raids we have escaped, altho' they were at William Seaton's, where they carried [off] everything he had.

I think, my dear Son, our future never was

The Battle of Nashville utterly destroyed Hood's army, with 6,300 Southern casualties (three times the federal loss).

as dark as now—the news from Hood's army is truly distressing.

I hear that some of our members of our Congress have moved that we should free our negroes. I have long thought that it would come to this sooner or later, the whole world is arrayed against us, and as far as the border states are concerned we should be none the worse off. France has said that if we would emancipate our negroes she would acknowledge our independence. France, England and Russia have set us a good example, and however repugnant it may be to be coerced, still I am sure we shall have to *submit* (I know how you will dislike this word) before foreign nations will acknowledge us.

When Mr. Weidmayer was in Washington the consul told him that Lincoln intended to take possession of Loudoun and perhaps Fauquier—the inhabitants would be permitted to take choice of either going North or South, and a few days since there were two Colonels at Armistead's, who told George the same thing. I only wonder as they have complete possession of this county they have not done it before.

As the Yankees are within a few miles of us, I will lay aside my pen until tomorrow.

Mary Whiting and her two little boys left us on yesterday for Richland, leaving Nina with us. Tell Mary that Miss [Nannie] Grayson was married on yesterday, notwithstanding the Yankees all around us, and at the same time thank her for her long and interesting letter.

I have been anxiously looking for Armistead's return that he may enlighten us with respect to what is going on in the world.

We are completely shut out, (perhaps however it is best for our peace of mind), and try to believe the adage that "no news is good news" —this saying is rather a paradox, I think. I do not think I have ever known so severe a December as this has been—the very elements appear to be against us.

I sincerely hope you and Mary are in comfortable quarters. Yesterday was the only clear day we have had this month. I was in great hopes that poor Mary would have had good weather for her journey, but this morning it is snowing very fast and bids fair for a deep snow.

I hope it will drive the Yankees to their winter quarters. We could see their camp fires from Seaton's Hill, and they were a little south of Hal's. Their object must be to find Colonel Mosby; they cannot expect to get much plunder, as they have taken nearly everything from us.

They do not make any distinction between friends or foes; they have plundered Fletcher and Hogue [sic] and the Quakers generally; as they have been accumulating for the last three years, they found considerable booty. They (the Quakers) sent a deputation to Washington; they were informed that they did not know anything about it, the order to fire etc. proceeded from Gen. Grant—they were very sorry that their friends should suffer, but unfortunately it could not be helped &c &c.

William Fletcher of Shirland Hall, Rector's Crossroads. The Hoge family (Quakers) lived at Woodlawn, now Atoka Farm, once the home of U.S. Senator John W. Warner.

1 Jan. 1865 Your letters by Mr. Kerfoot have just been received. I regret to hear your wound is so slow in healing. We ought, however, to be thankful that your general health is so good.

Richard Carter arrived at home a few days since but has been driven off by the Yankees. They must have a very large cavalry force to send such a number here.

Daniel Kerfoot, age 58, operated a post office and tollgate between Upperville and Piedmont. (1860 U.S. Census)

We got a letter from Clarence; he says our horses are starving for want of food, as the snow has deprived them of grass. The fact is, we shall have to get rid of some of our negroes (if things go on as they are at present). There [being] so many consumers and so very few producers.

Thomas Glascock (1814-1885), son of Aquilla Glascock, lived at Rose Hill near Rector's Crossroads.

I am told that Tom Glascock intends sending a part of his off; I have not heard where they are to go.

I think the present policy of the Yankees is to try and starve us out, or they would not remain passive so long at Richmond.

I saw Doctor Eliason on yesterday; so far the Yankees have not found Mosby. The Doct. says that Richard Carter told him that the probability was that Welby Carter's sentence would be revised. I sincerely hope that it may be so, on his Father's account as [well as] his own.

Richard Welby Carter, colonel of the 1st Virginia Cavalry, was cited by Rosser at the battle of Tom's Brook in October and cashiered for cowardice.

Well, as you will receive several letters from home I think (and I have no doubt you think so too) that it is time to close my salmagundi of a letter, but when writing to you I hardly know when to stop; and I sincerely regret that circumstances make them so doleful. I would wish you and Mary a happy New Year if it did not appear like mockery. We all join in love to you and Mary. As ever, my dear R., yr.

J.P.D.

[P.S.] You must not think I have forgotten to have a cape made for you. We have been surrounded by the Yankees for nearly a month, so that it was dangerous to leave the house. It is supposed they have returned from whence they came, but no person appears to know where that is. I have not yet been able to get the wool from the mountain to exchange for negro clothing. Moses has had a relapse, and I very much fear that it will go hard with him.

Mr. Weidmayer will write to Mary. I hope she will answer his letter by the first opportunity, as she knows how very sensitive he is.

You mention in your letter that you had to pay nine hundred dollars per month for your board in Southern currency or in bank notes. What is the difference between bank paper and Southern currency? and what is your pay? You know I have great dislike to your going in debt, and it is so hard to realize that our resources are cut off.

I do not recollect if I informed you that Henry Arthur [Hall] had moved to John deButts' farm—he was so hunted by the conscripting officers that he had to leave or join the army. He is very much soured against his former friends, as he knows they disapprove of his course, which has certainly been an unfortunate one.

I have not heard from your sister Julia for some time. Your letters are so much obliterated that it is hard to make them out. I find it hard to say farewell, but as Mr. Weidmayer will be waiting to take our mail to Mr. Kerfoot, I must bid you good-bye—love to Mary and accept, my beloved Son

the affectionate love
of your Father.

Julia lived with her husband, Samuel Roszell, in Wheatland, a hamlet near Hillsboro.

"You have done everything you could do for your country. It is now time to try and make some provision for your children. ... I do not believe ... that this war can be carried on much longer, and if the South should be conquered it will make a great change in our circumstances."

John Peyton Dulany to his son,
February 24, 1865

1865

As 1865 opened, Colonel Dulany was still recuperating in Charlottesville with his daughter Mary attending him.

The following letter to Mary from Nina Whiting, who was at Welbourne, has a note at the top: "Don't show this to Uncle Richard, it is badly written":

Welbourne Hall
Jan. 1st 1865

My Dear Mary

Today is New Years day. How many of us will live to see another? How much better prepared we would all be for another world if we only knew how long we had to live. I hope we may be able to keep the many good resolutions which we have made this day. How many I have made before only to be broken.

We received letters which you sent by Mr. Kerfoot, I am sincerely glad to hear of Uncle

Richard's improvement, I hope he rapidly recovers. We have all been very despondent about the success of our armies by the recent bad news which we have received from the South.

We have heard that one of our Senators votes for the abolishment of slavery in the South, as France will then recognize the independence of the Confederacy. I hope that our Congress will never consent to such an act of cowardice for it would be nothing else. Grandpa appears to be in favor of it, which greatly surprises me.

I hope that Uncle Richard may be able to write a cheerful letter to him as now Mama has left he is quite doleful. Dear mama left us last Thursday, which was an exceedingly cold day. I fear that the boys as well as herself suffered from the cold. She was extremely anxious to return home as she left Sister Julia and also Alice & Mary suffering from the full effects of the chills, fevers or Bilious fever which they had during the fall. Poor Mama hardly slept at all for the last three weeks, she has a heavy responsibility. I hope we may all be able to help support ourselves, but *what can we do?* Oh! what would I give to be a boy. At least I might go into the Army, where nothing is required but physical strength.

I suppose you have heard of my poor Father's death, he died on Saturday night the 17th of Dec. You may remember having heard me speak on how much he suffered from phlegm on his lungs and his not having strength to throw it off. Well: on Saturday morning he suffered a great deal with it, but after having taken a great quantity of cherry Pectoral and other expectorants, he appeared to be relieved and we thought him much better and I thought I had been needlessly alarmed. Poor Mama had no idea that he was dying. That morning Cousin Mit told him that she feared he would not be with us long, and that she had never seen him look so deathlike, but I was so accustomed to see him that I was not so conscious of it.

But I must return to where I left off—he grew gradually worse after dinner, and when the Dr. came I saw all in his face. Nothing could be done, though Father did not see it and asked him to come the next day, but two hours after he was in another world. He went to sleep and never woke again. I never thought that anyone could have died so easily. He was not aware that he was dying. I never shall forget the way he gazed in the face of each one of us, as if he wished to read our thoughts.

Oh what would I give if I could recall all the unkind speeches which I have made. How I wish I could beg his forgiveness, implore his pardon, but all is past—never to be forgotten. I wish he could have seen Uncle R—He said so often that he would give weeks, months of his life to see him for one hour. He loved Uncle R more than his brothers. I wish that his last days could have been free from care & anxiety; no one knows how much the idea of having his family penniless pained him. Excuse me for writing such a sad, mournful letter, but it is very hard to write cheerfully when one doesn't feel so.

I have not yet thanked you [for] the nice letter sent by Boyd Smith, it is pleasant to think that you are not forgotten when absent. Fan has been very unfortunate in not receiving any of the letters which you have written to her, be sure next time to select a safe messenger. You must excuse this horribly written letter but I have the most horrible pen and ink that I have ever written with, but promise you that I will procure a better one before I inflict you with another letter. With much love to Uncle Richard and yourself I remain your attached

Cousin Nina

On the back of Nina's letter, John Peyton Dulany wrote to Mary:

Jan 1st, Sunday night

My dear Child

Your letter sent by Mr. Kerfoot arrived this morning, and was welcomed as a New Year's gift. We had been quite uneasy for fear the Yankees would get to Charlottesville. Boyd Smith said you were getting homesick but I think he must have been mistaken as your letter is written in a cheerful tone.

I am glad that you have an opportunity of improving yourself. Don't forget the English Grammar, the most important of all, and you are just the age to appreciate the study of it. You don't say where you go to Church, and how often. I feel so thankful that you are with Papa, for though we miss you very much, I know you are a comfort to him, and that he will watch over your body & soul as none else can.

I was so very sorry you left your toothbrush, even the Yankee visit and worries the day you left could not make me forget the annoyance of your being without one. How do you get along with your few clothes? Your Aunt Mary is to send up dresses for you & Fan by Charlie Ford, who drove her down, and I will send yours to you by the first opportunity. If you hear of one let me know.

I received a letter from Arthur a day or two

Arthur Herbert

ago. It was a month old. He was very anxious
to know where your Papa was that he might
write to him. He said he had just got the books
Fan & you sent to William & himself, he said
nothing could have been more acceptable,
and desired his best love to you and thanks.
Did Richard ever get his? Christmas was very
much saddened

[Here the letter ends, no signature.]

Fanny Dulany to her father, Richard H. Dulany:

Sunday Jan. 1st. 1865

My Dear Papa

We received letters from Mary and yourself
this evening by Mr. Kerfoot, and as he starts
tomorrow I avail myself of the opportunity
offered. We also received a letter from Cousin
Clarence to his father. It seems very sad that
he should have been forced to leave him, when
he was so ill, and to think that he could not be
with him when he died. His (Cousin
Clarence's) letter was so affectionate,
expressing his great regret at not being able to
nurse him more. We all know how sad it is to
lose those who are dear to us, but it must be
still worse to be ever so far away from all to
whom we are fond of, with no one to comfort
or sympathize with you.

The Yankees have been raiding about last
week, and consequently I have not been at
Oakley during the Christmas week.

I suppose of course you have heard of Col.
Mosby's being wounded. He was sitting at the
supper table, at Mr. Lud. Lake's, when before
they knew anything of the Yankees, the house
was surrounded by them, and they were firing
in the doors, & through the windows, several
of them seeing a Confed. soldier in the room,

Two of Lake's sons, Ludwell, Jr.,
and William, served in Mosby's
command.

Mosby was taken to Aquilla Glascock's home near Rector's Crossroads[1] only a few hours after his wounding, where Drs. William Dunn and Talcott Eliason removed the bullet. From there he was moved to Glen Welby, then to Wheatlands, the home of Marshall Lake, remaining only a few days in each location to avoid the federal patrols.

rushed into it. The Col. had been wounded through the window, and when the Yankees saw him stretched on the floor pale and motionless, it was no wonder that they thought he was dead. They asked the Miss Lakes who he was; and after having declared to them that he was Lieu. Johnson of the 1st Reg., the Yankees robbed and left him.

After they had all gone, one of the Miss Lakes knelt by him and said "Poor Mosby, poor Mosby, how sorry I am that he has been killed," when to her great astonishment Mosby raised a finger to her lips, and told her to hush. They then found he had been playing opossum. He stayed there several days, went to Mr. Quilly Glascock [and] from there they have taken him toward Richmond, at least it is thought so.

I am glad that Mary enjoys herself so much, and hope she will have many pleasant rides on Maud. I have made a good many resolutions, which I will try to keep. I hope your arm will improve rapidly with such kind nursing. I would give anything in the world to be able to be with you, I am so dreadfully lonesome and Grand Pa doesn't like me to go to Oakley. Love to all. Your affec. daughter

Fanny Dulany

From the journal of Fanny Dulany:

Sunday, Jan. 1st 1865. I have kept a very irregular journal lately, but will try to write oftener this year, as I know it will be some pleasure to Papa to read when he comes back. We received letters from [him] & Mary today. He says that his bodily health is good, but his arm does not recover as rapidly as he expected it would have done, although he is as kindly treated as he possibly could be.

Wood is very scarce in Charlottesville & some kind person hearing that Papa would suffer for the want of it sent him a two-horse cart load. Just before Xmas one of his old friends came to see him, a Mr. Gilmore I think, & promised to send him a load of wood & a large turkey gobbler for a Xmas gift. Papa also told us that he had to pay $900 a month for boarding Mary, his servant & himself & [portion or page missing] are $100 a yard in Confed. [money].

Monday, Jan 2nd 1865. We commenced school today. After dinner Cousin Mit & I walked over to Mrs. Seaton's to see Aunt Mary. We found her quite sick, though not in bed. When we returned we found Cousin Richard deButts here.

Today after dinner Mr. Weidmayer, who had gone to carry letters to Mr. Kerfoot, returned with his head tied up with a handkerchief & a large spot of blood which had soaked through just above his forehead. We asked him to tell us what had happened to him, & he told us that in riding through Upperville at the upper end of town, he met a cart of wood which two boys were driving & who were accompanied by a soldier, to whom he bowed & rode on. He had not gone far when the two boys called after him in a very insulting way. He rode back again, when before he knew anything about it the soldier had ridden up to him, wrenched the whip out of his hand, & struck him with the butt end.

As a great treat Mr. Weidmayer gave us all a glass of punch tonight.

Tuesday, January 3rd 1865. Mr. Caleb Rector's funeral passed by here today. I have nothing else to say.

Caleb C. Rector was captured at Louisa Court House, died in Point Lookout Prison on August 16, 1864, and is buried in the Quaker cemetery near Unison, Virginia.[2]

Wednesday, Jan. 4th. 1865. Miss Sue came today & she, Cousin Mit, Mr. Weidmayer & I sang hymns until supper, after which she went away.

Thursday, Jan. 5th 1865. I read my first German lesson today and translated about ten lines of English into German. Mr. Weidmayer says that I pronounce very well for the short time I have been learning. It was my second lesson. I do not intend to let Papa or Mary know anything about my learning it because it will be so pleasant to give him a pleasant surprise when he comes home.

We heard this morning that the Yankees were pulling down houses in the neighborhood, so as to get bricks to build their winter quarters with.

Nina and I went to see old Uncle Read who is quite sick. I read the fifteenth chapter of St. Luke to him, which he seemed to enjoy very much.

Not long ago Mrs. Seaton was scolding her little nephew, Harry Randolph, who is between two & three years old. She said to him "look here young man if you don't behave yourself I will punish you." He threw his head on one side & saying the verse from Polly Hopkins, "Oh cruel, cruel Polly Hopkins, to beat me so, to treat me so." I think it was very smart in such a little fellow.

January 6th 1865. Cousin Mit went over to Mrs. Seaton's this morning in spite of the rain. She found Miss Sue quite sick & she has been ever so since she sang here the other evening. I have learned the tune of "Faded Flowers" from Miss Sue; I have also learned a new tune to the hymn "Softly now the light of day" which Cousin Mit & I sing together in the evening.

Saturday, Jan. 7th 1865. We have had

miserable weather today. It follows just this course, first it rains, then it snows then it thaws, then it blows. I gave Nina a music lesson this morning. She took the whole of "Don Juan." She plays it exceedingly well. I hope she will practice it. It will be so pleasant for she & I to play it together & besides it is such a beautiful duet.

I do miss Mary so much, when I wake in the night & find Nina is there instead of her I miss her & when I say my lessons in school I miss her & when I practice I miss her & I miss her in everything I do almost.

I think that verse in one of Mrs. Hemans poems is so very pretty—

Felicia Dorothea (Brown) Hemans (1793-1835), an English poet

The Deserted House
We miss them when the prayer is said
We miss them when the board is spread
Upon our dreams their dying eyes
See still and mournful sadness rise.

Sunday, January 8th 1865. What a beautiful day after yesterday's miserable weather, the ground is frozen hard. I was determined to take advantage of the good roads so after breakfast Mr. Weidmayer & I walked almost to the creek; it was perfectly delightful. When we returned we had service. How beautiful it is. I think some of the prayers, indeed all of them are perfect. What would I give to be a sincere Christian, such as one as Mama was or as Papa is, *a Christian Soldier.* I think it is the most beautiful title a gentleman can have. After services Nina, Julia & I took another walk. After dinner we had Sunday school. Miss Sue did not come as usual, I hope she is not unwell.

Here Fanny copied two long, melancholy poems, entitled "Only Waiting" and "Moonlight on the Grave."

Eliason served in the Invalid Corps after his wounding. He was paroled at Greensboro, N.C., on May 12, 1865.[3]

Monday Jan 9th. Cousin Mit went up on the Hill to see Cousin Maria Conway, she was more quiet than usual. Grand Pa received a letter from Cousin Richard Carter, he says that Rosser is an "unprincipled villain" [and] that he has treated Cousin Welby shamefully.

Tuesday Jan. 10th 1865. Nothing has happened today except that Cousin Rutledge came while we were in school.

Wednesday Jan 11th 1865. Dick and I went over to see Aunt Mary this evening to take her some letters which Mr. Ayres [sic] had brought from Richmond. He also brought letters from Papa & Mary. Hal received one & Grand Pa too, but as usual there were none for me. I have not received a single letter from Mary since she went away.

Thursday Jan. 12th 1865. What beautiful weather we have had today if it had not been so muddy. The sun shone bright and warm & there was only the least bit of wind. I was determined to take advantage of the beautiful day, so as soon as school was over Dick & I walked about the fields on the grass where it was quite dry, we stayed out until dinner was ready & then came in.

The following letter of John Peyton Dulany to Colonel Dulany appears to have been written over a four-day period:

12 Jan. 1865.
Welbourne

My Dear Richard,

Altho' I wrote you a long letter last week I must again trouble you with my difficulties and troubles. You have no doubt heard the Yankees have again taken up their winter quarters near Wheatlands [sic]. Their object

Wheatland, a hamlet near Hillsboro.

is either to depopulate Loudoun and Fauquier as they have done Fairfax, or to take possession of the houses for their own use. You will, I have no doubt, attribute all this to the fears of an old man. I sincerely hope it may turn out so.

We are completely at their mercy, having no troops to oppose them nor a likelihood of their being any, but my principal reason of writing now is to consult your wishes respecting your silver. It keeps me constantly uneasy. I should think if it could be sent either to Baltimore or Richmond it would be the best thing to do with it, but it would be running a great risk to try to send it to either place. I have had some conversation with Mr. Weidmayer—he would not like to undertake to carry it to Baltimore. Do try to advise me on the subject for I know not what is best, and the responsibility that I labour under is almost too much for me.

I do not think there was ever a man placed in a situation, who had so helpless a family to provide for, not an individual can I look to for advice or assistance. I thought at one time that I would not say anything to you of my troubles, as you have enough to think of, but it is such a relief to open our heart to one that we know will sympathize with us.

Did you ever know so severe a December as the last? I fear that our boys and horses will suffer very much.

Do you know if Clarence has been apprised of his father's death? I do not know how to direct a letter to him. Your sister left Welbourne about the first of the month for Richland with her two little orphan boys.

Charley returned last night. She says in her letter to me, "I found the children in better health than when I left them four weeks ago, tho' it will be a long time before they recover from the effects of chills and fever if they ever do. Will you not be surprised to hear that I did not reach Richland until the fifth day after I left you. The horse must have been broken down before we started on our tedious journey, as soon as she began to kneel in harness, I endeavored to hire a horse on the road, and was charged five dollars to be carried seven miles, of course I declined, and some hours after found myself lost in a trackless waste of snow; help came as it always does, when I most wanted it; a man appeared with a horse much stronger than mine, harnessed his horse to the carriage, led him for miles through the forest until he put me in the right road, and in a safe place, I offered him pay but he would not take a cent because he heard from Charley that I was in trouble." Thank God there is at least some little kind feeling left in this world. I began to think there was none.

We have been looking out for sometime for the arrival of Armistead [Conway], I miss him very much poor fellow, he will return to a Home of desolation and ruin with one inmate and she a maniac. Mittie went to see her and if the servant had not interfered I do not know what the consequences would have been, she (Maria Conway) got a large stick to strike her with. George thinks there is danger of her firing the house.

You say in your letter you hope to be home etc. I am afraid, my dear Son, it will be a long time before it will be safe to venture home. I can compare the Yankees to nothing but hungry wolves, they hunt both night and day—the worse the weather, the more active they are, frequently catching Mosby's men in bed. I should be in painful anxiety all the time you were [here]—the best arrangement would be for the children to meet you at Richard deButts' when you are well enough to travel.

At present there is no communication with Maryland. Mr. Weidmayer hopes that he will be able to get to Baltimore some time in March, [but] even when there it is very difficult to get anything over. Persons have to take an oath that what they buy is for their own use. Mary was very fortunate in getting many things that her family stood in need of.

I will send you a pair of pantaloons by the first safe opportunity. Say to Mary her Aunt Mary had purchased a dress for her, but she was afraid to send it from Richland for fear of the Yankees so it is hard to say when she will get it. Charlottesville, I fear, is too poor to supply her with one.

Do let me hear from you by every opportunity. I expect Major White to call in the morning, who will take charge of this letter, so I must bid you good bye. We all join in love to you and Mary. May our God bless and preserve you both is the prayer of

your affectionate Father
J.P.D.
16th Jan. 1865

From the journal of Fanny Dulany:

Friday 13 [January] 1865. Miss Sue came over today & spent it with us this evening. When her horse came for her I rode up to the gate & in coming back the horse, who was trotting right fast, fell down in the mud, but did not succeed in throwing me over his head, which seemed to be his object. I shall try to write a letter to Mary tomorrow if Grand Pa refuses to let me go to Oakley, which I expect he will. Cousin Welby deButts came from Mount Welby this evening. He brought no news.

Saturday 14th. We did not go to Oakley this morning as Cousin Mit was too busy to do so & besides the wind has commenced blowing again. I did not write to Mary, either for which I have no better reason to give than that I was too lazy to do so & that while I ought to have been writing I was knitting.

Here Fanny copies another melancholy poem, "The Vacant Chair."

Colonel Dulany continues his recuperation in Charlottesville. Letter of Richard H. Dulany to his sister, Mary Whiting:

University [of Virginia], Jan. 29th, 1865

My dear Sister

I received your letter last night—will send it to Father by the first opportunity.

Mary has just gone to church. I did not feel well enough to accompany her but will content myself with reading and with having a little talk with you.

I need not say how deeply and sincerely I sympathize with you, my dear Sister, in your great affliction. I know but too well what it is to be left alone in the world and to have a void in my heart that neither love of father, children, or country or all combined can fill. There is but one consolation: if we do our duty here we will before many years join those we love where there is no war, no sorrow, no separation, but one eternal rest peace and joy.

Oh, how ardently do I long to have that full and perfect assurance that my darling wife had of her acceptance with God; of her entire trust in her Saviour. Read the 151 hymn in your prayer book, it will give you a better description of my feeling than any thing I can write.

Do you think it is the privilege of every Christian to feel this perfect assurance of which I have spoken? See how selfish I am in thinking of myself when I intended to devote an hour to you and yours.

I am glad you hear frequently from Clarence—he is a noble boy and a good soldier. I wish very much it was in my power to promote him as he deserves. I had been told by Genl. Butler of South Carolina that Gen. Lee (R) intended to give me Rosser's Brigade as soon as Rosser could get a division—then I should have made Clarence Adjutant of the Brigade with the rank of Captain. My being unfit for duty at present will give Rosser the chance of putting some favorite in my place. I care but little for it except for Clarence's sake.

Gen. Matthew C. Butler

I shall never have the full use of my arm again, which makes me very helpless in some respects. If I can get on my horse with ease it is all I require. I shall take command of my Regmt. in March or April.

I heard from home a week ago. All well. Write as soon as you get this and let me know if there is anything I can do for you. I think I told you that I deposited seven (7) thousand dollars in Va. bonds with R.H. Maury for you about the commencement of the war. I expect to go to Richmond shortly and will send you Maury's receipt. We can get no funds now except Confederate which I suppose you could not use. Could you [use] tobacco to pay household expenses?

The Yankees you met were looking for Col. Mosby, who had been shot the night before at Mrs. Lake's and left as the party who wounded [him] thought he would die and did not know who he was until they got to their camp at night and examined his papers which they had taken from his pockets. Mosby was brought off by some of his men and is now at his father's doing well. He expects to be ready in two or three weeks to return to Loudoun. Are you troubled still now by the Yankees? If I could get a horse at Fredericksburg I would try and make you a visit before I return to the Army.

I see from the papers that Stephens, Hunter and Judge Campbell have been appointed commissioners to proceed to Washington to confer with the authorities of the U.S. Government on the question of peace. This has been old Blair's business at Richmond. God grant that they may make terms for an *honorable* peace and our *independence*, without such terms I am willing for war to [the] end of my life. I am not at all hopeful of the issue.

Give much love to each of the children by name and to Cousin Ellen—tell her that I received a letter from Burwell a few days since. All well at Clay Hill. Burwell had sent his family to Baltimore where they will remain until spring. The Yankees destroyed all of Burwell's food. He saved 125 sheep and cows.

He was far more fortunate than I have been. All my wheat has been burned with my barns and every head of stock driven off that could travel.

I fear you will find it hard to read my writing. I have still to hold my pencil between my third and fourth fingers.

Confederate commissioners to the Hampton Roads Peace Conference (February 6, 1865) were Vice President Alexander H. Stephens, Judge John Archibald Campbell, and Senator R.M.T. Hunter of Virginia. The meeting with Lincoln and Secretary of State William Henry Seward settled nothing. Francis Blair was the messenger from Lincoln who arranged the conference.[4]

Clay Hill was near Carter Hall, home of the Burwells of Clarke County.[5]

Tell Julia that if she still thinks it her duty to become a governess, and is willing to take charge of May and Fan to consider herself engaged from the receipt of this letter. I should want her to take charge of the girls, and the boys when they are more advanced except when they are studying the modern languages with Mr. Weidmayer. The terms would be three hundred dollars a year unless Mr. W should leave me—in that case, four hundred dollars. As to vacations &c, we can settle that when we meet. I should expect Julia to come to Va. in April if she has an opportunity. I can make all necessary arrangements when I hear from you.

Mary has just returned from church. She desires much love to you and all the family. She will write to Julia in a day or two. Ever your affectionate brother

R.H. Dulany

Partial letter of John Peyton Dulany to Richard H. Dulany:

There is a great deal of talk about peace in consequence of Mr. Blair and Sons having returned from Richmond. I feel sure that there will be no peace without the South is prepared to give up everything that they have been contending for—all the wise-acres (if we have any) say that the South is prepared to give up the negroes, but whether they will agree to reenter the Union is another question.

Did you ever see such a continuation of severe weather? The children have been enjoying themselves very much sliding over the ice. I never saw them in such health. Clarence gives a very unfavourable account of the horses in the Valley—there is neither corn nor hay to be procured, the horses have only straw and not enough of that.

4th Feb. '65 Mr. Norris has called on his way to Charlottesville and has promised to take you a pair of pantaloons and two shirts, and a frock for Mary, which I have no doubt will be acceptable. Norris, who is just from Baltimore, says Thomas's army from the South is passing down through Washington and Baltimore—I presume on their way to Richmond.

This rumor was untrue. Gen. George H. Thomas was in Tennessee with part of the Army of the Cumberland.

Welby Carter's court-martial had apparently been sent to Jefferson Davis for intercession. John Randolph Tucker is a Richmond attorney.

Armistead requests me to ask you to make enquiries respecting Welby's case, and let him know the decision of the President as soon as you can. Randolph Tucker can give you every information on the subject.

As ever my dear Son
Yours affectionately,
J.P.D.

[P.S.] Love to Mary.

In February, General Fitzhugh Lee invited Colonel Dulany to join a military court. Lee's letter to Colonel Richard H. Dulany:

Staunton, Feb. 2, 65

My dear Colonel,

I write to ask you how you would like a position as a member of the Military Court to be appointed for the Cavalry of this Dept. You know such courts are composed of 3 members with the pay rank and emoluments of Colonels of Cavalry and a Judge Advocate with the rank of Capt.

Very truly
Yours &c
Fitz Lee

Letter of Mary Dulany to her cousin, Julia Whiting:

Feb 4th, University of Va.

Dear Cousin Julia,

I received your letter dated Jan 1st a day or two ago, & only delayed answering it in hopes of being able to send you news from Welbourne, but as I have waited in vain for two weeks for a letter from home, I think I had better take this opportunity of writing, as Papa has gone to Charlottesville & I am here alone.

I will give you an account of the way in which I spend my time that you may know exactly how large a portion of it I devote to each study. I am in general dressed by eight & the first thing I do in the morning is to learn my algebra lesson, this takes about an hour or less. From nine until ten I study Italian, & from ten until eleven French, then I practice two hours and read one, we have dinner at two, and after dinner I draw until half past three and read again until four. From that time until six, which is our supper time, I am generally out of doors, then history again to seven when Mr. Minor calls me to go to Capt. Colston's to do my algebra with Annie. We usually stay there until half an hour after our lesson, returning to Papa's room about nine; from that time until half past ten we always have company—professors, students, soldiers, and some times, though not often, ladies.

At first I found it very difficult to keep the rules I had made for dividing my time; two or three visitors would come in and I would be obliged to put down my books, & as Mr. Minor says "try to improve my conversational talent" (I have never yet discovered that I had any), but by studying my lessons early in the morning

Possibly John B. Minor, law professor at the University of Virginia. It was he who surrendered the university to Custer.[6]

& drawing in the evening I manage to keep up right well now.

I visit very little, though I would like to do so. I know lessons & visiting will interfere with each other, & besides I see just as much company as is good for me, in Papa's room, perhaps a little too much.

Papa requests me to tell you that in the offer he made you in Aunt Mary's letter he spoke of money as it was before the war; you need not think that I persuaded him to make it. I did not know any thing about it until the letter containing it was written & sent. I need not tell you how anxious I am that you should consent to come to Welbourne, you know already how much I have always desired to have you for a teacher.

Papa's arm is rapidly improving, & I [am] glad to say that he will next spring return to the field, he has just received an offer from Gen. Fitz Lee of an appointment to a permanent military court, of course he will refuse it, he will write to the Gen. at once informing him of his intention of returning to his command. I inclose a copy of a paragraph, I saw in a Charlottesville paper soon after I arrived here, in which Papa gets credit for one more wound than he ever received.

From the Charlottesville *Daily Chronicle* (undated)

We are glad to inform our readers that the gallant commander of the 7th Va. Cavalry is again with us. This noble soldier is now suffering from the fourth wound he has received since the war. Col. Dulany was one of the most aristocratic & wealthy farmers in Va. At the beginning of the war he forsook his father, children, home, property, every thing to devote his time, talents, and if need be his life, to his country. "Of such stuff is the rebellion made," all glory & honour to such noble patriots!

As dinner is ready I must conclude. Ask Alice & Mary to write to me, & write soon yourself. I should be very glad to receive a letter from Neville.

>With best love to all.
>I remain Yours truly
>Mary C. Dulany

Partial letter of Fanny Dulany to her sister Mary:

February 11, Saturday, 1865

My dear Mary,

As Anna Bolling has been here all the morning, I have not been able to write to you but will try to do so now. After dinner, it being such beautiful weather overhead, Cousin Clarence, Nina, and I walked over to Mrs. Seaton's. We had a good deal of fun, and trouble in trudging through the snow, but were fully repayed by Mrs. Seaton, and Miss Sue's singing. Eva sang "I will arise" which you know is taken from the "Prodigal Son" very sweetly with her sisters. We stayed until after dark, and I wish you could have seen us coming through the cornfield, where there was no track and the snow more than a foot deep.

We all, except Nina, and Cousin Clarence, walked to Oakley two weeks ago in that sleety weather; it was almost like walking on ice all the way. I forgot to tell something that happened to me Friday before last. Cousin Welby Carter had just come, and cousin Mit sent Ellen in Mr. Weidmayer's room to tell us of his arrival. We all ran in the parlor, and I happened to be first; I saw someone sitting in the armchair and thinking it was Cousin Welby, ran up to him, and was just going to kiss him, when to my great surprise, the soldier sprang up and retreated to the sofa, and looked as if he wanted to go through the wall. I never felt so embarrassed in my life; I told him that I thought he was Col. Carter, and after asking him to excuse us, I retreated as fast as I could, into Grandpa's room with Cousin Welby and Cousin Richard deButts, who told us that when the Yankees went to Glen Welby they went in Miss Julia Forest's room, and as soon as they opened her trunk, she jumped in, she then told the Yankees she knew they were coming that day; and when they asked her how, she said that Puss had not been to prayers that morning, and whenever that was the case, something always happened.

Cousin Welby deButts came from the mountains Friday and said that a soldier, a Mr. Kennedy, had told them of my taking him for Cousin Welby.

[unsigned]

Letter of Colonel John S. Mosby to Colonel Richard H. Dulany:

Feb. 19th '65
Col. R.H. Dulany

Col.

Mosby resumed command the first week of March 1865.[7]

Your note has been rec'd—I expect to start to my command next Saturday & I will take pleasure in carrying any letters to your father—I am glad to hear of your recovery.

Your friend
Jno. S. Mosby

Richard Welby Carter was captured in February 1865. He was found hiding in an old chimney at Glen Welby, "a large, portly man in his drawers and stocking feet." A former slave who led the Federals to him identified Carter as his father.[8]

Upon capture, he was sent to Ft. Delaware Prison. Early said, "Had it not been for his strong [family] connections in Virginia, he would have been shot."

Letter of John Peyton Dulany to his son:

24 Feb. 1865
Welbourne

My Dear Richard,

I presume you have received ere this a letter I sent by Joseph Carr.

I have now to inform you that Welby Carter was on yesterday taken prisoner at Richard Carter's. His father tried to prevail on him to leave the neighbourhood, but he said that there was no danger.

On the day before Welby's capture the colonel of the 12th was captured. It really appears like derangement for men to run into danger so recklessly. I am in daily expectation of Welby deButts and Clarence Whiting being taken. Poor Welby gives me a great deal of anxiety; altho' I pay his board at Richard deButts' he will stay at Welbourne. They all appear to think that when here they are safe.

A detachment of the 8th Illinois Cavalry was searching for Mosby's men. Lt. Col. Thomas B. Massie of the 12th Virginia Cavalry, was captured near his home in Warren County on February 18, 1865.

On last Friday there was a great deal of heavy firing, and today (Wednesday 23 inst.) I believe they are firing either at Harpers Ferry or Washington in commemoration of some victory (I fear). I hear a great many unpleasant rumors, which I try to disbelieve, but must confess they make a depressing impression. I wish I were as happily constituted as someone I know who can believe anything that they wish will come to pass.

February 23, 1865, was a Thursday. The firing might have been a commemoration of George Washington's birthday on February 22nd.

My object, dear Richard, in writing is to beg you to consider the change that you mention—you have done every thing that you could for your country. It is now time to try and make some provision for your children. In the course of nature I can not remain much longer with them. I am nearly eighty years old and begin to feel the infirmities of age and it will be soon time for you to take the superintendence of them for, there is no one who can supply a Father's place. I do not believe without a great change in our favour that this war can be carried on much longer, and if the South should be conquered it will make a great change in our circumstances.

I know it is very unpleasant to take so sombre a view, but it is better to look at least at the possibility of it, and try and prepare ourselves for the worst. Major White called a few days ago on his way to Leesburg, and has promised to take my letter.

Charleston, S.C., was evacuated by Confederate forces under Lt. Gen. William J. Hardee on the night of February 17-18, 1865.

A man has this moment informed me that Charleston has fallen—can it be so? I fear you will think I am a bird of ill omen, as my letters are generally filled either with unpleasant facts, or anticipations, but I think under present circumstances it would be hard to be hopeful of coming events.

I received a letter from Sam Roszell [at Wheatland]. He informs me that Yankees, altho' encamped near him, have as yet done him no injury, they will all be well and have all the necessaries of life. I also heard from John deButts; he was quite well.

I frequently think of you and my dear little girl when I have the comfort of a fine fire this cold weather, and wonder how you are provided. If you should accept being a member of a court martial, will it be necessary for you to stay in Richmond, and if so would you have Mary with you? Tell Mary our neighbours are very merry, they are giving dancing parties all around us. I think it is somewhere said, "Those whom the Gods intend to destroy, they first make mad"; really those who can enjoy these merry meetings must have very little reflection.

I presume you have heard of a very gallant affair of Major Richards with forty men. He captured fifty-two of their horses etc., besides the wounded and killed. Unfortunately, however, the Yankees have picked up a goodly number of our soldiers, who left the army to recruit their horses.

On February 19, 1865, Maj. Thomas Gibson with 225 men attempted to capture some of Mosby's men, including Maj. Adolphus "Dolly" E. Richards, at Green Garden, his father's home near Upperville. The 14th Pennsylvania Cavalry split up, and some men got drunk in Upperville. Richards recaptured many of the rangers west of Ashby's Gap, at Mt. Carmel Church.

I hear the Yankees have taken all Mary Welby [Carter]'s meat and a large part of her bed clothing. I fear she and her family are in a very suffering condition, and unfortunately there are none to help her.

A Mr. Roberts has just called informing me that he will take my letter to Charlottesville. I must therefore close. I have written you a long letter and little in it, but that is nothing extraordinary. The fact is, my dear Son, when I take up my pen to write to you, I know not when to put it down.

Every one that you know in this neighbourhood is well. The few cattle that are in the county will be starved if the snow remains on the ground a few days longer.

All would join in love if they knew that I was writing. Love to Mary—we all miss her. Write to me as often as you have an opportunity. I do not get more than one half the letters you write, or the papers you send. I must bid you farewell. Believe me ever, my dear Son,

your affectionate Father,
J.P.D.

Letter of Richard H. Dulany to Mary Whiting:

University, Feb 26th, 1865

My dear Sister

You must excuse my using a pencil as I have no ink, and I find it much more difficult to use a pencil than a pen. Your letter of the 21st instant has been received, as well as two others in answer to mine.

You need not fear that I shall uselessly or recklessly throw away my life; the good God who has so mercifully spared it to my children and country, does not require that I shall hold arms in my hand to protect me still if he sees it best that I shall live through the war. There are too many persons halting now, when our cause requires every soldier in the ranks, for an officer not to be willing to make any sacrifice, that he may use whatever knowledge he may have gained so as to be able to use his influence in strengthening our army although he may be unable to wield a sabre or handle his pistol.

My general health is good and I think I am gaining some little strength in both my arms. If I get strength sufficient to mount my horse without too much difficulty I shall think it my duty to take command of my regiment, if not, I expect a place on a permanent court marshal [sic] for a Cav. Division. I shall go before the Examining board of Surgeons tomorrow so as to get a furlough for thirty or sixty days. Some time in March I hope to make a visit for a few days to our dear father, and afterwards, if the way is open, to Richland.

I saw one of my men and of Capt. McNeil's yesterday on their way to Richmond with Genls Crook and Kelley and an Adjt. Genl. whom they had captured in the midst of their troops at Cumberland. They with forty-five

Examined by the surgeons, Dulany was admitted to the Charlottesville General Hospital on February 27. He was granted a 30-day furlough per Special Order #58, March 5, 1865.[9]

On the morning of February 21, 1865, sixty rangers under the command of Capt. Jesse McNeill captured major generals George Crook and Benjamin F. Kelley from their hotels in Cumberland, Maryland. Both generals were later exchanged.[10]

men captured the Yankee pickets and reserve without firing a gun, then marched into Cumberland, halted at the hotel—got the General's horses from the stable and then woke the gentlemen themselves, made them get out of their warm beds, and marched them through a portion of their own troops and brought them off without losing a man. This is certainly one of the most daring affairs of the war.

Major Richards with thirty odd men ambushed a party of 125 Yankee Cav., after they had captured a commissary train and several of Mosby's men, and killed and wounded upward of twenty beside taking 57 prisoners and 90 horses. This was at Ashby's Gap a few days since. Richards (son of Jessie) has made several captures this winter.

I think you are right in staying on another year at Richland for the reason given in your letter, especially if the younger children are sent to Welbourne where Julia can instruct them. Nothing can be done in settling the affairs spoken of until we have peace. I have written father to send you Mr. Ward.

If nothing better offers by the close of the year you had better move to Grassland. If your cattle could be driven there they would be as safe as at any place in the upper country. You can have there "food and rainment" and therewith be content. With your sheep, a loom, and Alice, I should expect a full suit of clothes for my portion of profits. All well at Welbourne. Mary seems to enjoy her studies, although sometimes a little homesick; she and Fanny were never separated [here letter is torn] we meet with great kindness [letter torn] [P.S.] Clarence is at Welbourne and well. I hear he has accepted Col. Hopkins' offer to make him Adjt. of his regmt.

Col. Warren Montgomery Hopkins, 25th Virginia Cavalry.

Armed with a thirty-day furlough, the colonel and Mary left Charlottesville for Welbourne in early March. They were forced to ford the Rappahannock River and spent several nights in abandoned farm buildings before reaching home.

Dulany did not serve as a member of the court-martial, and while it had been his hope to return to his regiment as soon as possible, the severity of his wound was such that he could no longer serve in the field. He may even have tendered his resignation, as his service record notes, "Tendered his r" on January 30, 1865.

When the news came of the surrender at Appomattox Court House on April 9, he was at home, where he had to confront the ravages of the past four years—the destruction of most of his crops, his barn, several outbuildings and the mill.

On May 17th he went into Winchester, Virginia, and gave his parole. The war was officially over, but the difficult post-war period had just begun.

Partial letter of Julia B. Whiting to her mother, Mary Whiting, July 13, 1865:

The indictment for treason was dismissed in a circuit court in Richmond on February 15, 1869. The threat of seizure by the new Bureau of Refugees, Freedmen and Abandoned Lands never materialized.

Uncle Richard and Col. Arthur Herbert have been indicted for treason. I do not know where they will be tried. A party of cavalry served a writ upon Uncle Richard today confiscating his house & its contents, the land and everything on it.

In November 1865 the colonel and his family faced perhaps the worst moment of that year— the death of his sister, Julia Ann Dulany deButts Roszell.

Afterword

With their business interests in New York and Baltimore, the Dulanys did not suffer economic hardship, even immediately after the war. The colonel once again farmed the rich and fruitful soil of the Loudoun Valley, the mill was rebuilt, barns were raised. In later years Dulany sold off many parcels of land, but he accumulated others and eventually became one of the wealthiest men in the state.

Dulany never regained the full use of his arm, but despite his handicap, he often rode to inspect his farms, some of them some distance away. He continued his breeding of horses, hounds and cattle. At the Upperville Colt and Horse Show, the Tiffany cup was once again awarded to the winners. For years, he was Master of the Hounds of what was later called the Piedmont Hunt.

In the fall of 1866, in letters to his daughters, the colonel expressed an interest in a distant relative, Miss Jessie Duncan Turner (1847-1920), daughter of Rear Admiral Thomas Turner, Jr., U.S.N., and Frances H. Palmer of Philadelphia. In September he wrote to Fanny who, with Mary, was attending a convent school in Baltimore:

> Has Miss Turner paid you a visit yet? If she should come to the Convent you and May must meet her as if nothing had taken place between us. I have a sincere regard for her, and my friends have no right to suppose that she has acted unkindly towards me. She behaved as every true woman should do—finding she did not care for me as much as she thought she ought, she honestly told me so, and thus ended our conditional engagement.

A few weeks later, on October 10th, he wrote to Mary:

> Mrs. Powell wrote to Ida some days since that since she had
> been in Phila[delphia], she had become better reconciled to my
> disappointment. I wonder what she can mean. I do not think
> it possible that I could have mistaken in the high estimate I
> formed of Miss T. It may be that Mrs. Powell now thinks that
> there was to [sic] great difference in our ages—which is very
> probable although I should have willingly risked that
> difficulty—but this is only for your own eye.

While Dulany never remarried, Miss Turner wed someone nearer her own
age in 1873.[1]

At Welbourne, Confederate veterans were frequent visitors. Joe Johnston,
Dabney H. Maury and Gordon McCabe were known to have stopped by. Heros
von Borcke, on a return visit from Prussia, spent the night. There was copious
correspondence with others: John Brown Gordon, then a U.S. senator from
Georgia, wrote to propose a way to make more money (pointing out that he had
to maintain homes in Washington and Georgia); Wade Hampton bragged about
the big fish he caught up in Canada.

Dulany had an interest in veterans' affairs. He was a member of the Turner
Ashby Camp of the United Confederate Veterans in Winchester, and in 1890,
he was a marshal at the unveiling of General Lee's statue on Monument Avenue
in Richmond. A speech that survives is typical Dulany, deflecting the spotlight
from his own deeds to focus on the bravery of others—in this case, women.

> I cannot address you, as I never attempted to speak in public
> in my life, and it is now rather late to begin. Instead of a speech,
> I will relate two or three incidents which some of you witnessed
> with me, showing the courage & endurance of our Confederate
> women.
>
> In pressing some of Sheridan's men, who were burning
> almost every thing they could not carry off, we came to a
> handsome stone dwelling near which was a large mill and a
> barn. They were all in flames.

---

1   John McGill, comp. *The Beverley Family of Virginia: Descendants of Maj. Robert Beverley*
     (1641-1687) and Allied Families. Columbia, S.C.: R.L. Bryan, Co., 1956, pp. 334-335.

I saw no living thing except a flock of pigeons flying around the burning barn, and near the house a woman, standing with one child in her arms and another about three years old clinging to her dress—near them was a spinning wheel and a cradle. I rode up to the woman and asked if this was all she had saved from her home—she replied that she had saved a bundle of her child's clothes, but one of the soldiers had snatched it from her hand, and thrown it into the fire. She uttered no complaint.

Another incident regarded one of my neighbours. She had three sons in the army, the youngest but fifteen years old. In the first battle of Manassas, in the charge made by Col. Welby Carter on the Zouaves, one of these boys was shot through the hand so that he could not use his pistol. Some months after this I saw his mother. She said to me, "John is well enough to shoot some birds today; I think he should return to the army." And return he did—the next day.

The last incident regards the death of young VanMeter.[2] Gen. Rosser was on his march to capture Grant's cattle. The eleventh, I think, was in the front, and my regiment, the 7th, was following.

Hearing there were no obstructions between us and the enemy, Gen. Rosser gave his usual order, to move forward, and ride over any force they came up with! Unfortunately, the enemy got wind of our coming, and the eleventh, receiving a heavy fire, were thrown into some confusion.

Rosser ordered me to dismount my men and open the way for the mounted cavalry. You all know how long a regiment would be strung out when marching by twos in narrow roads at night. I dismounted my men as fast as they came up, and formed them in line, but before half had come up, I received a second order from Rosser to press forward & drive the enemy out. Rosser's impatience caused me to move in an oblique line, the left forming as we advanced. This drew the whole fire of the enemy on our right.

While urging the left forward, I saw in the dim light (it was

---

2   Milton VanMeter, private of Company F, 7th Virginia Cavalry, wounded September 18, 1864.

hardly day light) a number of the men on the extreme right go down. Thinking they had fallen to reload their guns, I sent the Adjutant to get them up and move them forward. In a few seconds he came back and said, "Every man down is shot—Lieut. Smith[3] is dead, and young Van Meter has both legs broken!"[4]

Having promised his father to look after this young man, I sent the Adjutant to get him back to the Ambulance corps; he returned saying that "Van Meter refused to be moved, but asked me to tell you, to let his people at home know that he died like a man." After his death I wrote to his mother, and received this reply—

"Col., if you feel, as you seem to do at the death of one almost a stranger to you—what must his Mother feel at the loss of her youngest son. But I assure you that I had rather a thousand times have lost him doing his duty to his country, than that he should have saved his life by neglecting it."

Many monuments have been erected to our dead comrades, but none so richly deserved as one that should be built to the Confederate women of Virginia.

In April 1866 he began to draft an account of the Laurel Brigade, as did General Hampton. With many blanks and crossovers, it obviously was never completed. In 1890, when William McDonald began to research and write his own history of the Laurel Brigade, he contacted Dulany for information. Dulany must have referred to his poor memory of events as McDonald replied:

Berryville, Va., March 29, 1890

Dear Colonel
    Yours of the 24th inst. just received. The MSS of Hampton's arrived yesterday. Your letter found me engaged in reading it. It is very interesting and will help me very much. I will take good care of it. All I wanted from you about your life in the army is what service you rendered that is: 1st. When you first

---

3   First Lieutenant Granville Smith was several times cited for gallantry, and Dulany called
    him an "attentive, efficient and gallant officer." (Armstrong, 228.)
4   He was shot through both thighs, which were fractured, and died the next day from his
    wounds. He is buried in Olivet Cemetery, Moorefield, West Virginia.

commanded your company (2) When made Colonel of the 7th, the different times (dates) and fights in which you were wounded & what periods you commanded the 7th & the brigade. These facts I need for a brief sketch of your service.

I would like to know also, I have often said, what was done by the brigade from Tervylians [sic] to Reams Station. You are supposed to know more about that than anyone else. ... But since you cannot get your MSS from Hampton I will have to do the best I can, though almost certain to do you and others injustice. ...

As to the treachery of memory & the danger of relying on personal recollections, that you refer to I agree with you perfectly, but there is no other way about the year 1864, and indeed some of the official reports of the previous [year] are not reliable.

Dulany attempted to get his papers from Hampton. They saw each other briefly during the dedication of General Lee's statue in Richmond, and when Hampton got back to Washington, he wrote to Dulany on July 4, 1890:

I regretted not having the opportunity of saying goodbye to you in Richmond & of thanking you for being with me then. But the crowd separated us & I missed you. I intended to tell you then that my daughter gave me bad news about my papers for she said that the mice had destroyed nearly all of them—a great loss to me! When I have an opportunity to do so, I shall make another search & I hope to rescue something.

While he never held public office, Dulany had deep interest in public affairs. He supported the restoration of home rule and the Democratic party. He supported financially the election of Grover Cleveland, and as a reward, the Welbourne post office was established in 1886, a mile from Welbourne on the Quaker Lane. It operated through June 29, 1907.

The children grew up and married.

Mary Dulany married an Irishman, Robert Neville, on November 1, 1876. When they returned from their honeymoon, they found a red brick Victorian mansion already built for them by Colonel Dulany on 500 acres of land that had once been part of Crednal. They christened the home Pelham, perhaps in memory of that sunny morning when young Mary surprised a gallant cavalier etching his name on a parlor window. Mary was an artist of some talent. In her trips to Europe she made many drawings and always wrote devotedly to her father at Welbourne.

On January 2, 1873, Fanny married J. Southgate Lemmon, a Confederate veteran from Baltimore. They lived in Baltimore with their nine daughters, but every summer mother and children came to Welbourne, where Fanny frequently acted as the colonel's hostess.

Hal inherited the Lady Hunter fortune, which made him one of the wealthiest young men in the state. He was considered one of its most eligible bachelors, though he never married. He was a prominent figure at the White Sulphur Springs, which, for a time, he virtually owned. He lived in Paris for several years, where he collected art and enjoyed big game hunting. He died at Welbourne on November 8, 1890, at age 37. Among the letters of condolence to Colonel Dulany are one from his old commander, General Rosser, and one from Mrs. Jefferson Davis.

Dick, the colonel's only surviving son, was married on September 5, 1877, to Eva Randolph, daughter of Major Innes Randolph, who composed the popular poem, "I'm a Good Ol' Rebel." The first stanza goes: "I'm a good ol' rebel, that's just what I am/For this fair land of freedom I do not give a damn."

As he aged, the colonel became to many people a living relic of the old social order, a throwback to the antebellum period, domineering and imperious, always immaculately attired in the stiff, formal clothes favored in the late Victorian period. To his grandchildren, however, he was "Mopapa," and they remembered his quiet sense of humor and genuine concern and kindness toward them.

The colonel rode each morning, and upon his return would enjoy a light breakfast with tea in the library served by one of his granddaughters. He died on October 31, 1906, his eighty-sixth year. A granddaughter found him slumped in the chair at his desk.

In his will, recorded at the Loudoun County Court House, he left Old Welbourne to Dick; Fanny got Welbourne. To his long-time servant, Alfred Hoe, he left a lifetime annuity. His death was front-page news in the Richmond *Times-Dispatch* and was noted in the Washington and Baltimore papers. The Warrenton *Virginian* of November 8, 1906, ran this obituary on page two:

> Colonel Dulany had a due regard for the business side of life. But there were things that he loved and that caused him to be loved more than most men. He loved the sunshiny places and the shady hill sides of Welbourne, he loved the cattle that fed on its fields, his horses, dogs—and above all he loved those who

gathered around the fireside—his family and his friends and the stranger within his gates. ... In that Heaven where he surely is, other angels may be beating the air with their wings, but the Colonel is on horseback.

He is buried in the family cemetery at Old Welbourne, within sight of the log and stone cabin in which he was born, laid to rest in the soil he defended.

Despite all of the public reaction to the news of his death, perhaps one of the most telling tributes came from a former servant, Julia Peters. She wrote to Mary:

Norwalk, Conn.
Nov. 9, 1906

My Dear Miss Mary,

Away out here in this state I saw a Washington paper and in it the death of the dear Col. I was so very very upset at being so far away that it was impossible for me to get there in time to see him laid away, as I felt that [I] should pay him that mark of respect, as I had grown up right under his eyes and can think of nothing but kindness on his part towards me. Dear Miss Mary I know how you feel and do wish I was near you, but I know the dear "Lord who shelters the shorn Lamb" will comfort you in this great sorrow—it seems there is nothing but sorrow [in] some shape all the time in the last few years and what ever comes to the family always hurts me sorely.

Please remember me to Mr. Dick and Mr. Neville.

I can't write any more

Yours lovingly
Julia A. Peters

Genealogical Charts

Several family members appear on more than one chart, and where this is the case, it is so noted.

DANIEL DULANY THE ELDER

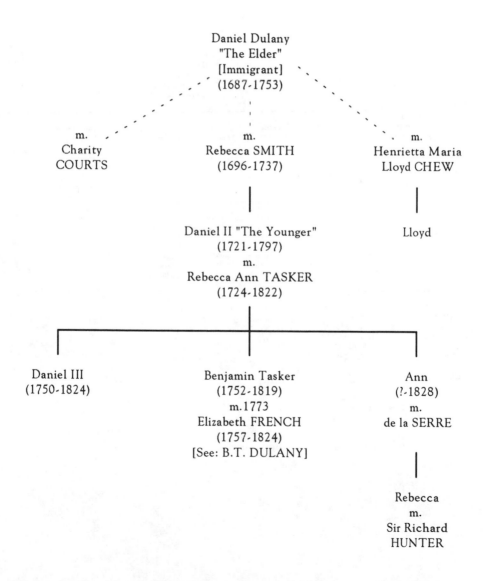

Daniel Dulany
"The Elder"
[Immigrant]
(1687-1753)

m.
Charity
COURTS

m.
Rebecca SMITH
(1696-1737)

m.
Henrietta Maria
Lloyd CHEW

Daniel II "The Younger"
(1721-1797)
m.
Rebecca Ann TASKER
(1724-1822)

Lloyd

Daniel III
(1750-1824)

Benjamin Tasker
(1752-1819)
m.1773
Elizabeth FRENCH
(1757-1824)
[See: B.T. DULANY]

Ann
(?-1828)
m.
de la SERRE

Rebecca
m.
Sir Richard
HUNTER

BENJAMIN TASKER DULANY

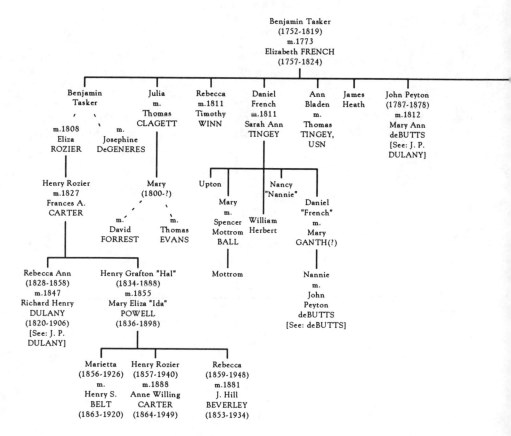

Benjamin Tasker
(1752-1819)
m.1773
Elizabeth FRENCH
(1757-1824)

Benjamin
Tasker

m.1808
Eliza
ROZIER

m.
Josephine
DeGENERES

Julia
m.
Thomas
CLAGETT

Rebecca
m.1811
Timothy
WINN

Daniel
French
m.1811
Sarah Ann
TINGEY

Ann
Bladen
m.
Thomas
TINGEY,
USN

James
Heath

John Peyton
(1787-1878)
m.1812
Mary Ann
deBUTTS
[See: J. P.
DULANY]

Henry Rozier
m.1827
Frances A.
CARTER

Mary
(1800-?)

m.
David
FORREST

m.
Thomas
EVANS

Upton

Mary
m.
Spencer
Mottrom
BALL

Nancy
"Nannie"

William
Herbert

Daniel
"French"
m.
Mary
GANTH(?)

Rebecca Ann
(1828-1858)
m.1847
Richard Henry
DULANY
(1820-1906)
[See: J. P.
DULANY]

Henry Grafton "Hal"
(1834-1888)
m.1855
Mary Eliza "Ida"
POWELL
(1836-1898)

Mottrom

Nannie
m.
John
Peyton
deBUTTS
[See: deBUTTS]

Marietta
(1856-1926)
m.
Henry S.
BELT
(1863-1920)

Henry Rozier
(1857-1940)
m.1888
Anne Willing
CARTER
(1864-1949)

Rebecca
(1859-1948)
m.1881
J. Hill
BEVERLEY
(1853-1934)

BENJAMIN TASKER DULANY

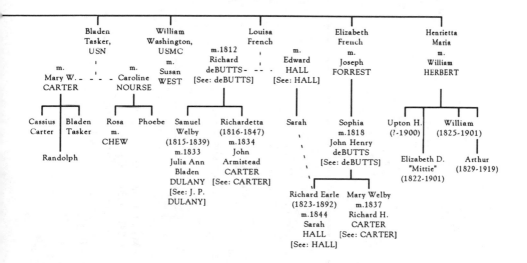

JOHN PEYTON DULANY

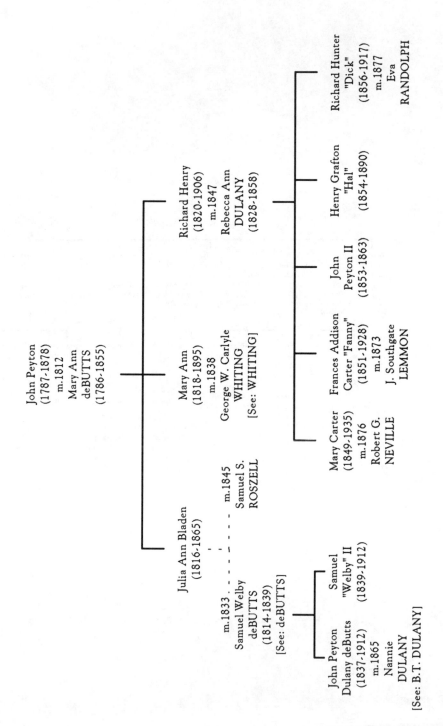

John Peyton
(1787-1878)
m.1812
Mary Ann
deBUTTS
(1786-1855)

Julia Ann Bladen
(1816-1865)

m.1833
Samuel Welby
deBUTTS
(1814-1839)
[See: deBUTTS]

m.1845
Samuel S.
ROSZELL

Mary Ann
(1818-1895)
m.1838
George W. Carlyle
WHITING
[See: WHITING]

Richard Henry
(1820-1906)
m.1847
Rebecca Ann
DULANY
(1828-1858)

John Peyton
Dulany deButts
(1837-1912)
m.1865
Nannie
DULANY
[See: B.T. DULANY]

Samuel
"Welby" II
(1839-1912)

Mary Carter
(1849-1935)
m.1876
Robert G.
NEVILLE

Frances Addison
Carter "Fanny"
(1851-1928)
m.1873
J. Southgate
LEMMON

John
Peyton II
(1853-1863)

Henry Grafton
"Hal"
(1854-1890)

Richard Hunter
"Dick"
(1856-1917)
m.1877
Eva
RANDOLPH

deBUTTS

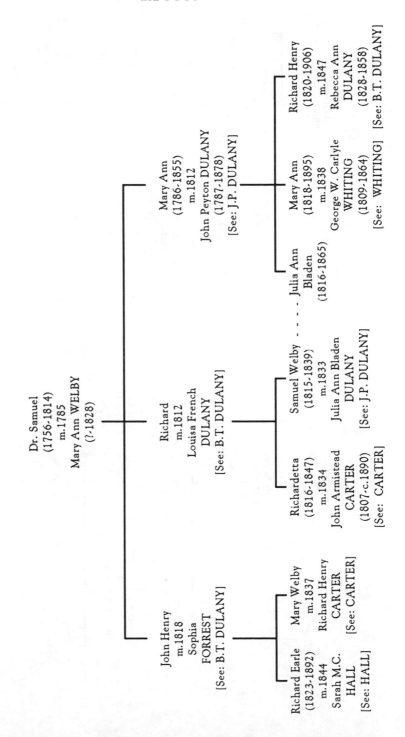

Dr. Samuel
(1756-1814)
m.1785
Mary Ann WELBY
(?-1828)

John Henry
m.1818
Sophia
FORREST
[See: B.T. DULANY]

Richard
m.1812
Louisa French
DULANY
[See: B.T. DULANY]

Mary Ann
(1786-1855)
m.1812
John Peyton DULANY
(1787-1878)
[See: J.P. DULANY]

Mary Welby
m.1837
Richard Henry
CARTER
[See: CARTER]

Richard Earle
(1823-1892)
m.1844
Sarah M.C.
HALL
[See: HALL]

Richardetta
(1816-1847)
m.1834
John Armistead
CARTER
(1807-c.1890)
[See: CARTER]

Samuel Welby
(1815-1839)
m.1833
Julia Ann Bladen
DULANY
[See: J.P. DULANY]

Julia Ann
Bladen
(1816-1865)

Mary Ann
(1818-1895)
m.1838
George W. Carlyle
WHITING
(1809-1864)
[See: WHITING]

Richard Henry
(1820-1906)
m.1847
Rebecca Ann
DULANY
(1828-1858)
[See: B.T. DULANY]

WHITING

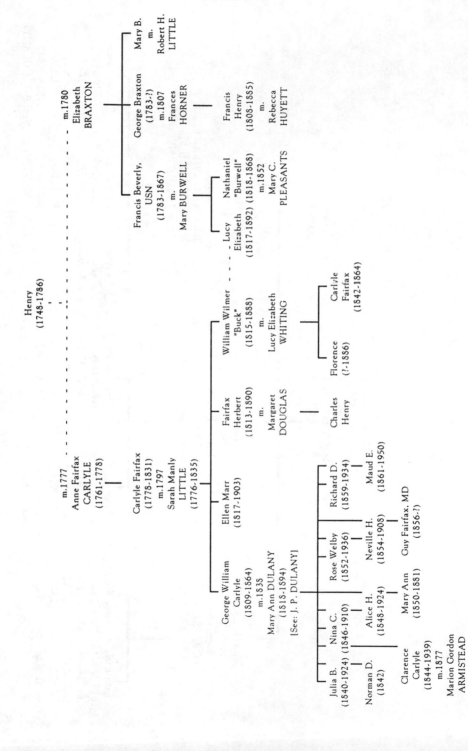

HALL

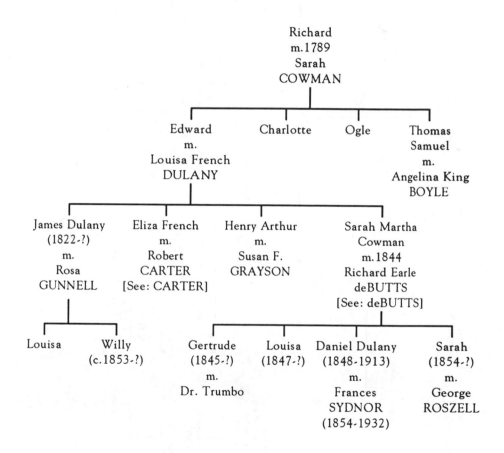

Richard
m.1789
Sarah
COWMAN

Edward   Charlotte   Ogle   Thomas
m.   Samuel
Louisa French   m.
DULANY   Angelina King
                             BOYLE

James Dulany   Eliza French   Henry Arthur   Sarah Martha
(1822-?)   m.   m.   Cowman
m.   Robert   Susan F.   m.1844
Rosa   CARTER   GRAYSON   Richard Earle
GUNNELL   [See: CARTER]   deBUTTS
                                          [See: deBUTTS]

Louisa   Willy   Gertrude   Louisa   Daniel Dulany   Sarah
       (c.1853-?)   (1845-?)   (1847-?)   (1848-1913)   (1854-?)
                     m.   m.   m.
                   Dr. Trumbo   Frances   George
                                     SYDNOR   ROSZELL
                                     (1854-1932)

CARTER

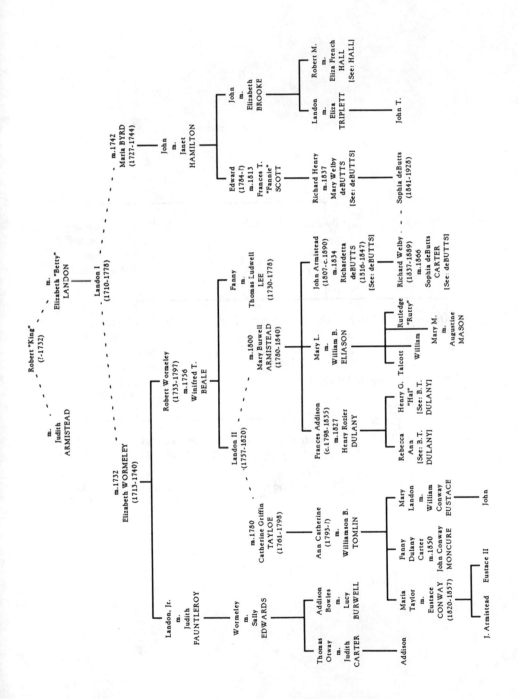

Notes

1861

1. Nan Netherton, et al., *Fairfax County, Virginia: A History* (Fairfax, Va.: Fairfax County Board of Supervisors, 1978), 315-16.
2. United States War Department, *The Official Military Atlas of the Civil War* (Washington, D.C.: Government Printing Office, 1891; Reprinted by Avenel, N.J.: Gramercy Books, 1983), plate VII. (Hereafter *Atlas*.)
3. Lee A. Wallace, Jr., *A Guide to Virginia Military Organizations 1861-1865* (Richmond: Virginia Civil War Centennial Commission, 1964), 47. (Hereafter Wallace.)
4. Mrs. Burton Harrison, *Recollections Grave and Gay* (New York: Charles Scribner's Sons, 1912), 3, 19.
5. Emily G. Ramey and John K. Gott, *The Years of Anguish: Fauquier County, Virginia, 1861-1865* (Warrenton, Va.: Fauquier County Civil War Centennial Committee and Board of Supervisors, 1965; Printed by the *Fauquier Democrat*.), 148-51.
6. Richard Lundgren, "A Genealogy of the Carters of Crednal," 1991, 56.
7. Nancy Chappelear Baird, ed., *Journals of Amanda Virginia Edmonds: Lass of Mosby's Confederacy* (Stephens City, Va.: Commercial Press, 1984), 52. (Hereafter Baird.)
8. Michael P. Musick, *6th Virginia Cavalry* (Lynchburg, Va.: H.E. Howard, Inc., 1990), 2. (Herafter Musick.)
9. Ibid., 117.
10. Ibid., 104.
11. Ezra J. Warner, *Generals in Gray: Lives of the Confederate Commanders* (Baton Rouge: Louisiana State University Press, 1959), 87-88.
12. Mary Dulany Lemmon White, granddaughter of Richard Henry Dulany, notation on original letter.
13. Wallace, 56; United States War Department, *The War of the Rebellion: Official Records of the Union and Confederate Armies* (Washington, D.C.: Government Printing Office, 1880-1901), Series I, Vol. LI, Part 2, 289. (Hereafter OR; all references Series I unless otherwise indicated.)
14. Compiled Military Service Record of Richard H. Dulany, National Archives, Washington, D.C. (Hereafter Dulany Service Record.)
15. Musick, 111.
16. Douglas Southall Freeman, *R.E. Lee: A Biography* (New York: Charles Scribner's Sons, 1931-34), Vol. I, 568-69.
17. Musick, 104.
18. Ibid., 111.

1862

1. Musick, 94.
2. *Atlas*, Plate VII.
3. Nan Netherton and Ruth Preston Rose, *Memories of Beautiful Burke, Virginia* (Burke, Va.: Burke Historical Society, 1988), 12.
4. Kevin Siepel, *Rebel: The Life of John Singleton Mosby* (New York: St. Martin's Press, 1983), 47.
5. Douglas Southall Freeman, *Lee's Lieutenants: A Study in Command* (New York: Charles Scribner's Sons, 1942-44), Vol. I, 99-109. (Hereafter *Lee's Lieutenants.*)
6. Musick, 113, 122.
7. *Lee's Lieutenants*, Vol. I, 306.
8. Wallace, 47.
9. Report of Col. John W. Geary, OR, Vol. V, 511-17.
10. Samuel P. Bates, *History of Pennsylvania Volunteers 1861-1865* (Harrisburg, Pa.: B. Singerly, State Printer, 1869), Vol. I, 445, 480.
11. Ibid., 427.
12. Baird, 89-90.
13. OR, Vol. XXIV, Pt. 1, 500.
14. Report of Lt. Joseph A. Moore, OR, Vol. XII, Pt. 1, 500-502.
15. Report of Col. Thomas S. Flournoy, OR, Vol. XII, Part 1, 733-34; John C. Donohoe, "Fight at Front Royal," *Southern Historical Society Papers*, Vol. XXIV, 1896, 131-39; Laura Virginia Hale, "'Stonewall' Jackson Gave North Its Worst Scare at Front Royal, Virginia, May 23, 1862," *Warren County Centennial Commemoration: Battle of Front Royal, May 19-20, 1962.*
16. Richard L. Armstrong, *7th Virginia Cavalry* (Lynchburg, Va.: H.E. Howard, Inc., 1992), 223. (Hereafter Armstrong.) For a sketch of Sheetz, see James B. Avirett, *The Memoirs of General Turner Ashby and His Compeers* (Baltimore: Selby & Dulany, 1867), 372-87. (Hereafter Avirett.)
17. Baird, 94.
18. Report of Thomas Munford, OR, Vol. XII, Part 1, 729-33.
19. Compiled Military Service Record of Henry G. Dulany, 6th Virginia Cavalry, C.S.A., National Archives, Washington, D.C.
20. Musick, 164.
21. Ibid.
22. Marietta Minnigerode Andrews, *Scraps of Paper* (New York: E.P. Dutton & Co., Inc., 1929), 19-21. (Hereafter Andrews.)
23. Avirett, 288-89, 384.
24. Thomas L. Livermore, *Numbers and Losses in the Civil War in America: 1861-1865* (New York: Indiana University Press, 1957), 87-88.
25. Robert K. Krick, *Lee's Colonels: A Biographical Register of the Field Officers of the Army of Northern Virginia* (Dayton, Ohio: Morningside Press, 1979), 97. (Hereafter Krick.)
26. Armstrong, 44.
27. Ibid., 43; Dulany Service Record indicates he may not have been a full colonel until March 23, 1865. Krick, 111, accepts the latter date.
28. For a sketch of Eliason, see Robert J. Trout, *They Followed the Plume: The Story of J.E.B. Stuart and His Staff* (Mechanicsburg, Pa.: Stackpole Books, 1993), 99-102. (Hereafter Trout.)

29. For a sketch of Farley, see John Esten Cooke, *Wearing of the Gray* (New York: 1866; Reprinted by Gaithersburg, Md.: Olde Soldier Books, 1988), 130-40.
30. Trout, 191-97.
31. Charles G. Milham, *Gallant Pelham: American Extraordinary* (Washington, D.C.: Public Affairs Press, 1959), 191.
32. Andrews, 63-64.

1863

1. Mark M. Boatner, III, *The Civil War Dictionary* (New York: McKay, 1988), 322. (Hereafter Boatner.)
2. E. Wilby Burton, *The Siege of Charleston, 1861-1865* (Columbia, S.C.: University of South Carolina Press, 1970; 1987 edition), 126-31. (Hereafter Burton.)
3. Boatner, 871.
4. Ibid., 405-6.
5. Ibid., 954.
6. Report of Gen. William Jones, OR, Vol. XXI, 747-48; Sanford C. Kellogg, *The Shenandoah Valley in Virginia 1861-1865: A War Study* (New York & Washington: The Neale Publishing Company, 1903), 83-84.
7. John O. Casler, *Four Years in the Stonewall Brigade*, Revised edition. (Dayton, Ohio: Morningside Books, 1982), 101.
8. For a sketch of Thomas Marshall, see Avirett, 276-317.
9. Musick, 116.
10. OR, Vol. XXV, Part 1, 34-35.
11. Ibid., 33.
12. Armstrong, 228.
13. Correspondence of William H. Strong, Jr., to Margaret Vogtsberger, October 22, 1993. For detailed accounts of the Herndon Station and Chantilly raids, see James J. Williamson, *Mosby's Rangers* (New York: Ralph B. Kenyon, 1896), 48-51. (Hereafter Williamson.); Hugh C. Keen and Horace Mewborn, *43rd Battalion Virginia Cavalry: Mosby's Command* (Lynchburg, Va.: H.E. Howard, Inc., 1993), 39-42. (Hereafter Keen and Mewborn.)
14. For details of battle, see *Lee's Lieutenants*, Vol. II, 457-66.
15. Musick, 157.
16. Armstrong, 160.
17. George M. Neese, *Three Years in the Confederate Horse Artillery*, Reprint (Dayton, Ohio: Morningside Books, 1988), 158. (Hereafter Neese.)
18. John S. Mosby, *Mosby's War Reminiscences and Stuart's Cavalry Campaigns* (New York: Pageant Book Company, 1958), 130-41.
19. Keen and Mewborn, 315.
20. Ibid., 350.
21. Ibid., 373.
22. Musick, 146.
23. OR, Vol. XXV, Part 1, 1107-8.
24. Boatner, 245, 273, 864-65.
25. Wilbur Sturdevant Nye, *Here Come the Rebels!* (Baton Rouge: Louisiana State University Press, 1965), 198-203.

26. Eugene Scheel, *The History of Middleburg and Vicinity* (Warrenton, Va.: Piedmont Press, 1987), p. 80-81.

27. Dulany Service Record.

28. Millard K. Bushong and Dean Bushong, *Fightin' Tom Rosser* (Shippensburg, Pa.: Beidel Printing House, Inc., 1983), p. 60.

29. William N. McDonald, *A History of the Laurel Brigade: Originally the Ashby Cavalry of the Army of Northern Virginia and Chew's Battery*, edited by Bushrod C. Washington (Baltimore: Sun Job Printing Office, 1907), 203-8.

30. Ibid., 208-13.

31. Robert J. Driver, *1st Virginia Cavalry* (Lynchburg, Va.: H.E. Howard, Inc., 1981), 159. (Hereafter Driver.)

1864

1. Thomas J. Evans and James M. Moyer, *Mosby's Confederacy: A Guide to the Roads and Sites of Colonel John Singleton Mosby* (Shippensburg, Pa.: White Mane Publishing, 1991), 100. (Hereafter Evans and Moyer); Williamson, 197.

2. Williamson, 476.

3. Jeffrey D. Wert, *Mosby's Rangers* (New York: Simon & Schuster, 1990), 164-71. (Hereafter Wert.)

4. Virgil Carrington Jones, *Ranger Mosby* (Chapel Hill, N.C.: University of North Carolina Press, 1944), 164-71. (Hereafter Jones.)

5. Armstrong, 129.

6. OR, Vol. XXXIII, 1117.

7. Driver, 227.

8. Keen and Mewborn, 290.

9. Evans and Moyer, 18.

10. See Briscoe Goodhart, *History of the Independent Loudoun Rangers 1862-1865* (Washington, D.C.: Press of McGill & Wallace, 1896; Reprinted by Gaithersburg, Md.: Olde Soldier Books, 1985), p. 123.

11. E.V. Smith and J.P. Burke, *The Civil War at Rio Hill* (Charlottesville, Va.: Self-published, 1988); Neese, 249-52.

12. For controversy concerning the raid, see *Lee's Lieutenants*, Vol. III, 334.

13. Trout, 188-91.

14. *Lee's Lieutenants*, Vol. II, 435.

15. John Divine, "Portrait of a Mosby Ranger," unpublished manuscript on John Peyton deButts. (Hereafter Divine.)

16. McDonald, 242-43.

17. Divine.

18. Wert, 98; Evans and Moyer, 94.

19. Keen and Mewborn, 339.

20. Diary of James Ward Woods, 7th Virginia Cavalry, Virginia State Library, Richmond, Va.

21. Armstrong, 238.

22. Ibid., 106, 123.

23. Frank M. Myers, *The Commanches: A History of White's Battalion, Virginia Cavalry* (Baltimore: Kelly, Piet & Co., 1871), 319.

24. Armstrong, 207.

25. Jones, 203, 212.

26. Armstrong, 240.
27. John W. Thomason, Jr., *J.E.B. Stuart* (New York: Charles Scribner's Sons, 1930), 124-26.
28. N.L. Atkinson, "At Welbourne Long Ago: How Grandfather Lost the Use of His Arm" *Fauquier Democrat*, 16 March 1978: A-11.
29. Musick, 113.
30. Armstrong, 250.
31. Evans and Moyer, 76-77; John H. Alexander, *Mosby's Men* (New York & Washington: The Neale Publishing Co., 1907), 119-28.
32. Wilfred Buck Yearns, *The Confederate Congress* (Athens, Ga.: University of Georgia Press, 1960), 96-99.
33. Evans and Moyer, 22. For details, see Jones, 246-50.
34. Keen and Mewborn, 325.

1865

1. Evans and Moyer, 22.
2. Musick, 148.
3. Ibid., 113.
4. Allan Nevins, *The War for the Union: The Organized War to Victory 1864-1865, Vol. IV* (New York: Charles Scribner's Sons, 1971), 268-69.
5. Keen and Mewborn, 216.
6. Ervin L. Jordan, Jr., *Charlottesville and the University of Virginia in the Civil War* (Lynchburg, Va.: H.E. Howard, 1988), 48.
7. Wert, 268, 274.
8. Gallagher, Gary W., ed., *Struggle for the Shenandoah: Essays on the 1864 Campaign* (Kent, Ohio: Kent State University Press, 1991), 99.
9. Dulany Service Record
10. For details, see Virgil Carrington Jones, *Gray Ghosts and Rebel Raiders* (New York: Holt, Rinehart & Winston, 1956), 356-62.

Bibliography

Primary Sources

Alexander, John H. *Mosby's Men*. New York & Washington: The Neale Publishing Co., 1907.

Avirett, James B. *The Memoirs of General Turner Ashby and His Compeers*. Baltimore: Selby & Dulany, 1867.

Barton, Randolph. *Recollections 1861-1865*. Baltimore: Thomas and Evans, 1913.

Blackford, Charles M. "The Trails and Trial of Jefferson Davis," *Southern Historical Society Papers*, Vol. XXIX: 1901.

Blackford, W. W. *War Years with J.E.B. Stuart*. New York: Charles Scribner's Sons, 1945.

Casler, John O. *Four Years in the Stonewall Brigade*. Revised ed. Dayton, Ohio: Morningside Books, 1982.

Cooke, John Esten. *Wearing of the Gray*. New York: 1866. Reprinted by Gaithersburg, Md.: Olde Soldier Books, 1988.

C.S.A. Congress. *Journal of the Congress of the Confederate States of America, 1861-1865*. 7 vols. Washington, D.C.: Government Printing Office, 1904-05.

Donohoe, John C. "Fight at Front Royal," *Southern Historical Society Papers*, Vol. XXIV, 1896: 131-39.

Gilmor, Harry. *Four Years in the Saddle*. New York: Harper & Brothers, 1866.

Goldsborough, W. W. *The Maryland Line in the Confederacy 1861-1865*. Baltimore: Guggenheimer, Weil & Co., 1900.

Goodhart, Briscoe. *History of the Independent Loudoun Rangers 1862-1865*. Washington, D.C.: Press of McGill & Wallace, 1866. Reprinted by Gaithersburg, Md.: Olde Soldier Books, 1985.

Harrison, Mrs. Burton. *Recollections Grave and Gay*. New York: Charles Scribner's Sons, 1912.

Johnson, Robert U., and Clarence C. Buell, eds. *Battles and Leaders of the Civil War*. 4 vols. New York: The Century Co., 1887-88.

McDonald, William N. *A History of the Laurel Brigade: Originally the Ashby Cavalry of the Army of Northern Virginia and Chew's Battery*. Edited by Bushrod C. Washington. Baltimore: Sun Job Printing Office, 1907.

Moffett, George H. "The Jones Raid Through West Virginia," *Confederate Veteran*, Vol. XIII, No. 10. October 1905: 450.

Mosby, John S. *Mosby's War Reminiscences and Stuart's Cavalry Campaigns*. New York: Pageant Book Company, 1958.

Myers, Frank M. *The Commanches: A History of White's Battalion, Virginia Cavalry*. Baltimore: Kelly, Piet & Co., 1871.

Neese, George M. *Three Years in the Confederate Horse Artillery*. Reprint. Dayton, Ohio: Morningside Books, 1988.

Rich, Edward R. *Comrades Four: During the Civil War, a Member of Company E, First Maryland Cavalry, C.S.A.* New York & Washington: The Neale Publishing Co., 1907.

United States War Department. *The Official Military Atlas of the Civil War*. Washington, D.C.: Government Printing Office, 1891. Reprinted by Avenel, N.J.: Gramercy Books, 1983.

United States War Department. *The War of the Rebellion: Official Records of the Union and Confederate Armies*. Series I. Washington, D.C.: Government Printing Office, 1880-1901.

Vandiver, Frank. "Letters from Veterans," *Confederate Veteran*, Vol. III, No. 11. November 1895: 335.

Wells, Edward L. *Hampton and His Cavalry in '64*. Reprint. Richmond: Owens Publishing Co., 1991.

Williamson, James J. *Mosby's Rangers*. New York: Ralph B. Kenyon, 1896.

Wise, John S. *The End of an Era*. Boston & New York: Houghton-Mifflin Co., 1899.

Secondary Sources

Andrews, Marietta Minnigerode. *Scraps of Paper*. New York: E.P. Dutton & Co., Inc., 1929.

Armstrong, Richard L. *7th Virginia Cavalry*. Lynchburg, Va.: H.E. Howard, Inc., 1992.

Atkinson, N. L. "At Welbourne Long Ago: How Grandfather Lost the Use of His Arm." *Fauquier Democrat*, 16 March 1978: A-11.

Baird, Nancy Chappelear, ed., *Journals of Amanda Virginia Edmonds: Lass of Mosby's Confederacy*. Stephens City, Va.: Commercial Press, 1984.

Bates, Samuel P. *History of Pennsylvania Volunteers 1861-1865*. Vol. I. Harrisburg, Pa.: B. Singerly, State Printer, 1869.

Berg, A. Scott. *Max Perkins: Editor of Genius*. New York: E.P. Dutton & Co., 1978.

Boatner, Mark M., III. *The Civil War Dictionary*. New York: McKay, 1988.

Boykin, Edward. *Beefstake Raid*. New York: Funk & Wagnalls Co., 1960.

Burton, E. Wilby. *The Siege of Charleston, 1861-1865*. Columbia, S.C.: University of South Carolina Press, 1970; 1987 edition.

Bushong, Millard K., and Dean Bushong, *Fightin' Tom Rosser, C.S.A.* Shippensburg, Pa.: Beidel Printing House, Inc., 1983.

Chappelear, B. Curtis. *Maps and Notes Pertaining to the Upper Section of Fauquier County, Virginia*. Warrenton, Va.: The Warrenton Antiquarian Society, 1954.

Dobson, Gwen, ed. *Middleburg and Nearby*. Researched and compiled by Vme. Edom Smith. Leesburg, Va.: Potomac Press, 1986.

Driver, Robert J. *1st Virginia Cavalry*. Lynchburg, Va.: H.E. Howard, Inc., 1981.

Evans, Thomas J., and James M. Moyer. *Mosby's Confederacy: A Guide to the Roads and Sites of Colonel John Singleton Mosby*. Shippensburg, Pa.: White Mane Publishing, 1991.

Freeman, Douglas Southall. *Lee's Lieutenants: A Study in Command*. 3 vols. New York: Charles Scribner's Sons, 1942-44.

_____. *R.E. Lee: A Biography*. New York: Charles Scribner's Sons, 1931-34.

Furlong, Roland Dulany. *Dulany-Furlong and Kindred Families*. Parsons, W.Va.: McClain Printing Co., 1975.

Gallagher, Gary W., ed. *Struggle for the Shenandoah: Essays on the 1864 Valley Campaign*. Kent, Ohio: Kent State University Press, 1991.

Hagey, King Albert, and William Anderson Hagey. *The Hagey Families in America and the Dulaney Family*. Bristol, Tenn./Va.: King Printing Co., 1951.

Hale, Laura Virginia. *Four Valiant Years in the Lower Shenandoah Valley 1861-1865*. Front Royal, Va.: Hathaway Publishing, 1986.

_____. "'Stonewall' Jackson Gave North Its Worst Scare at Front Royal, Virginia, May 23, 1862," *Warren County Centennial Commemoration: Battle of Front Royal, May 19-20, 1962*.

Higginson, A. Henry, and Julian Ingersoll Chamberlain. *The Hunts of the United States and Canada*. Boston: Frank L. Wiles, 1908.

Hubbell, Jay. *The South in American Literature 1607-1900*. Durham, N.C.: Duke University Press, 1954.

Jones, Virgil Carrington. *Gray Ghosts and Rebel Raiders*. New York: Holt, Rinehart and Winston, 1956.

_____. *Ranger Mosby*. Chapel Hill, N.C.: University of North Carolina Press, 1944.

Jordan, Ervin L., Jr. *Charlottesville and the University of Virginia in the Civil War*. Lynchburg, Va.: H.E. Howard, 1988.

Keen, Hugh C., and Horace Mewborn, *43rd Battalion Virginia Cavalry: Mosby's Command*. Lynchburg, Va.: H.E. Howard, Inc., 1993.

Kellogg, Sanford C. *The Shenandoah Valley and Virginia 1861-1865: A War Study*. New York & Washington: The Neale Publishing Company, 1903.

Krick, Robert K. *Lee's Colonels: A Biographical Register of the Field Officers of the Army of Northern Virginia*. Dayton, Ohio: Morningside Press, 1979.

Land, Aubrey C. *The Dulanys of Maryland*. Baltimore: Johns Hopkins University Press, 1955.

Livermore, Thomas L. *Numbers and Losses in the Civil War in America: 1861-1865*. New York: Indiana University Press, 1957.

McGill, John, comp. *The Beverley Family of Virginia: Descendants fo Maj. Robert Beverly (1641-1687) and Allied Families*. Columbia, S.C.: R.L. Bryan Co., 1956.

Milham, Charles G. *Gallant Pelham: American Extraordinary*. Washington, D.C.: Public Affairs Press, 1959.

Miller, J. Michael. "The Saga of Shuter's Hill," *Fairfax County Historical Society*, Vol. 19, 1993: 75-108.

Morgan, James Henry. *Dickinson College 1783-1933*. Carlisle, Pa.: Dickinson College, 1933.

Musick, Michael P. *6th Virginia Cavalry*. Lynchburg, Va.: H.E. Howard, Inc., 1990.

Netherton, Nan, et al. *Fairfax County, Virginia: A History*. Fairfax, Va.: Fairfax County Board of Supervisors, 1978.

Netherton, Nan, and Ruth Preston Rose, *Memories of Beautiful Burke, Virginia*. Burke, Va.: Burke Historical Society, 1988.

Nevins, Allan. *The War for the Union: The Organized War to Victory 1864-1865*, Vol. IV. New York: Charles Scribner's Sons, 1971.

Nye, Wilbur Sturdevant. *Here Come the Rebels!* Baton Rouge: Louisiana State University Press, 1965.

Ramage, James A. *Rebel Raider: The Life of General John Hunt Morgan*. Lexington, Ky.: University of Kentucky Press, 1986.

Ramey, Emily G. and John K. Gott. *The Years of Anguish: Fauquier County, Virginia, 1861-1865*. Warrenton, Va.: Fauquier County Civil War Centennial Committee and Board of Supervisors, 1965. Printed by the *Fauquier Democrat*.

Reniers, Perceval. *The Springs of Virginia: Life, Love, and Death at the Waters 1775-1900*. Chapel Hill, N.C.: University of North Carolina Press, 1941.

Scheel, Eugene M. *The History of Middleburg and Vicinity*. Warrenton, Va.: Piedmont Press, 1987.

Scott, Laurel Kathryn. "Piedmont Foxhounds: 150 Glorious Years," *Hunt Country Magazine*. January-February 1990.

Siepel, Kevin. *Rebel: The Life of John Singleton Mosby*. New York: St. Martin's Press, 1983.

Slater, Kitty. *The Hunt Country of America*. Cranbury, N.J.: A. S. Barnes and Company, 1967.

Smith, E. V., and J. P. Burke. *The Civil War at Rio Hill*. Charlottesville, Va.: Self-published, 1988.

Super, Charles W. *A Pioneer College and Its Background (Dickinson)*. Salem, Mass.: Newcomb & Gauss, 1923.

Thomason, John W., Jr. *J.E.B. Stuart*. New York: Charles Scribner's Sons, 1930.

Trout, Robert J. *They Followed the Plume: The Story of J.E.B. Stuart and His Staff*. Mechanicsburg, Pa.: Stackpole Books, 1993.

Wallace, Lee A., Jr., *A Guide to Virginia Military Organizations 1861-1865*. Richmond: Virginia Civil War Centennial Commission, 1964.

Warner, Ezra J. *Generals in Gray: Lives of the Confederate Commanders*. Baton Rouge: Louisiana State University Press, 1959.

_____. *Generals in Blue: Lives of the Union Commanders*. Baton Rouge: Louisiana State University Press, 1964.

Wert, Jeffry D. *Mosby's Rangers*. New York: Simon & Schuster, 1990.

_____. *From Winchester to Cedar Creek: The Shenandoah Campaign of 1864*. Carlisle, Pa.: South Mountain Press, 1987.

Wright, Louis B. *The Cultural Life of the American Colonies 1607-1763*. New American Nation Series, edited by Henry Steele Commager and Richard B. Morris. New York: Harper & Row, 1957.

Yearns, Wilfred Buck. *The Confederate Congress*. Athens, Ga.: University of Georgia Press, 1960.

Manuscripts & Papers

Brumback, Jacob H. Diary. Handley Library, Winchester, Va.

Compiled Military Service Record, Richard H. Dulany. National Archives, Washington, D.C.

Compiled Military Service Records, 6th Virginia Cavalry. National Archives, Washington, D.C.

Compiled Military Service Records, 7th Virginia Cavalry. National Archives, Washington, D.C.

deButts Family. Letters.

deButts Family. Papers. Virginia Historical Society, Richmond, Va.

Divine, John. "Portrait of a Mosby Ranger," unpublished manuscript on John Peyton deButts.

Dulany Family Bible.

Dulany Family Genealogy.

Dulany, Fanny Addison Carter. Letters.

Dulany, John Peyton. Letters.

Dulany, Mary Carter. Letters.

Dulany, Rebecca Ann. Correspondence to Mary Eliason. Diary.

Dulany, Richard Henry. Letters. Account books.

Fauquier County Deed Books. Fauquier County Court House, Warrenton, Va.

Loudoun County Deed Books and Wills. Loudoun County Court House, Leesburg, Va.

Lundgren, Richard J. "A Genealogy of the Carters of Crednal," 1991.

Rosser, Thomas Lafayette. Papers. Alderman Library, University of Virginia.

Strong, William H., Jr. "John Singleton Mosby 'Adventures to the Adventurous': A Tour of Selective Mosby Sites in Loudoun, Clarke, and Fauquier Counties, October 22, 1993," unpublished manuscript.

Suderow, Bryce A. "The Battle of Trevilian Station, June 11-12, 1864," unpublished manuscript.

_____. "The Cavalry in the Civil War: May 28, 30, 31 & June 1, 1864: Haw's Shop, Matadequin Creek and Cold Harbor," unpublished manuscript.

U.S. Census, 1860, Fauquier and Loudoun counties. Thomas Balch Library, Leesburg, Va.

U.S. Department of the Interior. National Register of Historic Places. Nomination
     Form, Welbourne, 1971.
Walter, Franklin Gardner, Co. A, 39th Virginia Cavalry. Diary. Handley Library,
     Winchester, Va.
Welbourne file. Thomas Balch Library, Leesburg, Va.
White, G. Howard. "A Retrospective of the Dulany Fortune," unpublished
     manuscript, 1983.
Whiting, Julia. Letters.
Woods, James Ward, 7th Virginia Cavalry. Diary. Virginia State Library, Richmond,
     Va.

Newspapers

Charlottesville, Va. *Observer*. 1864.
Richmond, Va. *Times-Dispatch*. 1 November 1906.
Warrenton, Va. *Fauquier Democrat*. 16 March 1987.
Warrenton, Va. *Virginian*. 8 November 1906.

Index

Military Units

A